T0382842

ROUTLEDGE LIBRARY EDITIONS: THE OIL INDUSTRY

Volume 7

THE OIL INDUSTRY IN INDIA

THE OIL INDUSTRY IN INDIA

Some Economic Aspects

BIPLAB DASGUPTA

Routledge
Taylor & Francis Group

LONDON AND NEW YORK

First published in 1971 by Frank Cass & Co. Ltd

This edition first published in 2024
by Routledge
4 Park Square, Milton Park, Abingdon, Oxon OX14 4RN

and by Routledge
605 Third Avenue, New York, NY 10158

Routledge is an imprint of the Taylor & Francis Group, an informa business

British Library Cataloguing in Publication Data
A catalogue record for this book is available from the British Library

ISBN: 978-1-032-55944-5 (Set)
ISBN: 978-1-032-56321-3 (Volume 7) (hbk)
ISBN: 978-1-032-56322-0 (Volume 7) (pbk)
ISBN: 978-1-003-43494-8 (Volume 7) (ebk)

DOI: 10.4324/9781003434948

Publisher's Note
The publisher has gone to great lengths to ensure the quality of this reprint but
points out that some imperfections in the original copies may be apparent.

Disclaimer
The publisher has made every effort to trace copyright holders and would
welcome correspondence from those they have been unable to trace.

THE
OIL INDUSTRY
IN INDIA

Some Economic Aspects

Biplab Dasgupta

School of Oriental and African Studies

University of London

With a foreword by Professor Edith Penrose

FRANK CASS & CO. LTD

1971

First published in 1971 by
FRANK CASS & COMPANY LIMITED
67 Great Russell Street, London WC1B 3BT

Copyright © 1971 B. Dasgupta

ISBN 0 7146 2583 3

PRINTED IN GREAT BRITAIN BY
STEPHEN AUSTIN AND SONS LTD., HERTFORD, ENGLAND

CONTENTS

LIST OF TABLES

FOREWORD

It was with very great pleasure that I accepted Dr. Dasgupta's invitation to write a preface for this study. The petroleum industry is one of the most important of all international industries, but it has until very recently received little attention from academic economists. This neglect is difficult to explain but, fortunately, it is at last being corrected, for over the past ten years some serious works on the international industry have begun to emerge. These are still suffering, however, from the absence of adequate studies of the national industries in individual countries on which to draw, and especially in the importing countries of Asia and Africa. Dr. Dasgupta's study helps to fill this gap, for it deals with one of the most important countries of Asia. It is greatly to be welcomed on that account alone.

India is neither an important crude-oil producing country nor an important importing country. Its total consumption in 1968 was only 13,000,000 tons, (that of Japan was 139,000,000 tons) and it imported 7,000,000 tons. Consumption has been growing at the rate of 16% per year, however, and will continue to grow as the country industrialises. Nevertheless, a study of the Indian petroleum industry, including the country's relationships with the international companies, has a greater significance than these modest figures would suggest. The Indian experience illustrates, both historically and for the present time, many of the problems that the international petroleum companies have posed, and still pose, for developing countries. The Indian situation shows the type of issue that must be closely analysed when the less-developed importing countries formulate their petroleum policies, Dr. Dasgupta has brought out these issues, particularly with respect to pricing, and he criticises impartially both the companies and the government when the occasion requires.

Although the international companies in India do not, by and large, come out very well from Dr. Dasgupta's historical review of their policies and activities in India, the spirit of his enquiry is not that of the "muckraker" or of one trying to demonstrate the inequity of "imperialism". Rather, it is a sober and documented historical enquiry into the facts of the past. It is clear that British colonial policy in India was not conducive to the development of an indigenous industry. On the one hand, the British oil companies, having found abundant oil in Burma and later in Iran did not have strong incentives to explore in India, but at the same time the British government did not permit foreign oil companies to explore for oil in the country. It is also clear that the pricing policies adopted by the international oil companies for products were highly discriminatory, depriving India of much of the advantage she might have obtained as an importer from the discovery and development of Asian sources of oil. Dr. Dasgupta's detailed analysis of these questions is a clear contribution to the history of the international industry, as well as to the history of the industry in India.

With the Abadan crisis it became clear to the companies as well as to the government, that it was risky for India to rely entirely on the import of products from this one source, and the oil companies finally agreed to the government's demand that refineries be established in India. These refineries were established under refinery agreements that gave the companies the right to import crude and, in effect, to determine the price of imports. The analysis of the consequences of this kind of arrangement has a widespread interest for other importing countries. The international companies naturally saw their activities in any one country in the context of the international logistic and financial problems they faced in discovering, producing, transporting, refining, and selling oil all over the (non-communist) world. Dr. Dasgupta's concern is with India and with India's development, and I think his researches do show that the vertical integration of the international oil companies, combined with their oligopolistic position, tended to be inimical to the economic interests of India.

It is often suggested that the less developed countries should not devote their own resources to searching for crude oil, nor indeed even to building refineries. Some twelve years ago India embarked on the establishment of a state-owned refining industry to operate along side the refineries of the international private companies. She also has engaged in extensive exploration for crude oil on her own account. Dr. Dasgupta's analysis of the India experience with the public sector in oil (and he is by no means uncritical) will be read with interest by governments of other developing countries.

School of Oriental and African Studies,   EDITH PENROSE.

University of London.

PREFACE

This book attempts to examine some of the major issues facing the oil industry of India today, particularly those relating to the prices of crude oil and refined oil products. Two historical chapters have also been introduced, primarily because the material covered in this book is not otherwise available in published form, and also because it is expected to help the understanding of the present situation. In view of the international character of the foreign oil companies which operate in India, detailed world background to the happenings in the Indian market have also been presented.

There are, however, several important omissions. Industries like natural gas, petrochemicals, pipelines, and coastal shipping, which are related to the oil industry, have been barely mentioned. Discussion on pricing is largely confined to wholesale export prices, and retail and inter-regional wholesale prices have been more or less ignored. There is no discussion on the detailed balance-sheets of the individual oil companies and their implication in the Indian context. Oil industries of the socialist countries have been examined only to the extent that these are related to the rest of the world, and India. The purpose of this study will be served if it succeeds in stimulating interest among the research workers in the economics of the oil industry.

This book relies heavily on secondary sources for data. Most of the book was written during 1963–66, when I was studying at the London School of Economics as a Ph.D. student. Official information on India was difficult to obtain because of the emergency rules which were then in operation. There were also difficulties in securing the copies of relevant reports and in maintaining correspondence with the officials in India. The international oil companies, on the other hand, are generally unwilling to volunteer information on costs and prices for obvious reasons. In the absence of detailed (as well as reliable) data, it was not possible to carry out quantitative analysis in a meaningful way. Although some demand-elasticities were calculated during the time of writing, these have not been incorporated into the book. The tables published in this book, particularly those relating to the pre-Independence years, should be taken only as rough approximations of the actual situation, in view of numerous adjustments which had to be made.

It needs to be stressed that a number of interesting developments have taken place in the Indian market, since the book was rewritten in 1968 for publication. To mention a few: the Madras refinery has now been completed; a third committee has been formed by the Government to investigate the price structure; the contract with Philips has been amended to allow the Government to purchase one-half of the crude requirement for the Cochin refinery from the sources of its choice; a part of the offshore Iranian crude of O.N.G.C. is being made available to the Madras refinery; the Government has imposed foreign exchange restrictions on the major oil companies in order to force them to accept a lower price—$1·28—for their Iranian crude, and Japan has agreed to meet a part of the kerosene requirements. Internationally, a new price formula for ocean freight has been introduced, and the spot rates have more or less returned to their pre-1968-war level. However, none of these facts conflict with my general observations and conclusions.

I am grateful to Professor Edith Penrose, who acted as my supervisor at the London School of Economics and stimulated my interest in the economic problems of the oil industry. I am also indebted to Professor P. R. O'Dell, and Mr. Hartshorn for their comments, and to the staff of the following libraries for their help: Shell Centre, India House, Institute of Petroleum, London School of Economics, and the British Museum. My thanks are also due to my wife, Arati, who helped me in the collection of statistical data and the compilation of tables.

School of Oriental & African Studies,   BIPLAB DASGUPTA.

University of London,

October, 1970.

CHAPTER 1

INTRODUCTION

Petroleum is a fascinating subject for intensive study. It is indispensable as a source of energy and accounts for two-fifths of the volume of world trade. No country can afford to do without this "liquid gold". Its use accompanies industrial growth and military strength. The comment made by Clemenceau, "A drop of oil is worth a drop of blood", is still appropriate, both in war and in peace time.

Petroleum has been in use for hundreds of years in the countries of the Middle East and Burma, but the techniques of production were primitive and the production small, until the second half of the last century. Wells were shallow and were dug only in places where oil seepages were known to exist. Most of its modern uses were unknown, and in its uses as illuminant or lubricating oil, petroleum occupied an inferior position to vegetable oils. The modern petroleum industry dates from 1859, when a seventy-foot well was drilled in Pennsylvania which located an oil deposit. Since then oil production has grown very rapidly, and many of its new uses have been developed. It has replaced coal (which even in 1937 accounted for 72% of commercial energy consumption) as the main source of commercial energy, and in 1967 was responsible for 49% of the total energy consumption.[1] Oil is still important as an item of household consumption, as an illuminant and as heating and cooking fuel. But its domestic use has now been completely overshadowed by its application as an industrial fuel, automotive fuel, fuel for jet aeroplanes, raw material for road building, and as solvents, lubricating oil, and also for hundreds of other different purposes.

Oil is extracted in crude form from underneath the soil, but requires to be refined before being suitable for most uses. The products produced through the refinery process are normally divided into three broad categories—light distillates, middle distillates, and heavy ends. Motor spirit or petrol belongs to the first category, while diesels and kerosene are described as middle distillates. Products like bitumen (also known as asphalt) furnace oil (also known as fuel oil), or lubricants belong to the third category and are sometimes described as Residuals. In the early days of the industry, kerosene was the most important oil product, but with the development of the automobile industry since the 1890s the consumption of motor spirit has assumed the leading place among the oil products, although in recent years the growth of diesel oil consumption has been very spectacular. As it will be examined in a subsequent chapter, the extent of the use of petroleum, and also the pattern of oil consumption, are directly linked to the nature and the degree of economic development of a country.

MAJOR OIL PRODUCING AREAS

From 1899 until the end of the 1930s, the United States was the leading producer, consumer, as well as exporter of oil. It still continues to be the leading producer and consumer, but the rapid growth of domestic consumption has reduced it to the status of a net importer of oil. As will be seen below, the international oil companies of United States origin play an extremely important role in the world oil arena. The United States (27%) is followed by the Soviet Union (16%), Venezuela (10%) Saudi Arabia (7%), Kuwait (6%), and Libya (5%) as the leading world producers of oil.[2] Historically, the Soviet Union was a formidable competitor of United States oil in the Eastern Hemisphere, and during 1898–1901 its production surpassed that of the United States. But between 1905 and 1926, and again between 1939 and 1958, the supply of Soviet (or Russian before 1917) oil was withdrawn from the world market for various reasons. In the following two chapters we shall see how the supplies from the Soviet Union led to a series of "price wars" among the major oil companies of the world, including India.

Iran (or Persia as it was previously known) entered the world market as a large producer of oil during the First World War, but the development of its oilfields was hindered by the restrictive marketing arrangements among the major oil companies. Despite its proximity, Iranian oil was not allowed to play its expected role in the Indian market until the beginning of the Second World War. It still continues as the major source of imported crude to India. The oilfields of Saudi Arabia were developed during the 1930s and those of Kuwait during the 1940s, but the latter has never played any important role, and the former not until recently, in the Indian market— despite their large supplies to the countries of Western Europe and Japan. On the other hand, Bahrein, which now accounts for less than one-fifth of 1% of world production, was among the chief suppliers of oil products to India during the Second World War and for some time afterwards.

The Middle East as a region is of extreme importance to the world oil industry, both as the supplier of 28% of world consumption and also because it accounts for more than 60% of the "proved" oil reserves to date; further exploration may increase this percentage figure. As distinct from the United States, or the Soviet Union, the rate of consumption in the Middle East is low (3% of world consumption in 1967) and almost the whole of its production is exported to other countries. Hence its importance lies not so much in being a current large producer, but in being the main exporter of oil and as the main source of a future supply of oil. The Middle East is followed at a great distance by Africa, particularly North Africa, as an important source of proved oil reserve. The development during the 1960s of the oilfields of Libya, Algeria and Nigeria, which together accounted for about 8% of world production in 1967, has produced stiff competition for the Middle East sources in the markets of West Europe, and, as we shall see later, has helped to transform the price structure of the world market for crude and products.

TABLE 1

WORLD OIL IN 1967
Unit: Million Metric Tons

Source: World Oil Statistics
(Petroleum Information Bureau)

	Crude Production	%	Refining Capacity	%	Consumption	%
W. Europe	21	1·13	539	26·48	455	23·1
Middle East	507	27·73	102	5·01	51	3·2
Iran	129	7·07	25	1·25	12	—
Kuwait	115	6·30	17	0·84	5	—
Saudi Arabia	130	7·08	15	0·75	—	—
Bahrein	3	0·19	11	0·52	—	—
Africa	146	7·96	33	1·64	33	1·5
Libya and Algeria	100	5·32	3	0·15	—	—
North America	545	29·78	615	30·22	664	40·0
U.S.A.	402	26·86	557	27·35	601	36·5
South America	257	14·03	229	11·24	114	7·0
Communist Bloc	316	17·27	318	15·63	260	15·6
U.S.S.R.	268	15·79	265	13·01	—	—
Far East and Australia	38	2·10	199	9·78	197	9·6
Japan	1	0·04	106	5·20	119	5·2
Indonesia	25	1·37	14	0·70	8	—
Brunei and Sarawak	5	0·28	3	0·15	—	—
India	5	0·28	17	0·82	13	0·9
TOTAL	1,830	100	2,037	100	1,774	100

It is also important to mention two other oil-producing areas, which are no longer significant in the world oil map of to-day, but which played very important roles in the markets of Asia before the

Second World War—Burma and South East Asia (Indonesia and Malaysia). The former was the main source of oil to India for about forty years until the Second World War, when its refining industry was destroyed. The civil war, which followed the end of the War, also disrupted the reconstruction of the oil industry, and reduced Burma to the position of a net importer of oil. In recent years the oil industry of Burma has made some progress towards reducing dependence on foreign imports, but is still unlikely to play any important role in future as an exporter of oil. The oilfields of Indonesia and Malaysia, which now account for $1 \cdot 4\%$ and $0 \cdot 3\%$, respectively, of world production, were at one time among the chief competitors of the American and Russian (later Soviet) oil supplies in the markets of Asia.

INTERNATIONAL OIL COMPANIES

No introduction to the world oil industry is complete without reference to the seven large international oil companies, which dominate the world oil scene and are collectively known as "majors". Each of these companies operates through hundreds of affiliates and subsidiaries, spread all over the world, and participates in almost every conceivable kind of activity associated with the oil industry— from exploration, and crude oil production, to refining, transporting, and marketing of oil products, as well as fertilisers and petro-chemicals. In 1966 these companies together produced 76% of crude oil outside the communist countries and North America, and shared 61% of the refining throughput.[3] Each of these companies is large enough to be classified among the top thirty joint stock organisations of the world, and the largest of these companies—Standard Oil Company of New Jersey—is also the largest business organisation of the world in terms of assets, which amounted to $13,887 million in 1966.[4] Five of these international companies are of United States origin—Standard Oil of New Jersey, Gulf Oil Corporation, Texas Oil Corporation, Socony Mobil Oil Company, Standard Oil of California, one British–Dutch—Royal Dutch Shell, and one British—British Petroleum.

As it will be seen from the two following chapters, each of these major oil companies, with the exception of Gulf, has played an important part in the historical development of the Indian oil industry. Standard Oil of New Jersey (known as Esso) at present owns a $2 \cdot 8$ million ton refinery at Bombay, and operates a marketing organisation for the distribution of the refined products. Standard Oil of California and Texas Oil operate jointly through Caltex in India, and own a refinery at Vizagapatnam, as also a marketing organisation. Royal Dutch Shell operates in India through Burmah–

Shell, which is jointly owned by the latter with the Burmah Oil Company, which is organisationally linked with British Petroleum, another major. Burmah Shell owns the largest refinery in India, and until very recently was the largest marketing organisation of the country. Standard Oil of New York (afterwards named the Socony Mobil Oil Company) was a partner in Standard–Vacuum or Stan-Vac with the Standard Oil of New Jersey until 1960, when the group was broken up into its constituents and the Indian business of the group was transferred to Standard Oil of New Jersey. Before 1960 the majors were the exclusive suppliers of oil to India—both crude and products—except for less than 1% share of Western Indian Oil, a private Indian organisation. The growth of the Indian Oil Corporation, a state-owned marketing company, during the 1960s, helped to reduce their share to about 55% in 1967. Besides their share in marketing, and refining, the majors also own one-half of the crude production of Oil India Limited, the producing organisation for the new oilfields of Assam.

The importance of the majors to the Indian oil industry can also be seen from their control over the production centres which are geographically close to India, particularly those in the Persian Gulf area. In most of these centres the production of crude oil is virtually monopolised by consortia of major oil companies. Kuwait Oil Company is jointly owned by British Petroleum and Gulf Oil, and some of the latter's share is sold to Royal Dutch Shell on a long-term basis. The consortium of Saudi Arabia, Arabian American Oil Company (Aramco) is owned by four U.S. majors, Standard Oil of California, Texas Oil, and Standard Oil of New Jersey, each owning a 30% share, and Socony Mobil the rest. 40% of the equity ownership in the Iranian consortium is vested in British Petroleum, 14% in Royal Dutch Shell, 6% in C.F.P. (a French company, with a 35% state ownership, which is sometimes called the "eighth major"), and 5% in Iricon (a group of nine small U.S. companies), while each of the U.S. majors owns 7%. Before 1951, Iranian production was the monopoly of the Anglo-Iranian Oil Company (or Anglo-Persian Oil Company), which is now known as British Petroleum. The consortia operating in Iraq, Bahrein, and Qatar, are owned by Royal Dutch Shell (23·75%), British Petroleum (23·75%), Near East Development Corporation (23·75%, which is equally owned by Standard of Jersey and Mobil), and the C. S. Gulbenkian estate (5%). The same consortium also owns the onshore oilfields of Abu Dhabi, a new producing area in the Persian Gulf; the offshore oilfields being under the ownership of British Petroleum and C.F.P., on a 2 : 1 basis. The only important producing area outside the ownership of the majors is the Neutral Zone between Kuwait and

B

Saudi Arabia, where a number of "independent" companies (that is those outside the organisational structure of the international majors) like Arabian Oil (a Japanese company), American Independent Oil (known as Aminoil) and Getty Oil (another U.S. company), own production, which amounts to about $1 \cdot 2\%$ of the world production, and less than 5% of the Persian Gulf production. The majors also own an overwhelming part of Nigerian production, and more than half of Libyan production.[5]

OLIGOPOLISTIC MARKET STRUCTURE AND PRICE WARS

The international character of these major companies, their vertically and horizontally integrated organisational structure, and also their joint ownership of crude production (and in some cases their joint ownership of distribution), have important bearings on the policies they follow in various sectors of the industry and in various countries. Except during the periods of price wars, which are characteristic of an oligopolistic market structure, these major companies have always tended to pursue a uniform price policy and an agreed market sharing arrangement between themselves. Both the actual amount of oil produced from a particular source and the actual amount sold to a particular market, by any of these international oil companies, have depended on the nature of agreement or understanding existing between these major interests, with respect to production and distribution. During the 1930s these agreements were formalised into written documents, although in other periods the majors have preferred to rely on tacit understandings.

An interesting feature of the history of the oil industry is the occurrence of price wars between conflicting marketing interests. As distinct from price competition, price war results in reduced prices only for a short period and, more often than not, is followed by the restoration of prices to the pre-price-war level. A price war is usually initiated by a company which is dissatisfied with the existing distribution of the market among various companies, and is used as a weapon to force its rivals to accept a re-distribution favourable to the company initiating the price war. The outcome of a price war is either the elimination of rivals from the market or, if the rivals are strong enough to withstand the pressure of reduced prices and loss, a new agreement which, again, either confirms the pre-price-war market-sharing arrangement or works out a new arrangement. In some cases price wars are initiated when it is thought that some of the provisions of a previous agreement are being violated by a rival who deserves punishment because of "unethical conduct". The price wars of 1898–1905, 1909, 1911, and 1928, which were fought among the major oil companies in the Indian and other markets, were always followed by agreements between conflicting interests about market-sharing arrangements and prices. The various cartel arrangements of the 1930s between the oil companies were necessitated by the conditions of over-production and economic depression in the world market as preventive measures against outbreaks of price wars between these majors.

The nature of price wars fought in the oil industry has changed considerably since 1928. The major oil companies have consolidated their collective position through a series of collaboration agreements, in production and distribution. Besides the joint ownership of the production of the Middle East, these companies have participated jointly in marketing in the Eastern Hemisphere though companies like Burmah-Shell, Caltex, and Standard-Vacuum, and have entered into long term crude and product sales contracts between themselves in order to correct the imbalance between demand and supply in various branches of the industry and in various parts of the world, within the same corporate framework. A price war, under these conditions, is prejudicial to the interests of all these majors, and is suicidal and self-defeating in purpose. In view of the enormous financial strength of each of these companies, such a price war would continue for an indefinite period of time, during which all the participants in the war would suffer staggering losses, more so because of the joint ownership of most of their production, while the result of the war would, in all probability, be inconclusive. Both their collective and individual interests dictate the need to refrain from costly price wars. Except for rare instances of very short term and highly localised price wars in the petrol trade, the price competition among the major companies themselves is now visible only when selling crude oil to the independent refineries; but even in this case the prices at which crudes are offered by various companies are not, strictly speaking, comparable since the prices are accompanied by varying credit facilities and freight rates.

The rivalry among the major oil companies has been replaced since 1928 by the rivalry between the major oil companies, on the one hand, and the independents, on the other. Before 1959, the competition of the independents was localised, because of the small-ness of their organisations and the virtual absence of non-major sources of crude oil in the Eastern Hemisphere. The majors took part in those price wars in order to bring the independents to their heels, and succeeded in either eliminating them from the market, or in forcing them to function as appendages to their corporate entities through long-term supply arrangements. Since 1959 such competition is no longer localised, and the independents have been strengthened by the finding of oil in the Neutral Zone, Libya, and Algeria under their ownership, coupled with the reappearance of the Soviet Union in the world market. The secular decline in oil prices in recent years bears testimony to the increased competitiveness in the oil market of today, although the majors are still the most important factor in the oil market.

Of the scores of independent oil companies active in the world market today, three—Philips, Standard Oil of Indiana, and Ente Nazionale Idrocarbouri—are active in the Indian market. Philips, although a newcomer in the world market, like Standard Oil of Indiana, is an established integrated oil company of the United States. It holds a one-third interest in Aminoil's Neutral Zone production, and through Aminoil, in Iran's Iricon, besides a small share in Libyan oil. It is a joint owner of the Cochin refinery of India with the Government. Standard Oil of Indiana, a bigger company than Philips, owns the Darius oilfield of Iran with the state-owned National Iranian Oil Company, and is a part owner of the Madras refinery of India. E.N.I., the Italian state-owned company, has been very active in curbing the influence of the majors in the Italian market with the aid of Soviet supplies, and has extended its activities to various countries in Africa and the Middle East, both in crude production and in refining. It has helped the Government of India with technical advice and in prospecting, in the past, without participating in exploration and refining. It needs to be emphasised at this stage that, although these independents are small in size compared to the majors, they are large corporate entities by virtually any other standard.

OIL EXPORTING COUNTRIES AND THEIR GOVERNMENTS

Revenue from oil is still the most important source of earnings—about nine-tenths—of the Governments of the oil producing countries. The amount of revenue received from oil operation depends on the arrangements existing between the oil companies and the Governments. The original concession agreements allowed for payments which were very small in relation to the large income generated from oil operation, and caused dissatisfaction among the Governments of those countries. The agreements reached between the companies and the Governments in the early fifties replaced the old system and allowed for equal sharing of profits from oil operations between the oil companies and the Governments. The new system came under pressure when the major oil companies reduced the posted prices of crude oil in 1959 and 1960 in order to meet the competition of the newcomers in the world market, which also reduced Government revenue per unit of oil exported. The

Organisation of Petroleum Exporting Countries (O.P.E.C.) was formed in 1960 in order to resist this downward trend in oil prices and also to improve the bargaining strength of the oil producing countries *vis-à-vis* the major international oil companies. Its membership includes Libya, Venezuela, and Indonesia, besides the major oil producing countries of the Middle East. Since its inception, this organisation has scored a numer of successes. Although the crude oil prices are declining in the world market, the revenues accruing to the oil producing countries are still calculated as if the oil were being sold at posted prices, which have remained unchanged since 1960. Because of this discrepancy between the actual price at which the oil is sold by the oil companies in the world market, and the posted price which is used for calculating profits, the share of the Governments in the total profits has exceeded 50%. The agreement of 1964 now enables the oil companies to deduct fixed discounts (which are far lower than actual discounts) from posted prices, for a limited period, for the purpose of calculating payments to the Government. But the 1964 agreement also provides for the elimination of marketing allowances and the exclusion of royalties as constituting a part of the 50% share to the Government. The programme of O.P.E.C. in regulating oil production in order to maintain its prices has not been successful, because of the conflicts of interest among the members of this organisation.

A new feature of the current world oil scene is the appearance of a number of state oil undertakings in the oil producing countries of the Middle East. In most countries new concession agreements provide for the partnership of the state undertaking in oil production and refining, and scores of non-major oil companies have taken part in oil exploration under conditions which are highly attractive from the point of view of the oil producing countries. Under these new arrangements the foreign partner bears the entire risk of oil exploration, but, once the oil deposit is located, the state oil organisation is allowed the option of a half share in the producing organisation in return for paying for the proportionate amount of exploration expenses in instalments. Although the aggregate production under these state organisations is still small, this is likely to grow in future.

OIL IMPORTING COUNTRIES AND THEIR GOVERNMENTS

The oil importing countries of the world can be conveniently classified into three groups: (1) those like the U.K., U.S.A., or Netherlands, whose interests as importers are overshadowed by their producer interests as mother countries of the large international firms; (2) those like West Germany, or the U.K., with a large coal industry, which are apprehensive about the prospect of mass unemployment following large oil imports at low prices; (3) consumer countries like Italy, Japan, or India, which are anxious to avoid large foreign exchange payments for oil imports. The countries belonging to the first two groups are, for understandable reasons, less concerned about high oil prices than those belonging to the third.

The main activities of the relatively more oil-conscious Governments of the countries belonging to the third group were associated with refinery construction, since this helped to economise part of the foreign exchange cost on oil, and to make the economy less dependent on foreign supplies. As it will be seen afterwards, this objective of self-sufficiency in refined products, on the part of the oil consuming countries, is in conformity with the refinery location policy of the major oil companies since 1951. But most of the disputes between the oil companies and the oil consuming countries have been centred around the question of the prices at which crude oil is imported, and the prices at which the oil products are sold in the domestic market by the affiliates of the major oil companies. The increased competitiveness in the world oil market since 1959 has favoured the oil importing countries by providing them with a range of choice among the sellers of crude oil, and with a scope for the diversification of the ownership of the refining industry.

In recent years the attention of the oil consuming countries of the Eastern hemisphere has been drawn to the field of oil exploration. Where the prospects of success within the country are considered limited, some of these countries have encouraged their nationals to launch similar programmes in other countries with large known oil deposits. The success achieved by Arabian Oil, a Japanese-owned company with limited previous experience in this field, in locating the Khafji oilfield in the Neutral Zone, has encouraged Japan to undertake similar programmes in other parts of the Middle East and in Indonesia. The Khafji crude is accorded priority in the Japanese market. Both the Italian and the Spanish oil undertakings have won concession rights in a number of prospective areas of the Middle East and Africa, although these have not yet located any significant deposit. The modest success of the consortium of E.N.I.-Philips-O.N.G.C. in Iranian offshore, and the recent agreement for Pakistan to undertake oil exploration in Saudi Arabia also deserve to be mentioned as attempts to supplement domestic crude production.

The state oil undertakings are more or less a normal part of the oil industry of many oil consuming countries, although their influence varies from one country to another. As yet there has been little attempt to co-ordinate the activities of the oil consuming countries in order to further reduce oil prices, or to discuss matters of common interest. Where the major oil companies work on the basis of tacit understandings among themselves supported by the respective countries of origin, and where the major oil producing countries of the third world are capable of taking concerted action through O.P.E.C., there is no similar organisation representing the interests of the oil importing countries. There is also little direct contact between the state organisations of the producing and consuming countries, independent of the international oil companies. Although no attempt will be made in this study to develop this theme, it is possible to visualise a situation where the producing countries, through direct exchange, would receive higher prices for their crude, and the consuming countries would pay lower prices for their imports, within the framework of a radically reorganised world oil industry structure.

AN OUTLINE OF THE INDIAN OIL INDUSTRY

The amount of oil consumption is still very low in India, and reflects the economic backwardness of the country. At thirteen million tons in 1967, the per head consumption was a mere one-fortieth of a ton: one of the lowest figures in the world. In comparison, the per head consumption in Japan in the same year exceeded one ton, and for most of the West European countries the corresponding figure ranged from one to two tons. Another feature of the Indian consumption figure is the relatively higher share of kerosene—about a quarter—in the aggregate figure, although in most developed countries the share of kerosene lies below 10%. This feature, again, reflects the slow rate of growth of industrial fuel consumption, in India.

For a long time Digboi (Assam) was the only source of domestic crude oil in India. Since 1953 a number of new oilfields have been discovered in Assam and Gujrat, and there are good prospects of locating more oilfields in the near future. Present domestic production is less than six million tons, and the refining industry of India needs to depend heavily on imported crude for its operation. The main source of imported crude is Iran, followed by Saudi Arabia and Kuwait, and a small amount is also imported from the Far East.

There are, at present, nine refineries in India. The oldest, at Digboi, is owned by Assam Oil, a subsidiary of Burmah Oil. Burmah Shell, Esso, and Caltex own one refinery each, the first two are located at Bombay, and the Caltex refinery is at Vizagapatnam (Andhra). Three Government-owned refineries are located at Nunmati (Assam), Barauni (Bihar), and Koyali (Gujrat), and each of these draws crude from the domestic oilfields. Cochin refinery is jointly owned by the Government, Philips Petroleum, and some Indian interests, and Madras refinery is jointly owned by the Government, American International Oil (a subsidiary of Standard Oil of Indiana) and National Iranian Oil. The proposed Haldia (West Bengal) refinery will be wholly owned by the Government, and built with the assistance of a French company. The aggregate refinery capacity is adequate to meet India's aggregate demand for oil. But, because of the phenomenon of product-imbalance, to be discussed in a subsequent chapter in detail, India imports kerosene and diesel, while producing surplus naptha.

The import of oil products is a monopoly of the Indian Oil Corporation, the state-owned company specialising in marketing and refining. It imports deficit oil products from the Soviet Union and sells a part of the surplus to Ceylon, Thailand, and a number of other countries. Within the country, it draws supplies from the state-owned refineries (which are now controlled by the Indian Oil Corporation) as well as from those owned jointly by the Government with foreign collaborators. The Indian Oil Corporation is now the largest oil marketing company of the country. Burmah Shell, Esso, and Caltex, which together controlled 99% of the market before 1960, are still responsible for more than half of the total oil trade, and draw supplies from refineries owned by themselves.

NOTES

1. Petroleum Information Bureau, "*Oil—World Statistics*", 1968.

2. The figures refer to 1967. *Ibid.*

3. Penrose (4), p. 78.

4. *Annual Reports and Financial and Statistical Supplements of the Standard Oil Company* (*New Jersey*), 1967.

5. See Longrigg, Penrose (4), Hartshorn for details.

CHAPTER 2

HISTORICAL REVIEW: PERIOD UP TO 1928

Period before 1886

Up to 1886 the consumers of petroleum in India were completely dependent on American imports, with very few exceptions.[1] Oil was not discovered in the Middle East until the beginning of the twentieth century, and its production was not significant before the First World War. Far East oil production did not start before 1890, and the Russain oilfield of Baku did not reach the height of its activity before 1886.[2] Since the Suez Canal was closed to the oil-carrying ships in those days for fear of disaster, the transport of oil from Baku to India was not an easy proposition. There was no domestic production of oil, and Digboi oilfield, which was discovered in the early 1880s, did not produce any significant amount of oil until 1921. We know of a number of hand-dug wells of Burma, which was administratively a part of India until 1936, but the production was extremely small. The United States, on the other hand, accounted for approximately 80% of the total crude oil production of the world, and most of the export trade in oil.[3] Despite her great geographical distance from India, the U.S.A. was practically the only source of supply of oil to India.

Of the total amount of oil supplied by the United States in those years almost the entire amount was in the form of kerosene. For example, in 1879 the value of kerosene imports from U.S.A. was $926,285 out of a total import of all oil products from U.S.A. of $935,910.[4] This, as will be discussed in detail in Chapter 4, followed from the very low degree of development of the factory system in India until the end of the First World War. The two most important industries were the jute and cotton industries which then hardly used any extensive mechanical process and used to sell intermediate products to the manufacturers of Britain and the U.S.A. There developed some demand for "Batching oil"—a kind of lubricating oil used by the jute industry—at a latter period,[5] but the demand for lubricating oil, in general, was extremely small. The painting of woodwork was considered to be a luxury of the wealthy few and for this and other purposes vegetable or animal oils were used more extensively than mineral oil.[6] The use of motor spirit was out of the question until 1904–5, when for the first time motor cars arrived in India.[7]

In the absence of an industrial sector of a significant size, the only use of oil was for consumption as an illuminant, which explains the demand for kerosene. It was not until the end of the First World War that the consumption of other products reached a respectable level compared to kerosene (see Tables 3–7), and even now kerosene is the most important of all oil products in India. Given the low level of consumption of motor spirit and lubricants and the low prices of fuel oil, the kerosene oil trade was the most profitable part of the trade of the oil companies operating in India, and almost all the rivalries and competition between them centred round the kerosene trade up to the price war of 1927–28.

From 1886 to 1905

IMPORTS OF RUSSIAN KEROSENE

By 1885 small consignments of Russian oil illuminants were reaching the ports of India, and in 1886 Russian oil made its effective entry into the market.[8] The very first cargo brought into Bombay was an outstanding success, and Russian exporters were flooded with orders from India.[9] How popular it became, and within so short a time, can be seen from the fact that, whereas in 1885–86 the Russian export was non-existent, in 1888–89 it almost equalled American kerosene exports.[10] There were a number of factors, geographical and economic, operating in favour of Russian exports to India.

Firstly, Batum, the exporting centre of Russian oil, was 120° longitude nearer to India than Philadelphia.[11] It took only thirty days to reach India from Batum, while the American exports needed $4\frac{1}{2}$ months to come to India.[12] This longer distance to the United States not only increased transport cost, but also other charges such as insurance, leakages, ocean loss, etc.[13] On the other hand, in view of the frequent changes made to the external value of currency during this period, Indian importers were less willing to enter into long term commitments.

Secondly, the cost of production of Russian oil was comparatively lower. Whereas the average yield of a well in the U.S.A. was only $4\frac{1}{2}$ barrels per day, the corresponding figure for Russia was 280 barrels.[14] The wages were low in Russia, and the refining cost was one-third of the American level. It was estimated in 1900 that the net cost price of illuminating oil (kerosene oil) leaving Baku was only half that of New York.[15]

A third factor which favoured the expansion of Russian kerosene export trade was the pattern of consumption of oil products in

Russia. The consumption of fuel oil was very high whereas that of kerosene was far below the level of production of kerosene necessitated by the production of fuel oil. Since there was no ready market for this surplus kerosene within Russia, the refiners were willing to dispose of kerosene in the world market at the price it would bring.[16]

However, despite these economic advantages of the Russian kerosene the larger proportion of the Indian kerosene market was still being supplied by the American oil until 1892.[17] One of the reasons was the supposed superiority of the American oil and also its decidedly better packing which maintained a favourable impression in the minds of consumers.[18] In reality there was possibly no significant difference in quality between the American and the Russian kerosene, although the latter smoked more.[19] The performance of the Russian kerosene was considerably enhanced afterwards by the introduction of cheap German lamps specially designed for service with Russian oil.

Furthermore, kerosene was then a very small market and the *per capita* oil consumption was less than one-fifth of a gallon.[20] The poverty and illiteracy of the people implied a limited need for the illuminants, and vegetable oils or animal oils were widely used for illumination purposes. The latter were produced by the villagers in their own gardens and could be used for many purposes in their day-to-day life.[21] "It is a matter of twenty or thirty years at most," wrote an expert on commercial problems in 1908, "since every European resident in India, and all the wealthier natives, employed either castor or coconut oil exclusively for house illumination."[22] However strange it may seem to many, not even the wealthier section of the country used kerosene in those days.

So, while because of the "snob appeal" of American oil it was consumed by the rich, most of the villagers were using vegetable and animal oils for illumination and the scope for expanding the market for Russian kerosene was limited unless it could be sold at prices within the means of the villagers, or at least a large part of them.

BULK OIL AND RUSSIAN IMPORTS

But, very soon a revolutionary change in the mode of transport of oil took place, which made Russian oil still cheaper to the Indian customers. In those days oil was either packed in tins or in barrels to be transported by ships.[23] For various reasons, however, trade in bulk oil was more economic than the alternatives of carrying oil in barrels or tins. The weight of a barrel amounted to a fifth of its oil-content on average, which increased considerably the cost of transporting oil. Again, when stowed in the ship's hold it was found that it took up more room because of shape than was economically permissible.[24] Case oil had to face the same difficulties, although to a lesser degree.

Secondly, the long journey from America, or even from Russia, caused considerable leakage to both of these two types of packages, especially in stormy weather. The exporting companies in those days were always flooded with complaints about these difficulties from the customers.[25]

Thirdly, the price of timber was also increasing in the world as a whole, which kept on pushing upwards the cost of transport of oil products.[26]

As against these difficulties of carrying cargo in sailing ships in barrels or tins, a tank steamer could carry a larger amount of oil at lower cost. It was estimated that one tank-steamer with a capacity of 20,000 barrels and making seven trips across the Atlantic per year was considered to be equal to more than ten sailing ships each carrying 5,000 barrels and averaging 2½ trips per year, in terms of cost. It was also estimated in 1888 that a tanker could transport oil at a quarter less cost than a sailing vessel carrying barrels.[27]

However, there were two difficulties in using tankers: one was the risk of disaster, and the other was the problem of getting a return cargo. The risk of explosion was reduced over the years and the problem of return cargo, although still serious, was less acute for the Russian exporters than for the American exporters. In the absence of a return cargo, which it was difficult to get for a tanker since most traders in other products were unwilling to use oil tankers at that time, Americans were liable to make larger losses if they employed tankers because of their long distance from India.[28]

As far as the Indian market was concerned, there was scope for further economies in the transport of oil from Russia to India if the Suez Canal could be used. Since the beginning of the 1880s, a number of oil companies, including Standard and Rothschild's Russian oil company, were interested in using this short route to India.[29] But they were refused permission owing to a number of disasters to the oil-carrying ships. Even after the success of Noble and other exporters of Russian oil with oil-carrying tankers in other parts of the world, the British Government, which had a controlling share in the Suez Canal Company, was opposed to allowing oil tankers to pass through Suez for various reasons.[30] So, it was not until a British merchant, Sir Marcus Samuel, took the initiative in persuading the Governors of the Suez Canal Company, that the canal was thrown open to the oil tankers.[31]

The first oil tanker carrying Russian oil reached India in 1892. From then onwards Russian exports of kerosene went on expanding with astonishing rapidity, and, by 1897–98, became responsible for 60% of total kerosene imported to India. (See Table 2.) The share of the United States declined to only 28% in 1897–98, and, as will be seen below, declined further with the entry of other competitors, like Burma and the Far East, into the Indian market.

BURMA AND FAR EAST SOURCES

Oil was discovered in substantial amounts in the Far East (in what is today Indonesia) towards the beginning of the 1890s. At the beginning, its supply was confined to the immediate neighbourhood of Sumatra—to Malaya, Singapore, and to some extent to China. But gradually the attention of the producers of this oil was drawn to the large Indian market, with increased production from their fields. By 1897–98, this source of oil accounted for about 10% of oil consumption in India.

The most important source of oil to India from 1905 to 1942, Burma, was administratively a part of India from 1886 to 1936. At the beginning the production was mostly from hand-dug wells, and the crude was processed in a primitive way.[32] But gradually its production and recovery methods improved. The fact that the kerosene of Burma was of inferior quality did not affect its sales, so long as the price was low. "The little tin lamps without chimney are great factor in this country and in those the amount of smoke, smell, or light does not seem to cut any great figure."[33] Again, Burma being a part of India, its exports to India enjoyed a certain amount of tariff protection, besides the fact that the proximity of Burma to India meant a comparatively low transport cost for its oil. So, very soon Burma's share in the Indian kerosene trade increased from 3% and 10% in 1898–99 and 1900–01, respectively, to 36% in 1904–05, and 48% in 1905–06. (See Table 4.)

COMPETING OIL COMPANIES

At this stage it is probably necessary to produce some details about the oil companies which were then operating in the Indian market. The only exporting company, until the arrival of the Russian oil, was the Standard Oil Trust of the United States. Founded by John D. Rockefeller in the third quarter of the nineteenth century as a company specialising in refining and pipeline transporting, it very soon became fully integrated with the growth of crude oil production under its ownership. By 1904 this Trust accounted for 84% of refinery output, 86% of total exports, and 85% of domestic sales of oil in the United States. Since the United States was then the largest producer and exporter of oil in the world, the dominance by the Standard Oil Trust of the United States market also conferred on it the leading position in the world market. The New York subsidiary of the Trust specialised in exports, and was the principal supplier of oil to India. The Trust was dissolved in 1911 by a decree of the Supreme Court of the United States, and thirty-three separate legal entities were created out of the original Trust under the same decree. As a result, the New York subsidiary was constituted as a separate organisation, and, after its amalgamation with the Vacuum Oil Company in 1931, became known as Socony Vacuum or Socony Mobil. (Hereinafter referred to as "Standard".) From 1933 to 1960 Standard's marketing operations in the Eastern market were integrated with those of Standard Oil of New Jersey, to form Standard-Vacuum (or Stan-Vac). In 1960 Stan-Vac was broken up into its constituents, and the control of its Indian market was transferred to Standard Oil of New Jersey. The latter (which operates in the Eastern Hemisphere under the name "Esso") is, incidentally, the largest oil corporation of the world of today. Two other offshoots of the Standard Oil Trust are also now active in India—Standard Oil of California (which operates through Caltex, in joint-ownership with the Texas Oil Company), and Standard Oil of Indiana (which operates through its subsidiary, American International Oil Company, a part-owner of the Madras refinery). The selling organisa-tion of the "Standard" in those days was not similar to that which they have adopted since. Standard, before 1893, played no part in the internal distribution of oil in India.[34] Most of the importing concerns in India were under British ownership, such as Ralli Brothers and Anderson Wright & Co. There were a few Indian importers too, of whom Bhajulal Mahado was relatively well known. None of these importing concerns was affiliated to Standard or other-wise linked organisationally. Their association with the big American giant was only of a commercial nature. And none of the importers of kerosene was big enough to set up a wide marketing network of his own all over India, neither had any of them had big storage facilities. Worst of all, the transport system was still in a deplorable condition and railways covered a very small fraction of the whole territory. Conveyance by animal-driven carts on village roads usually resulted in leakage in containers and involved considerable losses. So, most of the oil was sold, as well as consumed, in big towns. Sometimes an oil-case passed through many hands before reaching the ultimate consumer in the village.[35] The leaders of the Russian oil industry were Rothschild, the famous Paris banker, and the Nobles of Sweden. A group of English firms, owned by H. N. Gladstone and Alfred Stuart also had come to own a significant proportion of the Russian crude before the end of the last century. Besides these three groups there were a large number of Russian producers and exporters, notable among whom was Mentascheff.[36]

One of the first exporters of Russian oil in India were Messrs. Lane and Macandrew, a British firm associated with Rothschilds.[37] But the most important of all the exporters was Marcus Samuel & Co., another associate of Rothschild, who initiated bulk trade in kerosene to India. This company was founded in 1830 as a small East End business in Japanese ornamental shells. But very soon it developed into an import-export firm of a number of goods from pins to rice.[38] It was Sir Marcus Samuel who persuaded the Governors of the Suez Canal Company to allow the oil tankers to pass through the Suez Canal and it was he who in July, 1892, launched the first steam oil tanker, "Murex", to appear in Eastern waters, which carried Russian kerosene obtained from Rothschild on the basis of a ten-year agreement, to India. Within the first year of this shipment Russian imports increased by more than 30% and superseded American imports in amount.[39]

In order to facilitate his trade in kerosene, Sir Marcus Samuel set up a number of tank installations in the main ports of India and the Far East, including Calcutta, Bombay, and Madras, in agreement with independent traders. In India the company of Sir Marcus got favourable treatment from the Government because of its British origin,[40] but in the Dutch East Indies the entry of bulk oil was prohibited in order to protect the Dutch oil producers.[41] On October 18th, 1897, Sir Marcus made over the tank installations of his agents, together with his own tankers, to a new company, The "Shell" Transport and Trading Company.[42]

A third important British businessman exporting Russian kerosene to India was H. N. Gladstone, who, as we have noted already, became a producer of Russian oil in 1897.[43] Gladstone, a younger son of the great Liberal statesman, was the director of the Peninsular and Orient Steam Navigation Company and of Armstrong Whitworth & Co.'s shipyard. He was also the head of Ogilvy Gillanders & Co., which had a subsidiary organisation in Calcutta.

Of other exporters of Russian oil, Mentascheff was important. There were also a number of Indian importers: the biggest was the Bombay Company, which purchased the case oil directly from Batum, and provided its own transport to Bombay.[44]

The leading producer of Far East oil was the Royal Dutch Petroleum Company, which was formed in 1890 to produce, refine, and market the oil of Sumatra. Very soon it was able to unite the other Dutch East Indies producers under its leadership, against the competition of American oil.[45] Since 1897, Gladstone had been responsible for marketing in India a part of the Far East oil on behalf of Royal Dutch. But, by 1898, Royal Dutch had established its own tank installations at Calcutta, Karachi, and Madras.[46] Because of the declining rate of Far East production, in 1899 it set up a new company, Eastern Oil Association, in cooperation with Gladstone, on a two year contract, for selling Russian oil to India.[47] But, very soon Royal Dutch realised the importance of cooperation with Shell, which already had a large tanker fleet and a marketing organisation in the East, and, in 1896, also became a producer of oil in the Far East.[48] So, in 1902, an agreement was concluded with Shell and Rothchilds to form a new marketing company, Asiatic Petroleum Company, which took over the marketing activities of the parent companies in the East.[49] In 1907 Royal Dutch and Shell merged together to form the Royal Dutch Shell Group.[50]

The share of Far East kerosene rose slowly to about 10% of total consumption in India in 1897–98, but then fell rapidly to about 5% in the following four years, with the decline in production of the Far East.[51] Its exports to India grew again in 1903–04, with the increase in production, and in the following year it accounted for more than 20% of total consumption. (See Table 3.)

The leading producing company of Burma, the Burmah Oil Company, a British-owned firm, was formed as far back as 1871, but it was not until the conquest of this country by the British, in 1886, that the organisation could secure sufficient concessions, and was organised on a joint stock basis. The company was reconstituted in 1902, by distributing nine shares for each original share held.[52] The other producers of oil in Burma were insignificant in size, and were tied to Burmah Oil in marketing.

The contribution of Burma to Indian oil consumption was only 2% in 1897–98, but rose to 48% in 1905–06. From 1905 to 1942, Burma was the largest supplier of oil to India, until its refineries were devastated by the Japanese during the Second World War, and then its crude production was seriously interrupted by the civil wars.

However, the rise of Burma in the Indian kerosene trade was not accomplished very easily, since its rivals, particularly Asiatic, had well-established marketing organisations in the country. Its attempt to divert a part of its surplus kerosene production to the Far East markets, it is said, was one of the main factors behind the fierce price war which broke out in the Orient in 1897, and continued up to 1905.[53]

THE PRICE WARS OF 1897–1905

Between 1886 and 1897, the competition in the Indian market was not so much between American oil, supplied by Standard, and

Russian oil, supplied by Marcus Samuel and others, as between cheap kerosene and vegetable oils used as illuminants. The entry of the Russian kerosene broke the monopoly of Standard in the Indian oil market, but did not reduce the volume of trade in kerosene of Standard appreciably, as is evident from the published figures.[54] It was only after 1899–1900 that the latter started declining and that also partly because of the declining production of oil in the U.S.A. between 1897 and 1900. So, very soon, an equilibrium was established in the market between the American and Russian exporters and the basis of understanding between them was that the former was restricted to more wealthy consumers.[55] There was no "price war" between them in the accepted sense of the term, as a temporary reduction in price by a seller (or sellers) in order to drive its competitors out of the market, or to force its competitors to come to an understanding about market-sharing arrangements which are more favourable from its point of view, which is usually followed by higher prices in the market.[56]

The price war broke out in the Orient in 1897 as a four-cornered fight between Shell, Royal Dutch, Burmah Oil, and Standard and covered India and China as well as the rest of the South-East Asian market.[57] Although the war continued up to 1905, it was punctuated by local truces between two or more rival companies. The figures for imported bulk oil prices are not available for this period and the case oil prices for different brands did not show any definite downward trend.[58] Another confusing element was that almost all the competitors, including Standard, but not Burmah oil, were trading, at least in part, in Russian oil.[59]

However, it appears from historical accounts given in contemporary journals and other literature, that the price war was fought mainly between Royal-Dutch, Shell and Burmah Oil, and after 1902, between Asiatic Petroleum Company, the marketing organisation of Royal-Dutch/Shell, and Burmah Oil, and it covered almost the entire South-East Asian market. The former was particularly anxious about Burmah's exports to Malaya, Thailand, and the Dutch East Indies, and it was admitted that the main objective of this price war, from Asiatic's point of view, was to put a stop to these exports which threatened Asiatic's Far East markets.[60]

The main advantage of Burmah Oil in this price war was its cheaper price. To give an idea of the relative prices of different brands of kerosene, in 1904–05 the prices of "Chester" (American), "Rum" (the cheapest Russian brand), and "Victoria" (Burma) were Rs.4.0.11½, Rs.3.6.11., and Rs.2.12.5, respectively.[61] In order to meet this competition from cheaper Burma-kerosene, Standard produced a cheap brand from Kansas and Texas crude and introduced it in the Indian market under the name "Monkey". Royal Dutch also introduced a cheaper variety of kerosene, which was described as a "rubbish" in the official history of the said company.[62]

THE PRICE AGREEMENT OF 1905

However, it was soon realised by Asiatic that the price war against Burmah would not fulfil its objective,[63] and in 1902 on its behalf a delegation was sent to Burma in order to negotiate a truce. The delegation failed in its task since there was no agreement about the division of the Far East market.[64]

The price war continued up to 1905, when an agreement was reached between Asiatic and Burmah to share the eastern market. The whole of the eastern market was divided into three parts—East of 90°E meridian, west of 60°E and between 90°E and 60°E—the third, covering most of the Indian market. The agreement accepted the "superior geographical claim" of Burmah oil in this third part and stipulated that the latter should be allowed to market a maximum of 100,000 cases per week (or 195,000 tons per year) of kerosene in that area while Asiatic would only supplement Burmah's supply. The figure of 195,000 tons was arrived at on the basis of the sale figure of Burmah Oil in 1905. The rest of Burmah Oil's production, it was stipulated, could only be sold to Asiatic and Burmah Oil had to give up its marketing activities outside the area between 90°E and 60°E meridian. The effect of this arrangement was to assure Burmah Oil of its kerosene being sold in the Indian market, while relieving Asiatic of the fear of Burmah's competition in the Far East.[65]

Another agreement was reached, between Asiatic and Standard, at the same time, the details of which were never made public. Probably it was a temporary agreement about the division of the Indian market and was never reduced to writing.[66]

A number of reasons can be given why these competitors ultimately stopped the price war. Burmah Oil was suffering from three difficulties. Firstly, three-quarters of its sales in India were possible in the Eastern coast of India, while Western India accounted for less than a quarter of its sales.[67] In effect, the further a consumption centre was from Burma towards the west, the less became the comparative advantage of Burmah Oil over Russian oil in terms of transport cost. Secondly, by 1905, Royal Dutch and Shell were established as powerful traders in the Eastern markets. Particularly Shell, and after 1902, Asiatic, had a well-established marketing organisation in Western India, with Bombay as its centre,[68] and they had the means to sustain a lengthy price war with Burmah. Thirdly, Burmah Oil, it was reported, was weakened after 1902 because of an imprudent financial policy which it followed. In 1902 this company watered down its capital by issuing nine shares gratis for each share held and made no allowance for depreciation. This meant that almost the entire profit had to be paid out as dividend and nothing much could be saved ·to constitute a defence fund in the event of a price war.[69]

Asiatic was also suffering from a number of difficulties. The bulk of supply for India through Asiatic came from Russia. Unfortunately for Asiatic, there was a prolonged strike in the Baku oilfields of Russia in 1904, followed in 1905 by communal riots and terrorist activities. The production of this great source of mineral oil was stopped in 1906 and the damage caused was so serious that it took a very long time before Russian exports could recover from this shock.[70] Since the other source of supply of Asiatic, the Dutch East Indies production, was not reliable at that time, Asiatic had practically no alternative but to work out an agreement with Burmah Oil.

This agreement between Asiatic and Burmah Oil marked the beginning of the long-standing alliance between these two groups in the Indian market. As will be shown later, this agreement, coupled with the system of pricing of kerosene followed by this alliance, was partly responsible for the price wars of 1909–11 and 1927–28 between Asiatic and Standard in the Indian market. Another consequence of this agreement, in addition to the agreements bringing together Rothschilds, Shell and Royal Dutch, was to divide the companies operating in India into two principal groups—Standard on the one hand and Asiatic-Burmah on the other.

The role of Standard throughout this period was passive. Up to 1904–05 it was struggling to do its best to protect as much of its former market as possible, even at the cost of making marketing losses.[71] But with the decline in Russian supplies of Asiatic, Standard

TABLE 2

PRICES OF KEROSENE PER UNIT OF 8 IMPERIAL GALLONS
Source: Indian Trade Journal

Name of the Brand	1905–06	1906–07	1908–09
Chester (U.S.)	Rs.4.2.9½	Rs.4.7.6	Rs.4.10.2
Rising Sun (Russia)	Rs.3.10.6	Rs.4.1.6	Rs.4.3.11
Anchor (Russia)	Rs.3.6.8	Not available	Not available
Victoria (Burma)	Rs.2.11.5½	Rs.3.3.6	Rs.3.8.0
Gold Mohur (Burma)	Rs.2.14.6½	Rs.3.10.1	Rs.3.13.9
Cobra (Borneo)	Rs.2.11.9	Rs.3.5.4	Rs.3.10.5

was able to win back a large part of its former empire and entered into a number of long term contracts with local dealers in kerosene in order to guarantee a definite share of the market.

The cessation of hostilities between rival marketing interests following this agreement enabled the companies to increase prices of kerosene and the extent of price increases ranged from 12% to 18%. Table 2 gives figures for prices of kerosene of different brands in 1905–06, 1906–07, and 1908–09 would give us an idea about the extent of increases in prices following the price agreement.

From 1905–1928

EXPANSION IN BULK OIL TRADE

One of the important factors contributing to the success of the parent companies of Asiatic in the Indian market was their use of the bulk oil trade. In order to meet their challenge Standard undertook a number of steps. In 1893 it commenced business in India on its own, a head office was set up at Calcutta and a storage shed was built at Budge Budge, near Calcutta. But Standard did not decide to import bulk oil immediately, since there was the uncertainty of obtaining a return cargo. In 1898 the first two tanks for bulk storage of batching oil were set up and those for kerosene were established in 1901–02.[72] In February, 1904, kerosene was sent by oil tankers to India from the U.S.A. and a number of bulk stations were set up.[73]

Burmah Oil Company also, by that time, completed all the necessary arrangements for importing oil in bulk to India and in 1908 installations for bulk kerosene were erected at Calcutta, Madras, Karachi, Marmugao, Cochin, Cocoanada, and Chittagong. In those installations factories were attached for making tin containers.[74]

Between 1909–10 and 1912–13 the percentage of kerosene oil imported in bulk ranged from 71% to 80%.[75] In the market a differential of Rs.0.2.6 per Imperial gallon was maintained between the prices of bulk oil and case oil of the same quality.[76] But despite this price advantage of bulk oil, as we have noted, case oil survived in about a quarter of the market for the following reasons.

First, some brands of case oil were very popular in the market because of their quality. In the case of bulk oil there was always a possibility of adulteration, of mixing inferior quality with superior quality, by the retailers. There was no such fear for case oil.[77]

Secondly, for a completely different kind of reason tin oil was preferred. Almost everywhere in India the empty tins satisfied a number of needs in the domestic life of the people. They could be used for carrying water, for roofing or for keeping dried fish. They could also be used for turning out a number of articles which in

Europe were then made of iron, copper or tin. The container was no less important than the content.[78]

In order to meet this preference for the container by the consumers, despite the higher price of case oil, a number of packing establishments were set up where oil could be packed in brand new tins manufactured on the spot.[79]

TRADE IN OTHER PRODUCTS: UP TO 1927–28

As is evident from Tables 1–5, until the end of the First World War, trade in products other than kerosene was of minor importance. Between 1920 and 1927 there was a 55% increase in the consumption of all products, when kerosene consumption increased by only 32·6%. The share of kerosene in total consumption of oil fell during the same period from 60·3% to 56·5%. The fall in the importance of kerosene can be explained by the rate of growth of consumption of motor spirit and fuel oil, following the granting of protection to a number of domestic industries by the Fiscal Commission, constituted according to the recommendation of the Industrial Commission of 1918. This was a period of all-round industrial activity which expanded the market for petroleum products in India.

Before 1912–13 Far East sources were the exclusive suppliers of fuel oil to India.[80] Most of it came through the Asiatic Oil Company, while a small part also came through Standard. The latter drew its supplies from "Straits" (Singapore), which was neither a producing nor a refining centre, and the country of origin of this fuel oil is not known. Within a few years, after the entry of Persian fuel oil from the Anglo Persian Oil Company to the Indian market in 1912–13, the latter became the main exporter of fuel oil to India. In 1918, for example, Persia, Borneo, and the Straits supplied 79%, 10%, and 6% of fuel oil imports (see Table 7) respectively. The dominance of Persia in the Indian fuel oil market continued uninterrupted until the Abadan crisis of 1951, accounting for about 60% to 70% of total fuel oil consumption.

The growing market for motor spirit was almost exclusively supplied by Burmah Oil or its associates and subsidiaries in India and Burma and there was virtually no import from sources other than Burma before the end of the 1920s (see Table 5). However, before very long, Standard became interested in this highly profitable and expanding market which, as will be shown later, was one of the main causes leading to the price war of 1927–28.

The rate of growth of consumption for lubricating oil was never very high in India. Up to the middle of the first decade of this century, Standard was the sole supplier of both batching oil and other lubricating oils. With the rise of Burmah Oil, that monopoly in the Indian trade was broken, and the two companies reached an agreement to divide the market equally between them. But very soon they were faced with the threat of competition from the Asiatic group. Since none of the parties was willing to risk a price war so soon after an agreement was reached between them in 1905, a new agreement was signed by the three companies concerned. According to the terms of this agreement, the first 2,200 tons of lubricating oil were to be supplied equally by Asiatic and Burmah-Standard; seven-eighths of the next 800 tons were to be supplied by Asiatic.[81]

THE KEROSENE PRICE WAR OF 1909

In the trade of the most important oil product, kerosene, Burmah occupied the leading position, accounting for about 60% of the total consumption. Standard followed with 25% and Asiatic accounted for the rest, 15%. Standard's percentage of 25% remained approximately stable up to the middle of the 1930s, whereas the share of Asiatic fell after the First World War.[82] (See Table 4.)

The comparatively smaller share of Asiatic in the kerosene market was partly compensated by the sale of a part of Burma's oil through the marketing organisation of Asiatic, under the 1905 agreement, for which a certain commission was paid to the latter.[83] But the fact remained that Standard was importing to India more kerosene than Asiatic despite the comparatively superior geographical position of the source of supply of Asiatic, to that of Standard. It was estimated in 1906 that the freight from Borneo to Calcutta was only Rs.0.2.6. per unit of 8 gallons, while the ocean freight from Batum, the centre of export of Russian oil, to Calcutta was Rs.0.10.0. per unit. Again, the f.o.b. price of Borneo oil was Rs.11.4.0. per ton, whereas only the freight of railways between Baku and Batum was Rs.20.14.0. per ton.[84] We have noted already the transport advantage of Russian oil over American oil, and it is therefore remarkable that despite this huge difference in transport cost between U.S.-India and Far East-India ocean routes, Standard could still maintain its leading position in import trade in kerosene, ignoring the supply from Burma.

However, Asiatic was evidently not satisfied with its relatively smaller contribution to the Indian import trade in kerosene, and a number of price wars were fought with Standard, on its initiative, in order to improve its position in the import trade vis-à-vis Standard. The first such price war lasted for only six weeks in March–April, 1909.[85] The immediate cause of this price war was the supposed violation of the price agreement of 1905–06 by Standard. It was reported that, under the agreement, if there was a deficit in the production of Burma, other suppliers, instead of increasing their share in the trade, were expected to raise prices along with Burmah Oil. In 1909 there was a fall in the production of Burma, which coincided with the inflow of a large amount of cheap Rumanian and Russian kerosene to the Indian market,[86] through an independent marketing company, Indo-Burma Oil Company.[87] In order to prevent the expansion of the latter, Standard reduced its prices of kerosene which also resulted in an increase in the market-share of Standard.[88] This provided an excuse for Asiatic to initiate a price war against Standard.

The contemporary reports of this price war suggest that it was fought mainly in Karachi, Standard's most important market in India.[89] Within six weeks a compromise was worked out and agreement to increase prices of kerosene by 30% was reached.[90]

THE PRICE WAR OF 1910–11

A more serious price war broke out in August, 1910, and continued up to the end of 1911.[91] Asiatic confessed that the sole objective of the price war was to prevent the expansion of Standard's trade in kerosene.[92] A contributory factor was the overproduction of oil in the world market. According to one version this price war started when Standard demanded a higher quota of the gasoline market of Germany, which Royal Dutch refused to accept. In response, Standard cancelled all quota arrangements between them both in Europe and the Far East. Royal Dutch retaliated by initiating a price war.[93] A Government journal commented at that time that, "The popular belief is that the conflict resulted from overproduction, from the appearance of new competitors, and from consequent jealousy regarding supposed or expected encroachments in the spheres of conventional rights of the respective companies."[94]

This conflict between the two international companies did not remain confined to India alone, or to the Eastern market. It was in reality a part of the world-wide struggle between them with the objective of "the forcing of their more formidable competitors to come to an agreement with them for the parcelling out of the world's markets into well-defined spheres of influence".[95]

Regarding the course of events in India towards the end of May, 1911, Asiatic and Burmah Oil reverted to earlier price levels but, as Standard did not conform, a relapse took place within a month. Again, towards the end of September, 1911, another attempt was made by the same two companies to restore prices to the level at which they stood before the price war started. But, it was reported, Standard did not respond favourably to this gesture, and the prices were again reduced. The war was virtually over by the end of 1911, although no particulars of the agreement between them at its conclusion are available.[96] Probably the agreement about their respective shares in the Indian market was a mere part of the general agreement covering the whole world. But, as is understood from the quantity figures of Standard's kerosene trade in India, this price war produced no change in the percentage share of the kerosene trade of Standard.[97]

THE KEROSENE POOL OF 1919

As we have already noted, from 1905 Asiatic and Burmah Oil were working in close cooperation with each other in the Indian market and during the price wars of 1909 and 1910–11 Burmah Oil backed Asiatic's efforts to take away a part of Standard's trade in kerosene. In 1919 they decided to formalise the arrangements, which so far governed their relationship, into a Kerosene Pool along with a few other smaller companies. There were four contributors to the Pool: Burmah Oil, Asiatic, British Burma Petroleum Company and Assam Oil Company. Attock Oil Company was associated with the Pool, although it was not a formal contributing member.[98]

British Burma Petroleum Company, owned by British capital, was a producer of oil in Burma. However, it had no separate marketing establishment in India and Burmah Oil acted as its marketing agent in India.[99]

Assam Oil Company, formed in 1899 in order to exploit the oilfields of Digboi (Assam) discovered in 1890,[100] also owned a refinery in Digboi. Its production was very small and in fact was declining until 1921, when it was taken over by the Burmah Oil Company.[101] Since then the production of Digboi increased, but until very recently its kerosene production ranged between 5% and 10% of total consumption.

Attock Oil Company (now in West Pakistan) was formed in 1913 to exploit the oilfield of Khaur in Punjab.[102] 42% of its shares were owned by the Indo-Burma Petroleum Company,[103] and, its managing agent was Messrs. Steel Brothers.[104] The company owned a refinery at Rawalpindi where the crude oil obtained from its oilfields was processed. Its production, however, was very small. Until 1947 the production of kerosene by Attock accounted for less than 2% of total kerosene consumption in India (Table 4). Attock Oil was associated with the Pool in the following way. It had a well-defined economic area in the neighbourhood of its oilfields and no contribution was made to the Pool unless the production was in excess of that needed for that economic area. Within the said economic area Attock Oil used the marketing organisation of Burmah Oil for the sale of its products.[105]

The members of the Kerosene Pool controlled more than 90% of the total production of India and Burma. The only other important oil producer in Burma, as also a marketer in India, was the Indo-Burma Petroleum Company. But the latter was also associated indirectly with the Kerosene Pool through its part-ownership of Attock Oil. During the price war of 1927–28, Indo-Burma, although not a member of the Pool, supported the members of the Pool in their fight against Standard.[106] All along this company supported the price-leadership of the Kerosene Pool.

Kerosene secured by the Pool was sold through the marketing organisations of Asiatic and Burmah Oil. The system of pricing adopted by the Kerosene Pool and also its mechanism will be discussed in Chapter Six. It is sufficient here to note that this Pool brought together almost all the oil companies operating in India under the leadership of Burmah Oil and Asiatic against Standard.

THE RISE OF PERSIAN OIL

The most spectacular event of the period following the First World War was the emergence of the Anglo-Persian Oil Company (afterwards known as the Anglo-Iranian Oil Company, and now as British Petroleum) as an important supplier of oil to the Indian market. This company was formed by the Burmah Oil Company, (in cooperation with William Knox de Arcy, who discovered oil in Persia) in order to exploit the oil resources of this oldest centre of oil production in the Middle East. With the beginning of the First World War the Government of Britain purchased the majority of shares of this company, but Burmah Oil still maintained a substantial interest in its ownership.[107]

The most important factor contributing to the growth of exports from Persia to India was its proximity to the western coast of India. Ignoring Burma, by 1918–19 Persia accounted for 40% of the total import trade in all oil products. (Table 3.) During the twenties and thirties its share fluctuated from 22% to 62%, but most of the time it was around 40%. This great importance of the Persian source of oil products to India in quantitative terms was due mainly to its supply of fuel oil. As we have noted already, the rate of growth of consumption of fuel oil increased very rapidly after the First World War; almost the entire amount of which was imported. Persia accounted for 75% of the total import of fuel oil. A contributory factor was the fact that most of the fuel oil was consumed on the western coast of India for two reasons. Firstly, on the western coast, fuel oil was used as a substitute for coal; because of an acute shortage of railway wagons for carrying coal, only a small part of the coal produced in the country, almost all of which was concentrated in the east, could be supplied to the western coast. Secondly, one of the most important

consumers of fuel oil was the cotton textile industry, the largest
Indian industry, which was located in Bombay on the western
coast.[108]

However, despite the importance of Persian oil in the import
trade of all oil products in quantitative terms, its trade in India
was not proportionately profitable since its share in the trade of
kerosene, which was much more valuable than fuel oil, was small.
At the end of the war, in 1919–20, it supplied about 7%–8% of the
total kerosene consumption, but in the following years Persian
kerosene almost disappeared from the market until 1927–28.
(Table 4.)

THE SYSTEM OF PRICING AND PERSIAN KEROSENE

The two most important factors preventing the growth of the
Persian kerosene trade in the Indian market were the system of
pricing adopted by the Kerosene Pool and the market-sharing
arrangements between the different oil companies. As will be
discussed in detail in Chapter Six, the Kerosene Pool adopted the
"world parity system" for pricing kerosene in India, which was
based on U.S. Gulf f.o.b. prices, to which were added ocean freight
and other incidental charges in order to arrive at the ex-seaport
installation prices in India. Regardless from which sources they
were actually imported, they were always priced as if they had come
from the U.S. Gulf. One consequence of this pricing system was to
allow Burmah Oil, the parent company of Anglo-Persian, enormous
economic rent over and above its opportunity cost for the entire
production. A second consequence of this pricing system was to
make Standard's U.S. kerosene competitive with oil from other
sources since the latter, under this system, could not be priced lower
than the price of U.S. kerosene.

A third consequence of this pricing system was, given the demand
curve for kerosene and no change in factors capable of causing
shifts in the demand curve, to fix the quantity of kerosene which
could be absorbed by the market. So, if the level of demand for
kerosene at the given U.S. Gulf prices was 100, and the amounts
supplied by Standard, Burmah Oil, and Asiatic were 25, 60, 15,
respectively, there was no place for Persian kerosene, given the
system of pricing and the market-sharing arrangements.

The only way in which Anglo-Persian's geographical superiority
in relation to the Indian market could be made clear was through
lower prices. But there were two difficulties in following such a
policy. First, the responsibility for the distribution of Persian oil
products was vested with Asiatic and Burmah Oil, who were allies
of Anglo-Persian. Above all, Burmah Oil was its parent company,

but a lower price in India was going to reduce the economic rent of Burmah Oil. Secondly, because of the international character of the oil companies operating in India, every outbreak of price wars in India, as we have seen before, spread very quickly to many parts of the world, thereby inflicting, within a short time, heavy financial damages on all the parties concerned .

As a consequence, Persian kerosene had to be withdrawn from the Indian market pending an agreement with the Kerosene Pool. Such an agreement took place in early 1928 between Burmah Oil, Asiatic, and Anglo-Persian,[109] following which there was a sharp rise in the supply of Persian kerosene to the Indian market. (Table 4.) This increase was at the cost of a part of Asiatic's share in the market since Standard had no obligation to satisfy Anglo-Persian.

It will be evident from the following account that the question of the market-share of Persia was one of the chief factors leading to the price war of 1927–28.

THE PRICE WAR OF 1927–28

The immediate cause of the price war, which started in 1927 between Asiatic and Standard, was the introduction of Soviet oil to the Indian market. As we have noted already, Russian exports to India suffered a setback in 1905 and, with the outbreak of the First World War, totally disappeared from the Indian market. With the establishment of the Bolshevik régime in 1917 the properties of the oil companies in Russia—a large part of which was purchased by Royal Dutch, the parent of Asiatic in 1912, from Rothschilds[110]— was taken over by the Government. In the years following 1917, negotiations took place between the Government of the U.S.S.R. and the oil companies for settling the question of compensation which in the end proved fruitless. But, while the negotiations were going on, many international oil companies, including Royal Dutch/Shell, were trading in oil with the Soviet Government, part of which was brought to India by Asiatic.[111]

In 1926, according to Royal Dutch/Shell, it became clear that the negotiation for compensation was not going to succeed. Thus Royal Dutch/Shell stopped the purchase of Soviet oil and requested others, including Standard Oil of New York, to do the same. Standard did not pay heed to that request, and, according to Royal Dutch/Shell, "by making purchases independently, without insisting on the principle of compensation, jeopardised the chances of bringing home to the Soviet Government the necessity of making compensation, and they have encouraged them to continue their course of deposing, without redress, of other people's properties."[112]

It came to be known by the middle of 1927 that Standard had

concluded an agreement with the Soviet Government, at very low prices, to purchase 150,000 tons of kerosene a year, for three years.[113] Asiatic, the subsidiary company of Royal Dutch/Shell, considered this agreement to be immoral on the grounds that the oil had been obtained from properties from which the former owners had been expropriated without receiving compensation by the U.S.S.R. Government. Accordingly, Asiatic protested against this action of Standard and threatened to initiate a price war in the event of this oil being sold to India. Standard ignored this warning and continued its programme of importing Soviet oil to India.[114]

On 21st September, 1927, two days before the kerosene from U.S.S.R. was to arrive in Bombay, Asiatic announced a price cut of one rupee per unit of 8 gallons, to be followed by a further cut of Rs.0.4.0. per unit on the following day. Standard retorted with similar price cuts and within a very short period the price war was extended to Karachi, the stronghold of Standard's trade in India. Different markets were affected in different degrees by this cut-throat competition. In Bombay, very soon prices went down to about Rs.2.8.0. per unit below the original price. In Kathiawar and Kutch the prices were the lowest, and the cut was about Rs.3.0.0. On the other hand, in places further away from the western coast (where Standard's share was relatively high), the price cuts were not so big. In Calcutta the price cut was never bigger than Rs.1.4.0., and in Burma, where there was almost no trade of Standard, there was hardly any price-cut.

The severity of these price-cuts can best be understood with reference to the pre-price-war price level. Before the price war the average price of kerosene of superior grade—(Standard did not have any trade in the inferior grade)—was Rs.5.12.0. per unit. A cut of Rs.2.8.0. per unit implied a 43·5% reduction in price, that is, the prices were almost halved in Bombay. In Kutch and Kathiawar the reductions were more than 50% and 22% respectively, of the original price.

The price war was confined only to kerosene of superior grade and did not extend to either inferior kerosene or other petroleum products, since in the case of these products members of the Kerosene Pool exercised a virtual monopoly in the Indian market. However, the price war was fought very seriously by Asiatic and this was surely the fiercest of all price wars fought in India.

Although the price war was fought between Asiatic and Standard, the former received whole-hearted support from the companies directly or indirectly associated with the Kerosene Pool. The latter released Asiatic without any delay, from the stipulation of the Pool agreement to give six months notice before the dissolution of the Pool in order to help it fight the war as quickly as possible.[115] They also joined together and made a representation to the Government of India for protection against Standard's "dumping" and "unfair business practices".[116] It is also important to note that within a few weeks from the beginning of the price war, Burmah Oil wrote to its agents and dealers in India to cooperate with their counterparts of Asiatic in respective areas and declared that both of these two companies were, "out to take every unit of oil trade from the Standard Oil Company."[117] The only trading company of any importance in India and Burma declining to support the members and associates of the Kerosene Pool, Thilawa Refineries (Burma) Ltd., had no marketing activity in India,[118] and was closed down soon after the beginning of the price war.[119]

This active support of the members of the Kerosene Pool for Asiatic against Standard was purchased by the former in two ways. First, Asiatic allowed Anglo-Persian, the daughter company of Burmah Oil, to join the Kerosene Pool as an exporter at the cost of its own market share in exchange for the support of Burmah Oil for Asiatic in the price war against Standard. Secondly, Asiatic promised members of the Pool to compensate for losses suffered by them in the price war in exchange for their support. The loss suffered by the members of the Pool was measured as half the difference in the price of kerosene between India and China. The compensation was never paid since China's price level was almost equal to the price level in India. However, this assurance given by Asiatic about compensation for the loss suffered by the members of the Pool, was not made known until May, 1928, even to the Indian Tariff Board, which was then conducting an enquiry into the desirability of giving protection to the oil industry of India and Burma.[120]

Throughout the period of the price war, which continued up to the middle of 1928, Standard played a more or less passive role of following the price-cuts made by Asiatic in different areas.[121]

BOTH SIDES OF THE "STOLEN OIL" QUESTION

Besides the moral argument about "stolen oil", Asiatic objected to these imports of Russian kerosene on the ground that the price at which this oil was purchased by Standard was very low and uneconomic and Standard was intending to sell these products at uneconomic prices in India. If Standard succeeded in fulfilling this objective, Asiatic argued, that it would mean the virtual destruction of the home industry and the establishment of the monopoly of Standard. That would mean higher prices for the consumers in the future. It was in order to prevent Standard from fulfilling this objective, Asiatic argued, that the latter initiated the price war.[122]

As against this, Standard's reply was that in this case no moral principle was involved and they sought the permission of the U.S. Government before signing this agreement with the Communist Government of the U.S.S.R. On the other hand, it argued, Royal Dutch/Shell had negotiated until 1926 with the U.S.S.R. to obtain a monopoly of the Soviet oil trade. Since these negotiations had failed, the latter had decided to stop purchases of Soviet oil. Standard was also requested to refrain from further purchases by Royal Dutch/Shell, but it saw no reason to comply with this suggestion. Furthermore, Standard argued, since Royal Dutch/Shell had a large oil production in Rumania it was in a position to be fairly independent of the supplies of Russian oil. On the other hand, without an assurance of supply on favourable terms in the South-Eastern and Asian markets, given the declining trend in oil prices all over the world, Standard would be involved in heavy losses. Above all, since the domestic supply of oil in India was far short of the total demand at ruling prices, India was bound to import at least 30% of her needs from countries other than Burma. Since she must import, it did not matter from where she imported.[123]

As regards the effect of this price war on the domestic (including Burma) oil industry, (which, it should be emphasised, was owned by the British companies) two arguments were advanced by Standard. First, Standard never contemplated ruining the domestic industry by selling Russian oil at uneconomic prices. In fact it was Asiatic which initiated the price war and Standard was merely following Asiatic with similar price cuts. Secondly, Standard was not interested in the inferior kerosene trade of the domestic producers, while Asiatic was importing kerosene of inferior grade from Borneo and California to the detriment of the domestic producers.

However, after going through all the statements and counter-statements of the different oil companies in detail, we cannot but reach the conclusion that moral principles played a very small part in this price war. Probably the most important factor behind this price war, was the understandable dissatisfaction of Asiatic with its small share of the Indian kerosene trade, despite its geographical advantage over the U.S., the source of supply of Standard until 1927. To quote Mr. Heathcote, the representative of Asiatic before the Tariff Board of India, ". . . the Standard Oil Company knows that our arrangements with the indigenous oil companies make it very difficult for us to break prices and they have been steadily increasing their gallonage for the last several years and have got a share of the import trade much larger than they have in any other eastern country vis-à-vis the Asiatic, knowing that the Asiatic will not break prices while they have arrangements with the indigenous industry."[124]

This small share of Asiatic was further reduced by the entry of

Anglo-Persian to the Indian market through the Kerosene Pool. For a number of reasons Anglo-Persian's claim to a larger share in the import trade of India could not be dismissed very easily. It was the daughter company of Burmah Oil, it was a British enterprise, and it had a "superior geographical claim" to the Indian market. Since Standard was unwilling to make room for Anglo-Persian, and since, given an inflexible pricing system other things remaining the same, the quantity demanded was also a constant, Anglo-Persian's share could only be increased at the cost of Asiatic on the basis of an agreement between them. The only way in which Asiatic's geographical superiority over Standard could be proved was by lowering the prices, but this, Asiatic was so far unable to do because of the unfavourable effect of any price-reduction on Burmah Oil's profit.

The immediate cause of the price war was undoubtedly the introduction of Soviet oil to India by Standard. The latter was paying Rs.1.3.0. per unit of 8 gallons as ocean freight for kerosene oil imported from the U.S.A., which amounted to approximately 20% of the ex-seaport installation price.[125] This greater ocean freight provided some protection for the producers of the Far East and Burma and allowed them greater economic rent over and above their opportunity costs, besides the tariff advantage enjoyed by Burma's production. The decision of Standard to import Soviet kerosene implied a saving of 5,000 miles and a roughly 50% reduction in ocean freight, thereby reducing the natural advantage and predominance of the Burmah-Asiatic combine over Standard in the Indian market.

Another important cause was the threat of Standard's competition in the motor spirit trade in which Burmah Oil and Asiatic were enjoying almost 100% monopoly. The demand for motor spirit, as we have noted earlier, was growing very rapidly and all the companies were interested in getting a big share of that expanding market. In fact, Standard was already making arrangements for beginning motor spirit trade, which it actually began in 1930. The price war was initiated also probably in order to force Standard to come to an agreement about sharing the petrol market of India.[126] At the conclusion of the price war in 1928 there was probably an agreement about the motor spirit trade between Standard and Asiatic, which restrained the former from expanding beyond a small proportion of the total market in motor spirit. Throughout the thirties the share of Standard in the motor spirit trade never exceeded 5%. (See Table 3.) Again, it was reported in a Government trade journal, that the petrol pumps were set up by Standard "by arrangement with" Burmah Shell, the marketing company established by Burmah Oil and Asiatic, in 1928.[127]

THE TARIFF BOARD ENQUIRY

On 15th December, 1927, representation was made by seven oil companies to the Government of India for the protection of the "Indian" oil industry, in view of the "uneconomic" price war then continuing in India. The existing rate of tariff protection for kerosene products of India and Burma was Rs.0.1.6. per gallon, while there was no protection for motor spirit and other oil products. These companies now requested protection, for both kerosene and motor spirit, at least up to the sum of Rs.0.2.6. per gallon, and also asked for a complete ban on "dumping" of Soviet oil at "uneconomic prices".[128]

The Government of India acted very promptly in response to this representation and referred the matter to the Indian Tariff Board. The provincial Government of Burma immediately granted temporary exemption to the oil companies producing in India and Burma from the mining rules (all of which, but for one or two very small companies, were associated, directly or indirectly, with the Kerosene Pool) and agreed to the suspension of operations in proved but unremunerative territory.[129] The provincial Government of Burma also recommended enhanced tariff protection in advance of the enquiry of the Board of Tariff which, however, was rejected by the Government of India.[130]

On receiving instructions from the Government, the Tariff Board asked the companies to submit their views before the Board. Oral evidence was taken and the proceedings were continued from 24th April to 28th April, 1928 at Rangoon, and on 9th, 17th, 18th May, 1928 at Maynyo.[131] The report of the enquiry was submitted on 23rd June, 1928. There were two reports, the majority report of Dr. J. Mathai and A. E. Mathias, and the minority report of P. P. Ginwala, the President of the Board.

Both of these reports concluded that the application for protection was premature and that no satisfactory case had been made out by the oil companies for safeguarding the Indian oil industry against competition. After examining the financial position of the companies producing oil in India and Burma, both of the reports were satisfied that the present production of oil was not likely to be affected to any serious extent by the competition of Standard. As regards the question of the motor spirit trade, both concluded that since Standard was not going to initiate the motor spirit trade within two years there was no question of the price war being extended to the motor spirit trade. Both of the reports also strongly criticised the suppression of compensation for loss in the price war promised by Asiatic to the members of the Kerosene Pool. The minority report even went as far as suggesting that, "This failure to disclose material facts might alone have justified a summary dismissal of the application (for protection) in the interest of public discipline."

There were, however, differences in emphasis between the two reports. While the majority report calculated "world parity prices", the minority report refused to accept that term and calculated "American parity prices", for the purpose of comparison with ruling prices in India—although both were based on U.S. Gulf f.o.b. prices and produced similar results. The majority report concluded that "dumping" had been established, since the actual selling price of the Pool, the biggest seller, was below the world parity prices. The minority report, on the other hand, compared "American parity prices" with the price charged by Standard, since it thought that the best test whether there was any "dumping" or not was to take the price of the biggest importer of kerosene, Standard (not considering coast-wise imports from Burma), as the basis, and found that "dumping" had not been established. But this difference was not of much significance, since the majority report also agreed that, "dumping in the ordinary sense of the term could hardly be said to be established".[132]

The minority report, however, recommended the establishment of a domestic oil refining industry in order to curtail the predominance of the "oil ring" in the market, and also to allow the consumers to obtain oil at cheaper prices. It pointed out that whereas marketing and refining all over the world was controlled by the big oil trusts, the crude market was comparatively competitive in the U.S.A., and it made an attempt to establish that the setting up of a refining industry in India was economically feasible. As an alternative it also suggested price control or the establishment of a rupee-company with the monopoly on imports from cheapest sources in the world, subject to the control of the Government.[133]

After receiving the reports of the Tariff Board, the Government of India rejected the application for protection by the domestic oil companies. As regards the question of "dumping", the note published by the Government on the enquiry commented, ". . . the only company that could be considered to have sold imported kerosene at prices below world parity was the company which was working in closest alliance with the principal producer in India, and not the company against which the application for protection was originally directed."[134]

THE END OF THE PRICE WAR OF 1927–28

By the middle of 1928 it was reported in the Press that the price war had come to an end and an agreement had been reached between

D

the contesting parties.[135] The exact terms of the agreement were never made public,[136] but, from a number of secondary sources, some of the important elements in that agreement can be guessed. Before we consider the likely provisions in that agreement it may be of interest to know why ultimately the price war came to an end and how.

From the point of view of Standard, the agreement was accepted by them probably on account of fear at the possible outcome of the Indian Tariff Board's enquiry. There were a number of reasons for Standard to be afraid of not obtaining a favourable decision from a Board of Tariff constituted by the British Government of India. Since the beginning of the present century, companies of American origin had been trying to obtain permission to explore, refine or produce oil in India and Burma which was consistently refused.[137] During the present enquiry, some companies, in their statements before the Tariff Board asking for protection, referred to the "imperial policy" of protecting British enterprises in India from foreign competition.[138] Probably Standard also had in mind the majority shareholding which the British Government held in the Anglo-Persian Oil Company. We find from the reports and minutes of the proceedings of the open sessions of the Tariff Board enquiry, that the New York office of Standard was not cooperating whole-heartedly with the Tariff Board and the chairman of the Board frequently expressed his dissatisfaction with the non-cooperative attitude of Standard. So it is not unlikely that Standard was expecting an unfavourable decision from the Tariff Board and was only too glad to come to an agreement with Burmah Oil and Asiatic before the Tariff Board report was published.

But probably a much more important factor influencing the decision of the contestants in the price war to end the fight, was the spread of the price war to many markets of the world, including the U.S.A. and the countries of Europe. To quote from a contemporary account of this price war:[139]

"Just as when two powerful nations engage in physical war, the non-combatant countries may become involved in the material loss consequent on the dislocation of the world's affairs caused by every great war, so it is in the Petroleum industry. Immediate losses and the effects of the aftermath of the struggle will be suffered by every petroleum enterprise in the world."

In this war each party tried to broaden the sphere of the conflict. Royal Dutch/Shell took steps to compete more vigorously with Standard in the United States. Standard, on the other hand, intensi-fied the advertising of Ethyl fuel in the U.K. market, so, the price war spread to all the markets where both parties were competing.

In order to maintain their respective positions, other companies were also compelled to reduce the prices for their products.[140]

After a few months of this intensive price struggle, all the parties in the dispute realised the futility of the war and also the impossibility of gaining any decisive victory. Both the major parties were financially strong enough to hold out on their own for a long period to come. It was reported in March, 1928 that a special envoy of Royal Dutch/ Shell was proceeding very shortly to New York with the object of negotiating an amicable settlement to the dispute.[141] In July, 1928 it was known that agreement had been reached.[142]

Although the details of the agreement were not known it was clear that the agreement involved a settlement about the trade in Soviet oil. One of the suggestions given earlier by Royal Dutch/Shell to Standard was to share between them and Anglo-Persian a third each of the Soviet trade. At that time the point of disagreement was about a compensation fund of 5% for the former owners of Russian oil, to be contributed by the parties to the agreement.[143] In the final agreement also, there was probably a provision about the creation of a fund to indemnify, at least partly, the former owners. However, relative shares of the different parties to this fund are not known.[144]

With respect to India, there was probably no change in the share of Standard, as is understood from Table 2. In a contemporary pamphlet on oil it was stated, ". . . the Standard acknowledged the rights of the Shell-combine and consented not only to cooperate, but also undertook to limit its disproportionate trade in India."[145] However, as will be seen in the next chapter on the conditions of the Indian market during the thirties, there was hardly any reduction in Standard's share of the kerosene trade. There was probably an agreement on the part of Standard to limit the trade in motor spirit. (See p. 35.) It was also reported that Standard, as a compensation for these concessions, sought a restriction in the production of oil from the Indian fields. But this demand was categorically refused by Burmah Oil and others.[146]

This price war, which started in India but very soon covered the whole world is considered to be of immense importance to the history of the world petroleum industry, since it paved the way for a series of international agreements among the leading oil companies. It was reported in a document prepared by the U.S. Senate on the oil industry that as a result of this price war, "the relative positions of all international companies in the principal consuming markets of the world were jeopardised. Thus the stage was set for an international live-and-let-live policy. This was the background against which the first steps towards cartel control of world markets were taken in 1928."[147] (See also Chapter Four.)

TABLE 3

TOTAL OIL CONSUMPTION IN INDIA: 1903-04 TO 1946-47

Unit: Thousand Gallons

Sources: Review of Trade of India, Records of the Geological Survey of India, Indian Trade Journal

Year	U.S.A.	U.S.S.R. Russia	Rumania	Iran Persia	Bahrein	Iraq	Total Persian Gulf	Far East	Burma	Digboi	Attock	Others	Total
1903-04	11,915	57,321	—	—	—	—	—	—	42,729	2,276	2	11,286	125,529
1904-05	11,323	40,310	—	—	—	—	—	—	42,729	2,327	1	31,999	128,689
1905-06	28,125	7,767	3,512	—	—	—	—	—	50,680	2,460	1	25,315	114,348
1906-07	35,535	2,249	15,699	—	—	—	—	—	64,841	2,608	1	21,891	130,637
1907-08	32,916	9,418	16,284	—	—	—	—	—	68,607	2,841	1	21,541	151,023
1908-09	39,974	8,188	1,229	—	—	—	—	16,310	65,475	2,919	—	16,091	165,241
1909-10	48,997	3,585	—	—	—	—	—	12,158	85,940	2,953	1	11,510	166,373
1910-11	43,011	5,842	—	—	—	—	—	10,848	96,710	2,989	1	19,944	179,345
1911-12	69,275	2,923	—	—	—	—	—	21,951	93,627	3,209	1	13,268	204,254
1912-13	41,664	2,469	4,107	—	—	—	—	20,841	106,768	3,373	1	16,180	195,403
1913-14	51,672	1,079	—	—	—	—	—	24,671	109,000	4,220	1	17,601	208,244
1914-15	55,690	583	—	—	—	—	—	25,103	106,400	4,220	1	25,404	217,401
1915-16	52,440	—	—	—	—	—	—	26,320	111,498	4,095	226	17,224	211,803
1916-17	51,857	—	—	—	—	—	—	19,205	116,598	4,713	166	17,094	209,633
1917-18	34,371	—	—	—	—	—	—	9,143	113,155	8,411	558	19,283	184,921
1918-19	23,269	—	—	23,520	—	—	23,520	7,770	128,420	9,899	676	5,888	199,442
1919-20	57,318	—	—	35,762	—	—	35,762	40,718	118,324	10,610	103	10,698	273,533
1920-21	50,074	819	—	28,441	—	—	28,441	33,783	120,966	12,022	46	12,279	258,430
1921-22	51,623	—	—	51,386	—	—	51,386	13,490	149,525	8,578	54	6,472	281,128
1922-23	52,221	—	—	50,917	—	—	50,917	16,633	126,595	8,445	6,626	13,132	274,569
1923-24	57,977	8,004	—	60,102	—	—	60,102	31,127	149,505	9,904	10,625	11,692	338,936
1924-25	71,107	5,328	—	77,743	—	—	77,743	26,157	158,404	11,678	10,245	6,942	367,604

TABLE 3 (*continued*)

Year	U.S.A.	U.S.S.R. Russia	Rumania	Iran Persia	Bahrein	Iraq	Total Persian Gulf	Far East	Burma	Digboi	Attock	Others	Total
1925–26	72,290	4,311	—	72,098	—	—	72,098	36,313	154,553	16,857	7,242	15,398	379,062
1926–27	71,202	—	—	66,648	—	—	66,648	33,266	169,886	21,688	5,607	12,451	380,748
1927–28	62,497	19,502	—	95,754	—	—	95,754	39,038	171,810	22,088	9,601	15,647	435,937
1928–29	31,418	42,803	—	113,844	—	—	113,844	36,294	157,445	28,352	11,029	17,545	438,730
1929–30	40,800	36,845	—	110,149	—	—	110,149	32,800	176,372	30,185	17,288	27,174	471,613
1930–31	48,985	47,014	—	94,179	—	—	94,179	29,380	171,344	42,130	6,896	22,930	462,858
1931–32	43,489	41,461	—	88,181	—	—	88,181	32,413	173,111	49,991	5,002	11,086	444,734
1932–33	16,719	40,894	—	72,342	—	—	72,342	29,330	180,512	44,622	5,310	28,498	423,227
1933–34	16,614	42,494	21,793	62,934	—	—	62,934	37,444	179,195	47,495	3,812	4,944	416,725
1934–35	14,553	45,157	3,952	90,630	—	—	90,630	42,169	189,944	57,379	3,160	4,799	451,743
1935–36	15,633	50,526	1,013	116,656	—	1	116,657	38,150	187,465	61,097	3,093	4,807	478,441
1936–37	15,393	43,076	1,187	122,178	—	218	122,396	45,582	199,194	58,361	3,957	6,374	495,520
1937–38	23,552	20,903	2,284	131,671	5,748	48	137,467	71,820	212,370	59,146	8,945	6,450	542,937
1938–39	12,150	3,225	1,756	157,457	22,590	1,383	181,430	51,180	183,438	59,372	19,002	5,532	517,085
1939–40	18,423	—	2,513	142,292	52,855	3,011	198,158	59,023	180,564	46,213	27,100	4,223	536,217
1940–41	21,669	—	—	144,901	49,660	2,912	197,473	52,922	177,401	59,584	27,437	1,103	537,589
1941–42	17,044	—	—	191,201	62,889	11,453	265,543	33,233	135,112	59,605	31,701	2,851	545,089
1942–43	28,454	—	—	388,473	55,014	1,360	444,847	3,952	8,193	59,901	28,061	7,197	580,605
1943–44	32,037	—	—	491,376	48,634	—	540,010	—	144	64,801	21,346	1,358	659,696
1944–45	111,829	—	—	712,374	38,263	29	750,666	—	913	74,066	13,641	119,754	1,070,869
1945–46	212,874	2,461	—	810,270	63,242	—	873,512	3,411	—	62,762	11,663	3,323	1,170,006
1946–47	22,687	—	—	556,849	38,851	—	595,700	—	—	58,390	10,687	22,526	709,990

NOTES: (1) Figures for Burma up to 1936–37 do not include fuel oil, up to 1913–14 do not include motor spirit. (2) For Russia, up to 1932–33, only kerosene import figures are available. (3) For Attock and Digboi, 10% refinery loss and fuel consumption assumed. (4) Classifications are not complete. For example, the imports from Rumania before 1933–34 are not known separately. Between 1913–14 and 1932–33 the Far East figures only include "Borneo". (5) For the pre-World War period Rumanian imports refer to kerosene only. (6) Attock became a part of Pakistan after August 15, 1947. (7) Various other adjustments have been made to make the data uniform and comparable. (8) These points also apply to Tables 2–7.

TABLE 4

KEROSENE CONSUMPTION IN INDIA: 1897–98 TO 1946-47

Unit: Thousand Gallons

Sources: Review of Trade of India, Indian Trade Journal and Records of the Geological Survey of India

Year	U.S.S.R. Russia	U.S.A.	Far East	Burma	Digboi	Rumania	Persia	Bahrein	Attock	Others	Total
1897–98	50,634	23,985	8,138	1,709	—	—	—	—	—	38	84,504
1898–99	50,800	21,006	4,767	2,308	—	—	—	—	—	52	78,933
1899–1900	57,688	12,732	—	4,966	—	—	—	—	—	8	75,436
1900–01	67,351	5,102	143	8,269	—	—	—	—	—	6	80,871
1901–02	84,478	5,768	1,023	13,463	—	—	—	—	—	198	104,930
1902–03	71,125	9,229	808	35,206	—	—	—	—	—	289	116,657
1903–04	57,320	6,722	7,539	42,729	—	—	—	—	—	14	114,324
1904–05	40,304	7,477	27,193	42,729	1,445	—	—	—	—	1,216	120,364
1905–06	7,761	22,332	15,807	47,160	1,034	—	—	—	—	5,049	99,143
1906–07	2,249	28,836	18,432	61,834	1,598	3,512	—	—	—	9	116,470
1907–08	9,377	24,278	16,073	64,556	1,482	15,699	—	—	—	4	131,469
1908–09	7,004	33,915	26,378	62,278	1,514	16,284	—	—	—	—	147,373
1909–10	3,304	41,259	18,254	81,275	1,580	1,229	—	—	—	4	146,905
1910–11	5,842	34,839	15,893	92,076	1,551	—	—	—	—	24	150,225
1911–12	1,874	62,142	15,390	87,768	2,142	—	—	—	—	7	169,323
1912–13	12,469	31,877	16,187	100,579	1,714	4,107	—	—	—	996	167,929
1913–14	1,079	42,311	23,155	109,000	2,292	—	—	—	—	2,305	180,092
1914–15	583	47,240	30,449	100,400	2,574	—	—	—	—	2,319	183,565
1915–16	—	41,831	26,354	101,900	2,288	—	—	—	—	643	173,016
1916–17	—	39,303	8,773	107,000	2,692	—	996	—	—	35	158,799
1917–18	—	22,744	14	105,000	3,244	—	860	—	—	26	139,628
1918–19	—	9,844	18	117,000	2,940	—	2,892	—	—	1	132,695

TABLE 4 (continued)

Year	U.S.S.R. Russia	U.S.A.	Far East	Burma	Digboi	Rumania	Persia	Bahrein	Attock	Others	Total
1919–20	—	45,584	33,020	105,982	2,716	—	15,531	—	—	5	202,838
1920–21	819	35,641	16,804	104,536	2,548	—	3,926	—	—	2	164,276
1921–22	—	40,186	6,311	130,911	2,080	—	—	—	—	1	179,489
1922–23	—	39,068	9,153	122,754	2,259	—	2,091	—	1,104	—	176,429
1923–24	8,004	46,515	13,753	132,264	3,196	—	—	—	1,771	683	206,186
1924–25	5,328	54,224	11,042	137,885	3,900	—	1,385	—	1,708	1	215,473
1925–26	4,311	56,249	17,849	127,045	6,298	—	809	—	1,207	364	214,132
1926–27	—	55,222	8,413	137,687	9,458	—	—	—	935	51	211,766
1927–28	19,502	47,133	16,361	126,712	9,980	—	9,440	—	1,600	1,910	232,638
1928–29	42,803	14,009	13,528	112,052	11,976	—	32,062	—	1,838	2,258	230,526
1929–30	36,845	23,376	16,843	120,571	12,624	—	28,759	—	2,881	634	242,533
1930–31	47,014	21,290	12,375	113,728	15,790	—	18,214	—	1,149	—	229,560
1931–32	41,461	20,362	4,417	120,414	23,095	—	18,552	—	834	898	230,033
1932–33	40,894	3,675	2,079	126,397	24,077	—	6,559	—	885	6,487	211,053
1933–34	38,234	2,205	5,914	122,588	23,197	9,974	292	—	635	7,443	210,482
1934–35	43,363	858	14,777	127,776	29,817	2,788	6,770	—	619	90	226,858
1935–36	46,855	331	5,365	114,728	32,861	1,013	10,805	—	448	2,054	216,460
1936–37	40,770	185	13,784	127,565	33,900	506	6,696	—	943	268	224,617
1937–38	20,093	3,190	30,890	132,880	34,940	88	11,461	3,063	1,294	171	238,880
1938–39	—	1,305	17,549	114,075	34,298	1,753	30,273	11,056	3,983	87	214,379
1939–40	—	3,921	18,365	112,068	25,598	99	25,235	33,776	3,885	—	222,907
1940–41	—	442	15,182	117,918	34,789	—	10,828	27,513	3,629	—	210,309
1941–42	—	—	4,107	87,443	34,597	—	28,082	27,170	4,339	—	185,738
1942–43	—	—	7	5,656	21,731	—	66,869	21,403	4,425	—	120,091
1943–44	—	—	—	—	16,885	—	64,520	15,764	2,951	—	100,120
1944–45	—	—	—	29	16,449	—	84,200	11,419	1,494	575	114,166
1945–46	—	—	—	—	10,497	—	104,877	18,764	612	—	134,750
1946–47	—	—	—	—	13,984	—	131,945	13,863	502	—	160,294

THE PETROLEUM INDUSTRY IN INDIA

TABLE 5

Motor Spirit Consumption in India: 1914–15 to 1946–47

Unit: Thousand Gallons

Sources: Review of Trade of India, Records of the Geological Survey of India

Year	Burma	Other Imports	Digboi	Attock	Total
1914–15	4,000	52	218	—	4,270
1915–16	4,000	50	240	50	4,340
1916–17	6,631	15	367	37	7,050
1917–18	5,188	366	462	124	6,140
1918–19	8,453	52	449	150	9,104
1919–20	10,099	16	415	23	10,553
1920–21	14,639	2	471	10	15,122
1921–22	16,426	1	521	12	16,960
1922–23	16,085	1	662	1,472	18,220
1923–24	14,604	3	1,101	2,361	18,069
1924–25	17,672	4	1,505	2,277	21,458
1925–26	24,846	6	1,750	1,609	28,211
1926–27	29,516	4	2,933	1,246	32,453
1927–28	41,636	138	3,330	2,134	47,238
1928–29	41,770	168	5,186	2,451	49,575
1929–30	52,108	4,655	7,232	3,842	67,837
1930–31	51,101	8,836	9,088	1,533	70,558
1931–32	45,356	12,742	12,319	1,112	71,529
1932–33	46,650	5,117	12,927	1,180	65,874
1933–34	48,082	1,606	12,995	847	63,530
1934–35	55,389	1,483	15,981	702	73,555
1935–36	65,473	2,078	16,631	687	84,869
1936–37	66,124	9,747	14,987	879	91,737
1937–38	63,395	38,661	13,341	1,989	115,396
1938–39	40,060	44,088	14,105	4,223	102,476
1939–40	47,783	26,097	10,902	6,022	90,804
1940–41	34,790	34,303	12,338	11,928	93,359
1941–42	25,947	45,231	12,740	12,717	96,635
1942–43	989	116,227	14,394	11,283	142,893
1943–44	—	211,491	22,803	7,109	241,403
1944–45	—	528,158	26,421	3,845	558,424
1945–46	—	491,888	22,938	2,374	517,200
1946–47	—	156,330	21,044	2,165	179,539

TABLE 6

LUBRICATING OIL CONSUMPTION IN INDIA: 1905–06 TO 1946–47

Unit: Thousand Gallons

Sources: Review of Trade of India, Records of the Geological Survey of India

Year	Burma	Other Imports	Digboi	Attock	Total
1905–06	3,520	8,653	49	—	12,222
1906–07	3,007	9,535	261	—	15,143
1907–08	4,051	14,587	285	—	18,923
1908–09	3,196	10,001	407	—	13,603
1909–10	4,665	11,491	427	—	16,583
1910–11	4,634	13,653	331	—	18,618
1911–12	5,859	12,257	318	—	18,434
1912–13	6,189	15,257	346	—	21,792
1913–14	2,060	14,953	331	—	17,284
1914–15	2,967	14,356	435	—	17,758
1915–16	2,967	15,983	533	75	19,556
1916–17	2,967	18,638	626	55	22,331
1917–18	2,967	15,375	469	186	18,997
1918–19	2,967	19,077	747	225	23,015
1919–20	2,243	14,688	428	34	17,393
1920–21	1,791	18,560	459	15	20,825
1921–22	2,188	16,899	384	18	19,651
1922–23	1,941	18,060	382	2,209	22,642
1923–24	2,637	16,147	408	3,542	22,734
1924–25	2,847	20,705	429	3,415	27,396
1925–26	2,662	21,363	353	2,419	26,797
1926–27	2,683	24,721	377	1,869	29,650
1927–28	3,462	26,293	420	3,200	33,375
1928–29	3,623	27,323	342	3,676	34,964
1929–30	3,693	26,700	290	5,763	36,446
1930–31	6,515	25,681	347	2,299	34,842
1931–32	7,341	16,047	172	1,667	25,167
1932–33	7,405	17,274	179	1,770	26,627
1933–34	8,525	18,166	186	1,271	28,148
1934–35	6,779	19,248	171	1,124	27,322
1935–36	7,264	19,342	181	1,044	27,832
1936–37	5,505	19,222	—	985	25,712
1937–38	—	39,970	—	2,064	42,034
1938–39	—	32,761	—	1,881	34,642
1939–40	—	35,191	512	1,627	37,329
1940–41	—	42,840	182	1,775	47,797
1941–42	—	38,423	2,138	2,296	42,907
1942–43	—	27,776	4,167	2,787	34,731
1943–44	—	21,806	5,838	3,458	31,103
1944–45	—	23,704	3,596	2,906	30,205
1945–46	—	32,661	5,235	2,143	35,327
1946–47	—	34,903	337	986	36,226

TABLE 7

Fuel Oil Consumption in India: 1905-06 to 1946-47

Unit: Thousand Gallons

Sources: Records of Geological Survey of India, Review of Trade of India

Year	Bahrein	Persia	Iraq	U.S.S.R.	U.S.A.	Far East	Rumania	Burma	Digboi	Attock	Others	Total
1905-06	—	—	—	—	—	1,301	—	—	874	—	28	2,203
1906-07	—	—	—	—	—	281	—	—	819	—	72	1,172
1907-08	—	—	—	—	—	1,250	—	—	1,030	—	—	2,280
1908-09	—	—	—	—	—	2,863	—	—	922	—	52	3,837
1909-10	—	—	—	—	—	1,481	—	—	137	—	—	1,168
1910-11	—	—	—	—	—	7,006	—	—	152	—	96	7,254
1911-12	—	17	—	—	—	12,168	—	—	278	—	1,049	13,495
1912-13	—	—	—	—	—	11,068	—	—	192	—	—	11,277
1913-14	—	3,292	—	—	—	3,635	—	—	248	—	839	8,014
1914-15	—	7,655	—	—	—	1,010	—	—	402	—	1,163	10,230
1915-16	—	5,746	—	—	—	4,703	—	—	344	50	634	11,477
1916-17	—	4,372	—	—	—	11,352	—	—	363	37	3,946	20,070
1917-18	—	6,592	—	—	—	6,752	—	—	549	124	1,964	15,981
1918-19	—	20,628	—	—	—	2,930	—	—	466	150	4,040	28,214
1919-20	—	20,231	—	—	—	10,982	—	—	348	22	2,922	34,505
1920-21	—	23,111	—	—	—	17,022	—	—	361	10	6,626	47,130
1921-22	—	51,386	—	—	—	5,132	—	—	306	12	1,654	58,490
1922-23	—	50,917	—	—	—	10,197	—	—	294	15	1,433	62,856
1923-24	—	60,102	—	—	—	20,293	—	—	337	2,370	65	83,167
1924-25	—	77,670	—	—	—	12,370	—	—	396	2,277	134	92,847
1925-26	—	72,097	—	—	—	21,458	—	—	1,227	1,609	50	96,441
1926-27	—	67,576	—	—	—	22,827	—	—	2,117	1,246	179	93,945
1927-28	—	86,180	—	—	—	17,888	—	—	1,679	2,133	2,660	110,540

TABLE 7 (*continued*)

Year	Bahrein	Persia	Iraq	U.S.S.R.	U.S.A.	Far East	Rumania	Burma	Digboi	Attock	Others	Total
1928–29	—	81,616	—	—	—	22,074	—	—	3,975	2,451	5	110,121
1929–30	—	81,267	—	—	—	28,437	—	—	2,980	3,842	107	116,633
1930–31	—	75,681	—	—	—	29,306	—	—	4,493	1,532	1,362	112,374
1931–32	—	69,238	—	—	—	26,471	—	—	3,445	1,112	5,119	105,385
1932–33	—	65,567	—	—	—	26,003	—	—	2,308	1,180	12,958	108,016
1933–34	—	62,340	—	2,958	294	29,660	8,543	—	5,647	847	81	110,370
1934–35	—	83,428	—	912	308	25,205	1,164	—	6,892	886	246	119,041
1935–36	—	104,463	—	2,117	3	31,710	—	—	7,857	845	235	147,230
1936–37	—	107,129	218	2,306	13	30,059	—	—	8,122	1,063	3	148,914
1937–38	886	95,551	46	—	458	29,468	—	1,632	8,387	1,824	6	138,258
1938–39	1,580	101,237	1,383	845	—	22,888	—	2,949	7,770	8,154	1,107	147,914
1939–40	6,715	105,991	3,011	—	—	25,881	—	2,607	5,785	6,007	2,243	158,240
1940–41	8,242	122,481	2,765	—	—	22,812	—	2,022	7,069	6,435	863	172,689
1941–42	12,846	139,847	3,751	—	250	24,590	—	1,333	7,529	6,547	3,768	200,461
1942–43	13,034	223,747	1,360	—	110	2,841	—	7	12,458	6,193	1,523	261,273
1943–44	2,904	235,916	—	—	—	—	—	118	14,284	2,659	96	255,977
1944–45	1,455	263,860	25	—	162	—	—	7	24,243	2,430	6,656	298,837
1945–46	5,353	403,388	—	2,461	—	—	—	—	21,679	1,236	114	434,231
1946–47	8,188	338,526	—	—	—	—	—	—	19,070	1,269	46	367,099

NOTES

1. Watt (1), pp. 156–180.
2. Gerretson, vol. II, p. 103.
3. Torray and others, pp. 83–99.
4. U.S. (1), 1880, p. 73.
5. The jute industry requires the greasing of fibres with oil. Since Batching oil was much cheaper than jute, and the latter was sold by weight, the jute manufacturers intended that a percentage of oil must still be present in the finished product at the end of the manufacturing process (see Gerretson, vol. 3, p. 214). Between 1913 and 1941, the volume of trade in Batching oil was approximately equal to half the total consumption of lubricating oil (see R.T.I., 1913–41).
6. Watt (2), p. 811.
7. *The Stanvac Story* p. 7.
8. Gerretson, vol. 1, p. 214.
9. Gerretson, vol. II, p. 104.
10. Watt (1), pp. 177–180.
11. Gerretson, vol. III, p. 215.
12. Hidy and Hidy, p. 259.
13. Indian Tariff Board (1), pp. 17–18.
14. Hidy and Hidy, pp. 132–133.
15. Gerretson, vol. II, p. 107.
16. Gerretson, vol. II, p. 105 and Hidy and Hidy, p. 135.
17. Watt (1), pp. 177–180 and Gerretson, vol. I, p. 215.
18. The Government concerns, such as railways and defence establishments, only used American oil up to 1906. See, I.T.J., November 29, 1906, p. 339.
19. Hidy and Hidy, p. 134.
20. Total consumption of oil between 1885–86 and 1889–90 ranged from 20 to 25 million gallons when the population was about 150 million. See Watt (1), pp. 177–180.
21. Watt (2), p. 812.
22. *Ibid.*
23. Cargoes of American kerosene were packed in two five-American gallon tins to the case and were transported by sailing ships to Calcutta, from New York or Philadelphia (*The Stanvac Story*). For a number of reasons cases were preferred to barrels. The transport system in India was very bad in those days and since cans leaked less than barrels, they could be sent more easily to the far interior villages over rough roads. Furthermore, India being a hot country, tin containers withstood heat better than glued barrels. (See Hidy and Hidy, p. 124.)
24. Gerretson, vol. 1, p. 208.
25. *Stanvac Story*, p. 6.
26. Gerretson, vol. 1. p. 208.
27. Hidy and Hidy, p. 146.
28. The success of Sir Marcus Samuel, the founder of "Shell", in the Indian market, as will be discussed below, was partly due to the fact that he, being an established trader in many articles in the Eastern market, could always find enough valuable goods for carrying in his vessels in their return journey from India. See *The Petroleum Review and Mining Laws*, 29.9.1906, p. 128 and also Henrigues.
29. Gerretson, vol. II, pp. 214–217, and Henrigues, p. 79.
30. There were various reasons for the British Government's opposition, besides the fear of accident. Most of the tin plates used for packing both American and Russian kerosene was manufactured in South Wales, and a large part of the business of oil transport from Philadelphia was also in the hands of the British merchants. So, the use of the canal by tankers was opposed to the interests

of an important section of British businessmen. (See Gerretson, vol. I, pp. 215–6). Henrigues insists that the main reason behind the refusal was that the tankers were defective. (See Henrigues, pp. 91–92.)

31. Henrigues, pp. 85–86.
32. Gerretson, vol. III, p. 211.
33. Hidy and Hidy, p. 548.
34. *The Stanvac Story*, p. 8.
35. U.S. (3), p. xv, and De Chezeau and Kahn, p. 89.
36. A detailed discussion on the early history of the Russian oil industry can be found in Gerretson.
37. Gerretson, vol. II, pp. 103–104. Lane was instrumental in bringing about the alliance of Shell and Royal Dutch in 1902. (See Gerretson, vol. II, p. 191.)
38. For a lucid account of the development of this company from a modest beginning, see Henrigues.
39. Hidy and Hidy, p. 259 and Henrigues, pp. 82 and 95–96.
40. Gerretson, vol. I, pp. 222–226. However, Sir Marcus Samuel's "Tank Syndicate" was refused permission to set up tank installations in Burma in order to give protection to another British company, Burmah Oil. (Gerretson, vol. I, p. 230.)
41. *Ibid*, vol. I, p. 224.
42. *Ibid*, vol. II, p. 99.
43. *Ibid*, vol. II, pp. 98–99; vol. III, p. 230.
44. Gerretson, vol. III, pp. 135–36.
45. For a detailed account of the history of Royal Dutch, see Gerretson.
46. Gerretson, vol. I, p. 286.
47. Gerretson, vol. II, pp. 117, 149, 183.
48. Gerretson, vol. II, pp. 183–201.
49. Gerretson, vol. II, pp. 238, 245.
50. Gerretson, vol. II, p. 348.
51. See Torray, Moore and Saber.
52. Money, p. 3.
53. Henrigues, pp. 323–24, and pp. 361–62.
54. Between 1885–86 and 1888–89 Russian exports rose from nothing to 18 million gallons, but American exports in those four years were 20, 29, 25, and 21 million gallons respectively. See Watt (1) and also Table 2.
55. Gerretson, vol. I, p. 37.
56. Cassady (2), pp. 49–62.
57. Hidy and Hidy, p. 267.
58. I.T.J., 5.7.1906, p. 482. For three years beinning in 1896–97 there was a definite downward trend in prices for all brands of kerosene but from 1899–1900 to 1905–06 prices fluctuated within a certain range.
59. Hidy and Hidy, p. 267.
60. Gerretson, vol. III, p. 211.
61. I.T.J., 5.7.1906, p. 482.
62. Gerretson, vol. III, p. 211. "Deterding outdid it with an even more rubbish product." (Deterding was the chief of Royal Dutch during most of its formative years.)
63. Gerretson, vol. I, pp. 229–231.
64. Standard also supported this move of Royal Dutch. See Henrigues, pp. 453–454 and Gerretson, vol. III, pp. 211–212.
65. Gerretson, vol. III, pp. 168–169, 211–212.
66. Hidy and Hidy, p. 553.
67. Gerretson, vol. III, p. 212.
68. *Ibid*, vol. I, pp. 229–231.

69. *Ibid*, vol. II, pp. 340–342.
70. I.T.J., 5.7.1906, p. 482.
71. Hidy and Hidy, p. 549.
72. *The Stanvac Story*, p. 8.
73. Hidy and Hidy, p. 552.
74. *Commerce*, 3.12.1927, p. 1089.
75. I.T.J., 1909–10 to 1912–13.
76. I.T.J., 1927.
77. Gerretson, vol. I, p. 224.
78. Hidy and Hidy, p. 261.
79. Gerretson, vol. I, p. 224.
80. Because of the waxy nature of the crude of Burma it produced very little fuel oil. Again, as will be shown later, a large part of the fuel oil component was sold as "inferior kerosene".
81. Gerretson, vol. III, pp. 214–215.
82. Asiatic's source of kerosene was the Far East. U.S. imports were sold through Standard and, after 1927, also the exports from U.S.S.R. Of course, a part of kerosene for Asiatic also came from Russia, as also a part of Standard's supply came from the Far East, but the amount involved in both cases seems to be small. As we will see later, more than 90% of Burma's exports were marketed by Burmah Oil.
83. Asiatic received 3½% commission for the sale of the products of Burmah Oil. See Indian Tariff Board (2), pp. 125–126.
84. *The Petroleum Review and Mining Laws*, 17.2.1906, p. 122.
85. I.T.J., 25.5.1911.
86. Gerretson, vol. III, p. 299.
87. Indo-Burma Petroleum Company was formed in February 8, 1909 as the successor to a marketing concern owned by Messrs. Jamal Brothers & Co. The ordinary share capital was held by Messrs. Steel Brothers and Messrs. Jamal Brothers. The latter disposed of their shares in 1921. The company was managed by Messrs. Steel Brothers, who were also managing agents of Attock Oil Company, which produced and refined oil in the Punjab. Indo-Burma opened oilfields in Burma and had marketing and refining interests in India and Burma. See, Indian Tariff Board (1), p. 8; Indian Tariff Board (3) pp. 12–15.
88. Gerretson, vol. III, p. 299.
89. I.T.J., 8.4.1909, p. 28.
90. I.T.J., 13.5.1909, p. 153.
91. I.T.J., 23.5.1912, p. 275; 26.6.1913, p. 558.
92. Indian Tariff Board (1), p. 6.
93. Henrigues, p. 517.
94. I.T.J., 25.5.1911, p. 238.
95. *Manchester Guardian*, November 19, 1910, and also I.T.J., 15.12.1910.
96. I.T.J., 23.5.1912, p. 275.
97. Indian Tariff Board (1), Appendix 1.
98. *Ibid*, (1), pp.–12.
99. *Ibid*, p. 5.
100. Metre (1).
101. Indian Tariff Board (1), chapter 1.
102. Indian Tariff Board (3), p. 21.
103. *Ibid*, p. 12.
104. See note 87.
105. Indian Tariff Board (1), p. 12.
106. Indian Tariff Board (3), pp. 9–11.
107. See Longhurst for a detailed history of this company.

108. Jather and Beri, p. 20.

109. See *Annual Report of the Anglo-Persian Oil Company*, 1928.

110. Gerretson, vol. IV, pp. 136–137.

111. Indian Tariff Board (3), p. 81.

112. *Ibid.* Statement of the Royal Dutch/Shell Co. of 19.1.1928.

113. *Ibid*, p. 7.

114. Also for the following account of the price war, see Indian Tariff Board (1), Chapter II.

115. Burmah Oil's reply to the Tariff Board's decision against protection, in P.T., 6.10.1928, p. 593.

116. Indian Tariff Board (3), p. 7. The companies who made the joint representation were: Burmah Oil, Assam Oil, British Burma, Rangoon Oil, Attock Oil, Indo-Burma, Hessford Development Syndicate. Rangoon Oil was a subsidiary of British Burma, Hessford a subsidiary of Indo-Burma, and Assam Oil was the subsidiary of Burmah Oil. Burmah Oil was the marketer of the products of British Burma and Attock in India, while the last-named company was partly owned (42%) by Indo-Burma. This shows the interrelationship between the companies signing the representation. See also Indian Tariff Board (1), Chapter I.

117. Indian Tariff Board (3), p. 83.

118. *Ibid*, pp. 217–222 (statement by Thilawa Refineries).

119. Indian Tariff Board (1), Chapter I.

120. P.T., 6.10.1928, p. 593 and Indian Tariff Board (1), Ch. II.

121. Indian Tariff Board (1), Chapter I.

122. Indian Tariff Board (3), pp. 7–8.

123. Indian Tariff Board (3), pp. 81–90.

124. Indian Tariff Board (2), p. 167.

125. When the price was Rs.5.12.0. per unit of 8 gallons of kerosene, the ocean freight from the U.S.S.R. was Rs.0.11.0. "The representative of the Asiatic Petroleum Company has admitted that even though the Standard Oil Company were to import oil not from Russia but from Africa, Arabia or any country situated nearer to India than America, a price war would have been commenced by the Royal Dutch/Shell Group." (Indian Tariff Board (1), Chapter II.)

126. The joint representation of the seven oil companies to the Government also emphasised the possibility of Standard's competition in the petrol trade. (See Indian Tariff Board (3), pp. 1–7.) The report of the Indian Tariff Board on this issue concluded, "The Indian market for petroleum is rapidly increasing, especially for petrol . . . How this increase is to be allocated hereafter between the Standard Oil Company, which has mainly held the field in the import trade in India, and the Royal Dutch/Shell Group and the Anglo-Persian Oil Company with nearer sources of supply, seems to be the underlying motive of the price war." (See Indian Tariff Board (1), Chapter II.)

127. Review of Trade of India, 1929–30, p. 50.

128. Indian Tariff Board (1).

129. Indian Tariff Board (3), representation of the Burmah Oil Company, dated 14.4.1928.

130. *Ibid*, pp. 25–29.

131. Indian Tariff Board (1).

132. Indian Tariff Board (1), p. 22.

133. Indian Tariff Board (1), pp. 88–93.

134. I.T.J., 20.9.1928, p. 589.

135. P.T., 7.7.1928, p. 4.

136. U.S. (2), p. 198.

137. *Ibid*, p. 41.

138. For example the letter of Attock Oil Company to the Tariff Board dated 15.12.1927. See Indian Tariff Board (3).

139. P.T., 3.3.1928, p. 400.

140. U.S. (2), p. 198.

141. P.T., 3.3.1928, p. 400.

142. *Ibid*, 7.7.1928, p. 4.

143. Indian Tariff Board (2), pp. 93 and 133.

144. P.T., 11.8.1928, p. 245.

145. Money, p. 9.

146. P.T., 11.8.1928, p. 245.

147. U.S. (2), p. 199. See also Chapter Six.

CHAPTER 3

HISTORICAL DEVELOPMENTS BETWEEN 1928 AND 1968

The Uneasy Thirties and the War Period

BURMAH-SHELL AND STANDARD-VACUUM: ORGANISATIONAL CHANGES

The price war of 1927–28 showed that the existing organisation of the Kerosene Pool was not suitable for the alliance of Burmah Oil and Asiatic Petroleum, the marketing organisation of Royal Dutch. One of the difficulties was that the products of the Pool were sold through the separate marketing organisations of Burmah Oil and Asiatic. Apart from the fact that the existence of two parallel organisations involved duplication and unnecessary costs, they also contained seeds of disunity which could grow very rapidly in a world of over-production and low prices. So, very soon, two very far-reaching organisational decisions were taken by these two companies.

The first step was to form in 1928 a unified selling organisation, "Burmah-Shell Oil Storage and Distributing Company" (known as "Burmah-Shell"), jointly owned by Asiatic and Burmah Oil, to take over the selling activities of its parents.[1] It was similar to the Kerosene Pool in working principles but differed from the latter in that Burmah-Shell was selling all the major products including kerosene. Burmah Oil, however, maintained its own selling organisation in Burma, Assam, and Chittagong. In 1940 the selling organisations of Burmah Oil in the last two regions were brought under a new company, "Burmah-Oil Company (India Trading) Ltd."[2] The last company (hereinafter referred to as B.O.C.(I.T.)) still distributes oil in Assam where there is no selling organisation of Burmah-Shell. The other parent of Burmah-Shell, the Asiatic Petroleum Company, was subsequently renamed the "Shell Petroleum Company" and but for its link with Burmah-Shell, disappeared from the Indian market.

The second step was taken during the middle of 1928 when Burmah Oil purchased a large number of shares in the "Shell Transport and Trading Company", one of the two companies constituting the "Royal Dutch Shell Group".[3] The object of this partial financial merger was to cement the friendship between them and to remove any scope from mutual suspicion or misunderstanding.

E

Similar organisational changes also took place in the American camp. In July, 1931, Standard of New York and Vaccuum Oil Company, Inc., were merged to form Socony Vaccuum Oil Company.[4] Although this was an agreement covering the whole world, it had a number of favourable consequences for both oil companies in India. Vaccuum Oil entered the Indian market in 1890, but chose to specialise only in its high grade "Mobil" motor oil trade. But from the late 1920s it faced severe competition from "Shell Motor Oil" which was all the more serious because Vaccuum did not have a wide marketing network of its own in India.[5] The beneficial effect of the merger with Standard of New York was to provide "Mobil" with a big selling organisation. Standard also gained from the addition of a very popular item to its list of products.

Another important change came with the merger in the East of the selling organisations of Socony Vaccuum and Standard Oil Company of New Jersey, the largest corporate business entity in the world, under the name of "Standard-Vaccuum" (hereinafter referred to as "Stan-Vac").[6] Its effect on the Indian market was negligible, except for the change of name, since before this merger in 1933 Jersey had no trading activity in India. This combine continued up to 1960, when Stan-Vac was broken up into its constituents and New Jersey took over the control of the Indian market under the name of "Esso".

THE UNEASY RELATIONSHIP BETWEEN BURMAH-SHELL AND STANDARD

During the thirties Burmah-Shell continued, as successor to its parent companies, to be the chief trader and, even excluding imports from Burma, was responsible for more than half the total amount of all oil products imported. The proportion of all oil products imported by Standard, from the U.S.S.R. and U.S.A., was not higher than 32% of the total trade (excluding Burma's coast-wise exports) and even this smaller share was declining from 1933–34. (See Table 3.)

However, despite this much higher proportionate share of Burmah-Shell in the Indian oil trade, constant compaints appear in Burmah-Oil's annual reports during the thirties about "competitors". These complaints were partly the outcome of the declining demand for oil products in the market because of the economic depression of the 1930s which, whatever their relative proportions, affected the absolute trade activities of all the companies. But more important than this was the fact that Standard was supplying a higher percentage of imports in terms of value, excluding Burma. As an example, while in 1932–33 Standard was responsible for only 24% of the import trade, quantitatively, it received more than 67·3% of the total value of imports.[7] This discrepancy between value and quantity percentage figures can be explained by the fact that Standard was mainly importing more valuable products like kerosene, lubricating oil or motor spirit, while, excluding Burma, the chief import item of Burmah-Shell was fuel oil, which was cheap. (See Table 10.)

To consider kerosene first: Standard's supply amounted to about 24·6% in 1928–29, and 24·8% in 1929–30. These figures were slightly less than the 25% share of Standard in the kerosene trade before 1927–28 (see Table 9).[8] However, since more than 70% of this kerosene came from the U.S.S.R., Burmah Oil was still suspicious of Standard's motives and was in constant fear of a price war initiated by Standard on the basis of cheap Russian supplies. There were rumours of such a price war in the business world. However, it could hardly be believed that the lessons of the 1927–28 price war were forgotten so soon.[9] Standard was obliged to pay full respect to the world parity price system and also not to exceed its one-quarter share of the market for at least two years.

In 1930–31 and 1931–32 Standard made attempts to expand its share in the kerosene trade, probably forced by the conditions of over-production in the United States, and its share in those two years became 29·8% and 26·9%, respectively. The result was that given the world parity price for kerosene and the declining schedule of demand for kerosene (the consumption index dropped from 135 in 1929–30 to 117 in 1933–34, with 1913–14 = 100; see Table 4), plus the priority given to Burma's production in India within the framework of Burmah-Shell, the share of Persia and the Far East was reduced, to the utter discomfort of the Burmah Oil–Anglo Persian–Royal Dutch/Shell alliance. The chairman of Burmah Oil expressed his bitterness in the following words, "Our arrangements with our friends the Anglo Persian Oil Company and the Royal Dutch Shell Group have until recently provided us with the necessary breathing space, as their imports have gradually dropped out to yield to the indigenous production (i.e. productions of Burma and India) the outlet in India it has required . . . that margin has now, however, been exhausted, and . . . the time has arrived when we must require other importers of foreign oils to hold back to the extent necessary for India's indigenous production to find its market in India itself."[10]

Understanding that this warning was not enough, Burmah Oil sent one of its leading men to the United States to hold discussions with other exporting interests, particularly Standard Oil of New York (Socony). This conference enabled Burmah Oil's representative, Mr. Watson, "to harmonise relations in the Indian market with our only important American competitors and to secure their cooperation in the principle of indigenous prodction's first call on the indigenous outlet,"[11] in the words of the chairman of Burmah Oil.

That the understanding was achieved with Stan-Vac is proved partly by a drop in the latter's share of the market in kerosene to 21·12% in 1932–33. However, there were also other factors operating to reduce the share of Stan-Vac in the Indian trade. One was the control imposed by the Government of the United States on crude production to stop over-production, which very sharply reduced Stan-Vac's imports direct from the U.S.A. The other reason was the complete stoppage of imports from the U.S.S.R. after 1938–39, because of wartime needs for kerosene in the U.S.S.R. So, the share of Stan-Vac in the kerosene trade gradually declined to 10% in 1937–38 and then below 1% for the period until the end of the Second World War. (See Table 9.)

As regards motor spirit, Standard entered the petrol trade of India in 1930 and, by arrangement with Burmah Shell, established a number of petrol pumps all over India.[12] But Standard's (or, its successor in India, Stan-Vac's) share in the motor spirit trade was never above 4%; the rest being supplied by Burmah-Shell from Burma, Assam and Attock, and a marginal amount from Persia. (See Table 5.) Even this small share of Stan-Vac could not be maintained after 1936–37, when its Russian supply was stopped.[13]

It was, however, in the lubricating oil trade that Stan-Vac had its highest proportion of the total Indian trade, amounting to about half the total.[14] This trade of Stan-Vac was based on supplies direct from the U.S.A. Burmah-Shell, on the other hand, supplied most of the lubricating oil from Burma and the U.K., the latter enjoying a tariff advantage over other exporting countries because of Imperial preference.[15]

The fuel oil trade was virtually a monopoly of Burmah-Shell which imported about 70% of its supply from Persia and the rest from the Far East, ignoring a small amount from Burma. (See Table 7.)

Within the framework of Burmah-Shell, we notice a gradual increase in the supply from Persia of almost all oil products and a consequent reduction in supply from the Far East. Between 1927–28 and 1939–40, excluding trade in Burma and Indian oil, the Far East accounted for 17% of the total trade in oil products, while Persia contributed about 46%. (See Table 4.)

EMERGENCE OF CALTEX

The most important incident during the thirties, from the point of view of inter-company relationships, was the emergence of Caltex as a major supplier of oil to India. This company, a jointly-owned subsidiary of two major American companies, Standard Oil Company of California[16] and Texas Oil Company,[17] owned the oilfields of Bahrein, a small but important oil producing island on the Persian

Gulf. Oil was discovered at Bahrein in the early thirties, but the oilfields were not properly developed until 1936–37.

With the growth of the production of Bahrein, Caltex decided to set up its own marketing organisation in India, although in the earlier part of its life it sold the oil of Bahrein to India through Stan-Vac. "As Bahrein is the nearest point of supply to western India, it was natural and normal," stated the chairman of Caltex, "that we should establish distributing facilities for the full line of our products in that market. . . ."[18] In 1937–38, Caltex's share of the Indian market, excluding the trade with Burma, was 2·2%, but in the following two years it rose to 8·8% and 18·7%, respectively. In 1939–40, Caltex supplied 41% of the kerosene trade and 34% of the motor spirit trade, ignoring the trade of Burma with India. (Tables 4 and 5.)

This rapid rise of Caltex to a major producer within three years, could, under normal circumstances, provoke a price war with the existing marketing interests. In fact the chairman of Burmah Oil in the Annual Report of 1936, gave a warning to the producer of Bahrein oil, "All that I wish to emphasise today is that you cannot put more than a pint into a pint without overflow."[19] But everthing was settled very soon without any price war and Caltex was accommodated into the Indian market structure.

One important reason behind this restraint shown by Burmah-Shell despite the entry of a rival was possibly the realisation that Caltex was too favourably situated in relation to the Indian market to be driven out very easily. The very cheap cost of production of Bahrein oil[20] was also a factor which weighed against any decision to initiate a price war. But the most important explanation can be found in the happy coincidence, from the point of view of Burmah-Shell and Caltex, of the emergency of Caltex with the withdrawal of the U.S.S.R. supply from the rapidly expanding Indian market. (See Tables 3–7.) The fact that Caltex expanded its market at the cost of Stan-Vac, while allowing Burmah-Shell to take full advantage of India's growing demand, was probably the biggest single factor influencing Burmah-Shell's tolerant attitude towards Caltex.

Caltex, for its part, promised to pay the full subscription for membership to the Indian oil cartel of Stan-Vac and Burmah-Shell and agreed to respect the world parity system. Its main demand was, "with increase of domestic demand in Russia and failure to maintain her export position, and the decline in Roumania as well, a natural, normal market should be secured for Bahrein production without any disturbance to normal marketing conditions."[21] Since its demand was fully met, Caltex had no objection to joining the other two big companies. It was only Stan-Vac's market which was reduced for a number of reasons during the last three years of the thirties. The complete stoppage of Russian supply could not be made good by supplies from the U.S.A. due to tanker difficulties, Government control and, above all, rising demand in the U.S.A. And surely, no price war could be decisively won by Stan-Vac against Caltex in India, the cost of production and transport being so low in the case of the latter.

BURMAH-SHELL'S PRICE WAR WITH THE INDIAN INDEPENDENTS

There are records of a number of small Indian traders who were very active in the thirties; the most important of these companies was the Western India Oil Distributing Company (W.I.O.D.C.) which was registered in December, 1932.[22] Its main activity was the importing of kerosene and petrol from Russia and Rumania. Among its sponsors were some very well-known Indian businessmen, such as Phiroze Sethna and Hussein Bhoy Lalljee. Throughout the thirties it fought a series of price wars with Burmah-Shell. In 1941 its installations were taken over by the Government for war purposes and were not returned until 1949. The company started regular trading again in 1957.[23]

Among other companies, National Petroleum Company specialised in the diesel trade, while Bombay Petroleum Co.[24] entered into the kerosene market. There are also records of another company, named Northern India Oil Company,[25] with a registered office at Lahore.

It is very difficult to establish what proportion of the Indian market was occupied by these importers. The three products which they used to import were motor spirit, diesel, and kerosene, but their supply was not regular. Their sources of import were the U.S.S.R. and Rumania, who could supply oil products at prices below world parity since the entire production of the former and a large part of the latter were outside the control of the large international oil companies which adhered to the world parity system of pricing based on U.S. Gulf and divided the world oil market between themselves.[26] We notice a significant rise in 1933–34 in imports of kerosene from Rumania to 10 million gallons, which was slightly less than 5% of the total kerosene trade. (See Table 3.) It could be that a large part of this amount came to India via these small importers, but this cannot be proved from statistics. In subsequent years imports from Rumania were not higher than 3 million gallons. Again, although most of the Russian kerosene and motor spirit was sold through Standard Vacuum in India, part of it was also imported by these independent importers. In 1935–36, one of these independents imported about 0·55 million gallons of Russian oil.[27] Some of these importers took advantage of the loopholes in the Indian customs tariff and paid the lower fuel oil scale of duty for their imported kerosene.[28]

However, the amount of trade done by these traders could not be very significant because of two difficulties. First, these concerns had no marketing network in any part of the country to compare with those of the established international companies. Secondly, the supply of oil from the U.S.S.R. and Rumania was irregular and so they were unable to sustain the big overhead cost of a marketing organisation anywhere in the country throughout the year. Thus, their supplies could never reach the interior part of the country and were mostly confined to the ports of western India, particularly Bombay.[29]

But whatever the exact proportion of the market supplied by them, continuous reference to their activities in the Annual Reports of Burmah Oil during the thirties at least proves that their activities were of much greater significance than the volume of business achieved by them.[30] Whenever these companies tried to push their oil at cheap prices, Burmah-Shell attempted to restrict their trade by offering its products at still lower prices. This discreet price war continued throughout the thirties and kept the price of petrol in Bombay, where the competition was most severe, at about 15% lower than the price in Calcutta.[31] The prices were raised again to higher levels by Burmah-Shell as soon as the supplies of these independent importers were exhausted or the latter were driven out of a market through cut-throat competition.[32]

The attitude of Burmah-Shell towards the small Indian importers was in marked contrast to the tolerant attitude which it adopted towards Caltex. This difference in attitude followed from the fact that while Caltex was an affiliate of two major international oil companies adhering to the world parity price and agreeing to the price-leadership of Burmah-Shell, the Indian importers were "independents" from the international oil companies and could freely follow a flexible price policy at a much lower level than the world parity price. Again, any price war fought against Caltex was bound to be a very expensive affair because of the vast financial resources and international character of the latter. But the price war against Indian independents could be carried on only in a small number of ports without producing any adverse effect on the profitability of the business in the rest of India.

The use of a "price-weapon" by Burmah-Shell was subject to much criticism by the nationalist press of India.[33] There were demands for legislation to fix minimum and maximum prices for kerosene and motor spirit in order to deprive Burmah-Shell of its "price-weapon" against the independents.[34] In fact the situation then in India was not dissimilar to that in many other countries. In Goa,[35] a Portuguese colony on the western coast of India, as also in New Zealand,[36] the Government fixed maximum and minimum oil prices in order to make it possible for the small independent companies, receiving supplies from Russia or Rumania, to survive against the competition of giant international oil corporations. No such legislative action was taken in India. Yet the prices at which these independents offered oil in India were so low that some of them could survive severe cut-throat price wars with Burmah-Shell for a considerable period, and, as we have seen already, at least one of them, Western India Oil, continued its activities until the beginning of the Second World War when it was forced out of business by the Government.

THE DEPRESSION AND THE OIL COMPANIES

The world-wide economic depression of 1929–30 did not affect the consumption of oil products until after 1930–31, and the magnitude of its effect as also its duration, varied considerably from one oil product to another. The consumption of kerosene was the most affected, and its index declined from 135 in 1929–30 to 117 in 1933–34 (with 1913–14 = 100). (See Table 3.) For most of the period, kerosene import price indices were, on average, lower than the average wholesale prices in eight years. Its recovery, after 1935–36, was very slow, erratic, and was not complete until the end of the Second World War.

But the effect of the depression was not as serious on other oil products. As is clear from Table 15, the average price indices for other oil products were higher than the wholesale price index for all commodities. Thus, despite the economic depression, and the lower absolute level of oil prices, the relative prices of oil products could be maintained at a higher level because of the oligopolistic nature of the Indian market and the consequent downward rigidity in prices.

Motor spirit was the least affected of the major products. In 1930–31 when consumption of all other products was declining, motor spirit consumption showed a small increase. The following year the expansion in consumption was halted, and, in the year after that the depression showed its presence in consumption figures. But within two years the depression was over and a phase of rapid expansion initiated. This coincided with the recovery of the import trade in motor vehicles, which expanded from 9,000 in 1932–33 to 25,000 in 1934–35 and 32,000 in 1937–38.[37]

There was little effect of the depression on fuel oil consumption.

Between 1930–31 and 1933–34 consumption was less than the 1929–30 figure but was more than the consumption of any other year in the past. (See Table 7.) From 1934–35 onwards it was again rapidly increasing. The insignificance of the depression on fuel oil consumption followed from the insignificant effects of the depression on the two large consumers of fuel oil; the railways and the cotton textile industry.[38]

The lubricating oil trade was considerably affected by the depression which persisted up to 1937–38. Jute batching oil consumption was severely handicapped by a long sustained depression in the jute industry, whose index of profit fell from 100 in 1928 to $11 \cdot 1$ in 1937, and, even in 1941, it was only $46 \cdot 8$.[39] The trade in other lubricating oil products improved with increasing industrial activity and war preparations.

Taxes on oil products were increasing almost throughout the thirties. Even as early as 1933 Burmah Oil was bitterly complaining that high taxes "render it almost impossible to conduct the indigenous oil industry profitably".[40] In 1934 excise duties were $24 \cdot 65\%$ of the gross proceeds of Burmah Oil from kerosene,[41] which led Burmah Oil to complain that it was acting merely as a "tax-collector".[42] But, despite these expressions of dissatisfaction with the rate of taxation on oil products, which in 1938 accounted for $39 \cdot 85\%$ of the total proceeds of Burmah Oil from Indian trade,[43] this was much smaller than the rate of taxation at the present time on oil products in India or in the U.K.[44]

However, alongside these complaints about taxes, we find expressions of satisfaction and self-congratulation about the company's performance in the Annual Reports of Burmah Oil. One such statement is quoted below.[45]

"Even in the case of the most powerful and long-established of the leaders of the American oil industry one has seen profits eliminated, depreciations and amortisations reduced, and dividends—when paid at all—paid out of such 'savings' or out of reserves or capital realisations. In the same circumstances your company, on the other hand, has still been able to maintain satisfactory distributions while continuing to depreciate and amortise soundly and add further to already substantial reserves."

During the thirties, at least £200,000 was contributed each year to the Reserve Fund, which, by 1935, amounted to £9,000,000, in addition to a field expenditure equalisation reserve of £1,000,000. Between 1926 and 1938 dividends were three times 30%, once $27\frac{1}{2}\%$, twice 22%, twice 21%, four times 20%, once $17\frac{1}{2}\%$, and once 15%. Furthermore, twice during this period capital bonus of $33\frac{1}{2}\%$ (in 1933) and 50% (in 1937) were paid.[46]

The following table gives the net (after deducting all expenses and taxes) profits of Burmah Oil during this period.

TABLE 8

NET PROFITS OF BURMAH OIL: 1929–1939

Source: Annual Reports of the Burmah Oil Company

Year	Amount (£)	Year	Amount (£)
1929	3,437,472	1934	1,657,218
1930	2,736,000	1935	2,276,913
1931	1,869,495	1936	2,955,448
1932	1,058,153	1937	Not known
1933	1,754,068	1938	4,015,246

It is clear from these figures that net profit declined considerably during this period. But the annual average net profit for the whole period was 36%, when expressed as a percentage of total capital employed. This, obviously, was a very good performance considering that the general indices of industrial profit in India for these years were very low.

As regard other companies, Attock Oil Company suffered from losses for a number of years. But towards the end of the 1930s it started paying out dividends.[47] Assam Oil Company also made good all losses and paid back all debts before the end of the thirties.[48] Nothing is known about the financial position of Caltex and Standard-Vacuum in India during this period.

THE SUPPLY OF OIL DURING THE SECOND WORLD WAR

The supply of petroleum products to India was regulated during the Second World War by a committee in London, appointed by the Government of the U.K., which planned the amount of oil to be supplied to the different countries belonging to the British Empire. In India, the prices continued to be fixed on the basis of the U.S. Gulf prices, subject to two variations: first, a committee, under the chairmanship of the General Manager of Burmah-Shell, Mr. Lawson, and composed of the representatives of the oil companies, was set up. This committee pooled the total amount of oil available and the average price was worked out after every six months.[49] Secondly, prices fixed by this Pool were subject to the approval of the Government.[50] As regards the lubricating oil trade, the Central Government set up a Central Lubricants Advisory Committee in Calcutta, with sub-committees in Bombay, Madras, and Karachi,[51] which was entrusted with the job of regulating sales in accordance with the defence policy of the Government. The oil companies were bound to follow the instructions of this committee. For the distribution of oil from western India to the eastern border, where the war operations against Japan continued for a number of months, two pipelines were constructed by the military authorities.[52] But these pipelines were dismantled very soon after the war.[53]

The Second World War affected the pattern of the Indian import trade profoundly. Since a large part of the oil was now needed for military purposes, only a small part was made available to the civilians. But even this smaller civilian consumption could not be maintained. The fall of Burma to Japan in 1941 deprived India of her biggest and nearest source of supply. Supply from the Far East virtually disappeared after 1942. The supply of oil from the U.S.A. became uncertain with most of the oil tankers taken over by the U.S. Government and because of the high risk of a journey of more than three months at sea during the war. So, India came to rely mostly on the Persian Gulf countries for oil, and, during the last three years of the war, supply from this source ranged between 75% and 94% of the total import of oil. (See Table 3.) It is interesting that the urgency of war gave the opportunity to Persia, Bahrein, and Iraq to supply their natural and economic market without any oligopolistic restrictions. Efforts were also made to boost refinery outputs and crude production of Attock and Digboi, which partly succeeded. (See Table 3.)

The problem of supply was most acute in the case of motor spirit, for which the demand for war purposes was enormous, while the supply was drastically cut with the loss of Burma which contributed about 96% of the total trade in the pre-war period. Although there was a five-fold increase in motor spirit supply over the war years, this was still far short of demand at ruling prices. The Government took a number of measures in order to curtail civilian consumption of motor spirit. (See Table 5.)

First, tariff as well as excise duty on motor spirit was increased by 50% within two years, in two steps, partly to reduce consumption and partly to finance war expenditure.[54] Secondly, from August 15, 1941, rationing was introduced. Private motorists were allowed to have a basic ration of 200 miles per month and the total civilian consumption was 25% less than 1940 consumption.[55] From January 1, 1942, the civilian consumption was reduced to 60% of the 1940 level, and the basic ration of private motorists was reduced to 100 miles per month.[56]

The Government also decided to popularise the mixture of power alcohol, produced from sugar and motor spirit, and made it compulsory in certain sugar-producing provinces.[57] The motorists were, however, reluctant to use petrol mixed with power alcohol as they thought it to be injurious to their machines. In any case, it was not very popular and was uneconomic outside the sugar-producing areas. Even in 1946 this mixture accounted for less than 2% of the total motor fuel consumption.[58]

A more acceptable substitute for motor spirit was charcoal gas. The Government encouraged conversion of motor vehicles to producer gas by giving advances and certain tax concessions, and also by liberally granting import-quotas for steel needed for this conversion.[59] A number of factories were also established for facilitating this conversion. To ensure reliability of these plants the Government decided to examine a sample plant of each make through the War Transport Board, and also checked the calorie value and the dust content of the charcoal gas through the latter.[60] As a result of these measures, about 30% of the total number of motor vehicles in India were converted to producer gas by early 1944.[61]

As regards kerosene, its supply was drastically reduced during the war, due to the low priority given to it for military reasons. The total amount of kerosene available to India was much less than half of India's pre-war requirements. (See Table 4.) The situation became worse for the consumers of kerosene because even the domestic refineries of Digboi and Attock also erected new plants to extract a higher proportion of motor spirit.[62]

The overall effect of this reduction in supply of kerosene was disastrous for the consumers who had few substitutes for kerosene. Electricity was in use only in some towns and cities and the effect of the reduction in supply, the imposition of rationing by provinces from 1943, and the 20% increase in customs duty (which was now equal to the excise duty with a greater increase in excise duty)[63] was to compel many of the consumers to fall back on vegetable and animal oils. These products were now available in larger amounts because the highly developed Indian export trade in essential oils suffered a setback due to the war.[64] Black marketing in kerosene was widespread, even in villages, and the actual price of kerosene paid by the ultimate consumers became enormously high.

The Post-Independence Period

OIL SHORTAGE AND FOREIGN EXCHANGE CRISIS

Although the Second World War ended in 1945, wartime rationing of oil products, particularly of motor spirit and kerosene continued until the second half of 1950.[65] The most important political event of the time—independence, and the partition of India into India and Pakistan—produced no qualitative change in the oil economy of India.[66] Attock's oil now went over to Pakistan, but since its production, as also the production of Digboi, which is a part of India, was very small, it produced no perceptible change in the import-orientated oil trade of India.[67] During the first three years following independence, local production of oil products ranged from 5% to 10% and, in subsequent years, it fell to less than 5% until the beginning of a new phase in refinery construction in 1954.[68]

The shortage of oil was due to a number of factors. On the consumption side, increase in civilian consumption more than compensated for a decline in military needs for oil. For kerosene and lubricating oil, a higher level of consumption was the reaction to the wartime suppression of consumption. The higher consumption of fuel oil accompanied a higher scale of industrial activity; the demand for motor spirit was high because the railway system had yet to recover from the shock of the war and also because of the need for dispersal of refugees from Pakistan.[69] So, whereas 2,000,000 tons of oil was adequate for undivided India before the war, now the consumption exceeded 3,000,000 tons, despite rationing. (See Tables 3 and 11.)

On the supply side, because of the shortage of oil in the world market, the country was completely at the mercy of the major international petroleum companies for the supply of oil. The latter used to indicate the amount available for each quarter of a year to the Government which the Government had to distribute through a rigorous rationing system.[70]

A further obstacle to the inflow of oil to India was the small foreign exchange reserve of India, which was dwindling over the years. The value of imports of major oil products increased from Rs.309,000,000 in 1947–48 to Rs.833,000,000 in 1953–54 (see Table 12)—as a result of high oil prices, a higher level of consumption and the currency devaluation of 1949.[71] Although the Government took timely decisions to bringing oil imports under a license-system[72] and also to prohibit imports of oil from the dollar area,[73] with which the balance of trade was very unfavourable, the position of the foreign exchange fund was still precarious.[74]

OBJECTIVE OF SELF-SUFFICIENCY IN OIL PRODUCTS

It was as early as 1928 that the President of the Tariff Board advocated very strongly the case for an oil refining industry based on imported crude, but this suggestion went unheeded. The companies were not interested, because their refineries of the U.S., Persia, and the Far East were capable of satisfying India's two million tons annual demand. From their point of view it was not an attractive proposition. Again, contrary to the current trend, the refineries were then generally located near the oilfields, as against the consuming centres.[75]

But the question of refinery construction assumed a new significance during the years following the Second World War. Besides the balance of payments problem and the growing level of consumption of oil, many people in India resented the almost complete dependence on foreign supply. An important factor was also the "security-consciousness" of a vocal section of the population in the prevailing cold war atmosphere of world politics.[76] This feeling was continuously nourished by hostile relations with Pakistan. The importance of oil in the event of war and the uncertainty of supply from foreign countries encouraged the idea of self-sufficiency in oil production.

Besides refinery construction two other plans considered by the Government for saving foreign exchange and ensuring self-sufficiency were the erection of a synthetic oil plant and the development of a power alcohol industry. In one respect these two were more desirable from the point of view of national self-sufficiency compared to the refineries. Both of these two industries could draw their raw materials from within the country[77] while the refineries were to be dependent on foreign crude oil. Ultimately, it was found that the power alcohol industry could be more economically utilised in ways other than producing motor spirit,[78] and the cost of synthetic oil from coal was too high,[79] and, only the refinery programme could be pursued to the end.

In 1949 the oil companies of Britain and the United States, which were active in the Indian market, sent, at the request of the Government of India, a technical committee to India, in order to study "at their own expense", the "cost conditions" of a refinery project.[80] The report submitted after three months advised against any such project, and estimated an annual loss of Rs.20,000,000 if such a project were undertaken.[81] They were, however, prepared to consider a request for building refineries—one each in Bombay and Vizagapatnam—only if allowed to sell the products at a price 10% above the "world parity price". The Government turned down the proposal, and the whole subject of refinery construction was shelved for the time being.[82] But, within two years, the major companies amended their stand on this question, and agreed to build refineries even without making any further appraisal of the so called "cost conditions".

The decision of the companies on this question was without any doubt influenced by the developments in Iran, where the government of Mosaddeque took over the 25,000,000 ton giant oil refinery at

Abadan, after the disputes between the Anglo-Persian Oil Company and the government could not be resolved through negotiations.

The importance of Abadan, the great 25,000,000 ton refinery of Persia (Iran), to India was threefold—it was sterling oil, it supplied 70% of India's requirements,[83] and its proximity to India minimised the strain on tanker-capacity of Burmah-Shell, the seller of Persian oil in India. Although the latter tried its best to maintain the level of supply to India, the tanker freight was higher and the transport of oil products from the Far East and the U.S. was troublesome. There was an acute shortage of motor and aviation oil in India.[84] Above all, it involved the purchase of a large quantity of dollar oil products, which put a heavy strain on India's foreign balance.

For a number of reasons the "Abadan crisis" exposed the marketing activities of the international oil companies to a serious risk. It was not only that the business was less profitable because of higher transport cost. Any gap between demand and supply at current prices could make way for other competitors to the Indian market. The most feared of those likely competitors was the National Iranian Oil Company, the state oil undertaking of Iran, which was looking for marketing outlets.[85] Actually a company was set up in Calcutta in 1951, to refine Iranian crude oil and market Iranian products.[86] Any shortage of supply in the Indian market was going to be advantageous to this competitor. Again, such a competitor was not likely to pay any respect to the world parity system and could supply crude at a very low price for the proposed refinery.[87] Given the concern of the Government for foreign exchange, such a move might be warmly backed by the Government. Any refinery set up in India was sure to get priority in the allocation of foreign exchange. So, it was to the interest of their marketing subsidiaries not to allow any refinery to be set up by any company outside the international group of seven major companies. Furthermore, the Government was giving serious consideration to a plan for setting up a refinery on its own.[88]

The importance of the Abadan crisis in influencing the decisions of the oil companies on this question can be appreciated from the following remark made by the chairman of the Burmah Oil Company in 1951: "Events at Abadan, from which we have drawn the greater part of our petroleum products since we lost our Burma production, have caused us to review our future supply position, and we have decided to build a refinery at Bombay in conjunction with Shell to supply a large part of our requirements for the Indian market."[89] To quote from an article which appeared during this period in *Petroleum Press Service*, "the existence of nearby Abadan rendered such proposals (i.e. those to build refineries in India) economically unattractive. The closing down of Abadan altered the picture."[90] Similar observations were also made by other petroleum journals, including *Petroleum Times*, at that time.[91]

Very soon agreements were reached between Burmah-Shell, Standard Vacuum, and Caltex on the one hand, and the Government on the other, and between 1954 and 1957 three refineries were built, two by the first two companies at Bombay and the third one by Caltex at Vizagapatnam. A second phase of refinery construction was started in 1959, when three public sector refineries were constructed in Noonmati, Barauni, and Koyali. (See Chapter 8.)

THE GROWTH OF THE PUBLIC SECTOR IN OIL

The industrial policy resolution of 1948, which divided the industries into four groups according to the degree of control to be exercised by the Government, specified that all the new units in the oil industry would be set up only under Government ownership, unless specially authorised by the Government. But for seven years after the declaration of that resolution, there was no public sector unit in the oil industry, although permission was given to the private foreign companies to build refineries under their exclusive ownership.

In December, 1955, the Oil and Natural Gas Division was created as a part of the Ministry of Natural Resources and Scientific Research. Very soon it was formed into a commission and in October, 1959, the Oil and Natural Gas Commission became a statutory body under an Act of Parliament.[92] Its main function was the exploration and production of crude. From 1958 onwards, with the assistance of Russian experts, O.N.G.C. disocvered a number of oilfields in Gujrat and Assam.

A second crude-oil producing company, Oil India Limited (O.I.L.), was formed in 1959 to exploit the oilfields of Nahorkatiya-Moran-Hugrijan (Assam), discovered in 1953–56 by the Assam Oil Company, in partnership with Burmah Oil.[93] The latter, the parent company of Assam Oil, was not allowed to exploit, refine or market the oil of Assam alone. A pipeline was constructed from oilfields to the refineries by O.I.L., but the refineries of Nunmati (Assam), and Barauni (Bihar), erected to process the crude of these new oilfields, were constructed by the Government with the assistance of Rumanians and Russians and owned exclusively by the Government. These two refineries, and subsequently the Koyali refinery of Gujrat, were brought under the ownership of a state-owned company, Indian Refineries Limited, formed in 1958.[94]

The Government entered the sphere of marketing in 1959, when the Indian Oil Company was formed.[95] At the beginning, the main objective of the Government was to supply oil products to the state enterprises, which accounted for 10% of total oil consumption in India, through Indian Oil Company (I.O.C.).[96] Subsequently, a greater role was assigned to it and I.O.C. was expected to take over at least half the import trade of the country.[97] Besides the import trade, the products of state refineries are also sold through I.O.C. In future, when the refineries partly controlled by the Government in collaboration with foreign companies came into being, their products would also be sold through the state-owned Indian Oil Company. From the middle of 1965, under pressure of the foreign exchange crisis, the Government prohibited import trade by private oil companies and the import trade is now a monopoly of I.O.C. The latter imports from the U.S.S.R. and Rumania at cheaper than world average prices and the price is payable in local currency.[98]

Thus the Government of India is now participating in almost all the different sectors of the oil industry—from crude exploration and production, to processing, transporting, refining, and marketing. Since September, 1964, I.O.C. and Indian Refineries Limited have been merged together into one company, the Indian Oil Corporation,[99] but the crude production and exploration activity of O.N.G.C. is still independent of the downstream activities of the Indian Oil Corporation. This might be an initial step towards the vertical integration of all the Government oil agencies under one corporation like E.N.I., Petrobras or Pemex, the state oil organisations of Italy, Brazil, and Mexico.[100]

THE GOVERNMENT'S CONFLICT WITH THE MAJOR OIL COMPANIES

The expanding role of the Government in the affairs of the oil industry and the branching out of the public sector into different segments of the oil industry led to a series of conflicts with the established major international oil companies. The latter were now more or less united under the leadership of Burmah-Shell against the threat of state control or the competition of the state enterprises. No price war was fought among themselves after 1928 and hostility against the Government over the role of these companies and the Government in the development of the oil industry took the place of inter-company rivalry.

One of the first conflicts was over the question of exploitation of Nahorkatiya oilfields, discovered in 1953 by Assam Oil, Burmah Oil's subsidiary. As we have seen before, the Government refused the latter any right to refine or market this oil and only allowed joint-ownership in crude production. This was contrary to the marketing interests of Burmah Oil, whose loss of import trade in oil products (as a proportion of total consumption) consequent to the discovery of this oilfield more than offset its share in the profit

F

of Oil India. Burmah Oil strongly criticised this policy in the following words of its chairman: ". . . Our main difficulty has been to reconcile the development of the valuable oilfield we have discovered with the Government's restrictive policy towards this kind of private enter- prise." As a protest against this "restrictive policy", Burmah Oil suspended its exploratory activities in India for a while.[101]

On the part of the Government, on the other hand, there was a feeling that the major oil companies were not taking enough interest in exploratory activities. There was also widespread resent- ment that companies were unwilling to share their technical knowledge with the Government and also that they were providing few opportunities for the training of Indian personnel.[102]

The second, and more important, cause of the conflict was also the feeling on the part of the Government that the companies were charging "excessive" prices for the import of oil by taking advantage of their monopolistic position in the Indian market. (A detailed discussion of the pricing system is to be found in Chapters Six, Seven, Eight, and Nine.) The conflict came to a head when the major companies refused to refine Russian crude oil, secured at very cheap price by the Government, in their refineries in 1960.[103] A third cause of conflict was the refusal of the Government to allow expan- sion of refining capacity under the ownership of the established major international companies unless the latter agreed to scrap the refinery Agreements of 1951 and 1953 and also to import crude oil at prices comparable to the offers made by the Russians.[104]

The result of these conflicts was, at least temporarily, disastrous from the point of view of the major companies. During the early 1960s the Government took a number of steps to destroy the monopolistic position of the Burmah-Shell–Caltex-Esso group, which was already weakened after 1959 as a result of the competition of the Russians and the "independent" international oil companies in the world market, and also by the emergence of state oil enterprises in many countries of the world.[105] The major companies were denied the opportunity to build any new refinery partly because of their reluctance at the beginning to agree to the Government's majority shareholding in the Company, and partly as a reflection of the Government's policy of curtailing their monopolistic control. The import trade in oil products was made an exclusive privilege of the Indian Oil Corporation from 1965 and the target of making the corporation the leading marketing company of India was achieved by 1967. The latter is expected to increase its market share from $35\frac{1}{2}\%$ in 1967 and 43% in 1968, to more than half the total sales by 1971.[106]

The major companies, however, did not give up without a fight. As soon as the first consignment of Russian High Speed Diesel reached Bombay in August, 1961, they started a new kind of price war. Since the importing company, I.O.C., had no retail outlets, it could only sell to the bulk consumers, particularly state transport enterprises. The major companies, in a bid to retain their business, offered prices even lower than those quoted by I.O.C. for its Russian products. As a result, a large part of I.O.C.'s supply was unsold for a period of time which also created storage problems. The latter, in its turn, then offered even lower prices which were below economic level and secured some business.[107] However, the price war did not last very long. At any rate, the objective of the price war was surely very limited and the oil companies were not unaware of the serious risks to which their large investments in India were exposed by these conflicts with the Government. It seems that the main objective of the price war was to put pressure on the Government to reject the proposals of the oil price enquiry committee of 1961, which prescribed a lower schedule of prices for imported products.[108] From 1st June, 1962, the major companies, as also I.O.C., adopted Damle prices for products.[109]

This brief price war of 1962 probably marks the end of an era of price wars, between various groups of companies and between state-owned and the private foreign-owned companies. The leadership of Burmah-Shell in the Indian market has been taken over by the Indian Oil Corporation and the price wars have been made superfluous by Government action. The policy of limiting imports to the amount necessary for bridging the gap between domestic consumption and output, has guaranteed for each marketing company a share of the market which is related to its refinery output, and which cannot be increased though price wars. In the case of Indian oil, its share equals the output of the refineries which are either partly or wholly owned by the Government, plus the amount of import trade. From the point of view of the major oil companies, the only way left to expand their market shares is to increase the aggregate refinery capacity under their ownership. That is why these companies are so eager to seek permission to expand their refineries and to participate in further refinery construction. Their recent willingness to accept majority shareholding of the Government in a jointly built refinery, and also to agree to I.O.C. distribution of oil products of such a refinery, reflects their anxiety to increase sale of crude, even without a corresponding increase in its share of the oil products market.[110]

Government policy has also undergone changes over the past five or six years. Whereas Mr. Malaviya was adamant in his refusal to allow expansion of refinery capacity under the ownership of the major oil companies, such expansions have been allowed since his departure from the Indian Government, on grounds of national emergency and foreign exchange shortage. The Indian Oil Corporation has worked out arrangements under which oil products are bartered with the major oil companies in order to facilitate their distribution. Its appearance in the Indian market has now been accepted by the older oil interests and a policy of "live and let live" is being followed by all concerned.

TABLE 9

KEROSENE OIL TRADE: PERCENTAGE SHARE OF DIFFERENT COMPANIES 1928-29 TO 1938-39

Unit: Thousand Gallons.

Source: Annual Review of Trade of India

Year	Standard Oil Co.		Burmah Oil		Asiatic Pet. Co.		A.P.O.C.		Total Consumption
	Total	Percentage	Total	Percentage	Total	Percentage	Total	Percentage	
1928–29	56,812	24·64	125,866	54·60	13,528	5·87	32,062	13·91	230,526
1929–30	60,221	24·83	136,076	56·11	16,843	6·94	28,759	11·86	242,533
1930–31	68,304	29·75	130,667	56·92	12,375	5·39	18,214	7·93	229,560
1931–32	61,823	26·88	144,343	62·75	4,417	1·92	18,552	8·06	230,033
1932–33	44,569	21·12	151,359	71·72	2,079	0·99	6,559	3·11	211,053
1933–34	40,439	19·21	146,420	69·56	5,914	2·81	292	0·14	210,482
1934–35	44,221	19·49	158,212	69·74	14,777	6·51	6,770	2·98	226,858
1935–36	47,186	21·80	148,037	68·39	5,365	2·48	10,805	4·99	216,460
1936–37	40,955	18·23	162,408	72·30	13,784	6·14	6,696	2·98	224,617
1937–38	24,093	10·09	169,114	70·79	30,890	12·93	11,461	4·80	238,880
1938–39	1,305	0·61	152,356	71·07	17,549	8·19	30,273	14·12	214,379

TABLE 10

PRICES OF OIL IMPORTED TO INDIA: 1927 TO 1935

Unit: Pound per Gallon

Source: Review of Trade of India

Year	Kerosene		Batching Oil		Other Lubes		Fuel Oil		Wholesale Price Index
	Price	Index	Price	Index	Price	Index	Price	Index	
1927	0·04694	100	0·05010	100	0·1294	100	0·01650	100	100
1928	0·03999	85	0·04832	96	0·1316	102	0·01507	101	98
1929	0·04084	87	0·05387	108	0·1232	95	0·01435	91	95
1930	0·04040	86	0·05327	106	0·1143	88	0·01477	87	80
1931	0·03926	84	0·05333	106	0·1113	86	0·01494	90	65
1932	0·03441	73	0·05761	115	0·1242	96	0·01459	91	61
1933	0·02878	61	0·04848	97	0·1090	84	0·01423	88	59
1934	0·02789	59	0·04872	97	0·0915	50	0·01324	86	61
1935	0·02789	59	0·03764	75	0·0892	49	0·01243	80	62

TABLE 11

IMPORTS OF MAJOR OIL PRODUCTS TO INDIA: 1947–48 TO 1964–65

Unit: Thousand Tons

Source: Monthly Statistics of Foreign Trade of India

Year	Diesel	%	Fuel Oil	%	Kerosene	%	Lube	%	Motor Spirit	%	Total
1947–48	335	14·5	763	33·0	643	27·8	218	9·4	353	15·3	2,312
1948–49	297	14·8	728	36·3	378	18·8	204	10·2	400	19·9	2,007
1949–50	531	18·1	860	29·3	719	24·5	231	7·9	592	20·2	2,933
1950–51	514	17·1	845	28·1	830	27·7	164	5·5	649	21·6	3,002
1951–52	631	18·2	878	25·3	920	26·6	196	5·7	840	24·2	3,465
1952–53	610	18·3	687	20·7	968	29·1	246	7·4	814	24·5	3,325
1953–54	649	17·9	833	23·0	1,082	29·9	153	4·2	902	25·0	3,619
1954–55	758	21·3	646	18·1	1,222	34·2	227	6·4	717	20·0	3,570
1956*	241	18·2	29	2·2	794	60·0	163	12·3	96	7·3	1,323
1957	326	17·0	13	0·7	1,131	59·1	292	15·3	151	7·9	1,913
1958	256	17·9	33	2·3	907	63·3	162	11·3	75	5·2	1,433
1959	270	16·6	32	2·0	1,036	63·8	200	12·3	87	5·3	1,625
1960	520	33·0	43	2·7	711	45·1	229	14·5	74	4·7	1,577
1960–61	281	17·1	73	4·4	888	54·0	315	19·1	89	5·4	1,645
1961–62	349	22·2	168	10·7	707	45·0	237	15·1	109	7·0	1,570
1962–63	459	16·7	204	7·4	1,750	63·7	232	8·4	102	3·8	2,747
1963–64	569	21·3	351	13·1	1,282	48·0	387	14·5	83	3·1	2,672
1964–65	378	20·2	301	16·1	844	45·0	286	15·3	65	3·4	1,874

*From April 1 to December 1, 1956

TABLE 12

VALUES OF IMPORTS OF MAJOR OIL PRODUCTS TO INDIA: 1947-48 TO 1964-65

Unit: in Million Rupees

Source: Monthly Statistics of Foreign Trade of India

Year	Diesel	%	Fuel Oil	%	Kerosene	%	Lube	%	Motor Spirit	%	Total
1947-48	25	7·8	35	11·0	91	28·5	80	25·1	88	27·6	319
1948-49	29	8·9	40	12·2	65	19·9	84	25·7	109	33·3	327
1949-50	68	13·0	60	11·5	151	28·9	81	15·5	163	31·1	523
1950-51	69	12·7	49	9·0	177	32·5	70	12·9	179	32·9	544
1951-52	90	13·0	58	8·4	192	27·7	110	15·8	244	35·1	694
1952-53	94	12·5	55	7·3	219	29·2	131	17·4	252	33·6	751
1953-54	109	13·1	80	9·6	275	33·0	60	7·2	309	37·1	833
1954-55	129	15·9	62	7·7	281	34·7	87	10·8	250	30·9	809
1955-56	54	12·5	10	2·3	195	45·2	81	18·9	91	21·1	431
1956*	42	12·7	3	1·0	175	53·0	70	21·2	40	12·1	330
1957	57	11·1	3	0·6	253	49·6	133	26·0	65	12·7	511
1958	46	12·3	7	1·9	206	54·9	83	22·1	33	8·8	375
1959	49	11·8	6	1·4	227	54·4	100	24·0	35	8·4	417
1960	59	16·0	7	1·9	171	46·5	101	27·4	30	8·2	368
1960-61	45	9·6	9	1·9	228	48·4	153	32·5	36	7·6	471
1961-62	52	10·0	18	3·4	279	53·6	130	25·0	42	8·0	521
1962-63	66	11·7	19	3·4	323	57·2	116	20·5	41	7·2	565
1963-64	80	11·9	28	4·2	355	53·0	186	27·8	21	3·1	670
1964-65	62	12·8	23	4·8	233	48·2	137	28·4	28	5·8	483

*From April, 1956 to December, 1956

NOTES

1. *P.T.*, 2.6.1928, p. 993.
2. *Ibid*, 6.1.1940, p. 5.
3. *Ibid*, 6.10.1928, p. 592.
4. Socony Mobil Oil Company, p. 32.
5. Indian Tariff Board (3), letter from Vaccuum Oil Company, dated 8.3.1928, to the Central Board of Revenue, New Delhi.
6. Socony Mobil Oil Company, p. 32.
7. *Records of the Geological Survey of India* and *Review of Trade of India* relevant years.
8. In this table we assume, as before, that all the Russian and U.S. kerosene imported by India was sold through Standard, all the Far East exports through Asiatic, Persian oil through Anglo-Persian, and the rest of the kerosene trade was done by Burmah Oil from the production of Burma and India owned by the latter and its associates.
9. P.T., 22.3.1930, p. 490.
10. P.T., 13.6.1931, p. 835.
11. P.T., 10.6.1933, p. 599.
12. *Review of Trade of India*, 1929–30, p. 50.
13. Russian supply was highest in 1935–36 when 16,000,000 gallons of motor spirit were exported to India, as against the total Indian motor spirit consumption of 84·9 million gallons in the same year. It stopped from 1936–37. See *Review of Trade of India* of relevant years.
14. *Ibid.*
15. P.T., 23.9.1933, p. 148; 16.12.1933, p. 726.
16. A subsidiary of the Standard Oil Trust before its dissolution, Standard Oil of California very soon established itself as a leading oil corporation in the U.S. market. Its major achievement was the discovery of oil in Bahrein and Saudi Arabia during the 1930s. But, because of its lack of a marketing organisation in the Eastern Hemisphere, it decided to share the ownership of Bahrein crude with Texaco in "Caltex" and that of Saudi-Arabian crude with Standard Oil of New Jersey, Socony and Texaco in "Aramco". See De Chazeau and Kahn and Skinner's *Oil and Petroleum Year-book.*
17. Formed in 1902, Texas Oil Company (Texaco) soon became one of the largest U.S. oil corporations. It exapnded its marketing facilities enormously in the 1920s. The main reason behind Standard Oil of California's decision to form a joint company with Texaco to exploit and market its discoveries in Bahrein was to get the advantage of Texaco's marketing organisation in the Eastern Hemisphere. See James.
18. P.T., 14.8.1937, p. 200.
19. *Ibid*, 13.6.1939, p. 755.
20. The average cost of production of Bahrein crude was 12 cents per barrel, against 76 cents per barrel cost of production of U.S. crude, in 1955. See U.N. (2), p. 14.
21. P.T., 14.8.1937, p. 200.
22. E.W., 21.4.1960, p. 545.
23. Government of India (1), pp. 11–12.
24. Western India Oil Distributing Company, p. 16.
25. P.T., 5.5.1934, p. 494.
26. U.S. (2), pp. 236–250.
27. P.T., 13.6.1936, p. 751.
28. P.T., 9.6.1934, p. 619.
29. P.T., 10.6.1939, p. 753.

30. Burmah Oil Company's Annual Reports published in P.T., 14.6.1930, p. 1061; 13.6.1931, p. 835; 10.6.1933, p. 599; 9.6.1934, p. 619; 15.6.1935, p. 705; 13.6.1936, p. 751; 12.6.1937, p. 779; 10.6.1939, p. 753.

31. Burmah-Shell took over the independent active in Calcutta in 1939, and raised the price of petrol from Rs.1.2.0. to Rs.1.3.0. per gallon immediately. In Bombay, where the competition was much stronger, the price was kept at a low level of Rs.0.15.0. for most of the 1930s. See, Western India Oil Distributing Co., p. 9 and *Review of Trade of India* of relevant years.

32. For example, after the entry of Western India Oil to the Delhi market, the price of petrol there was brought down from Rs.1.11.0. to Rs.1.5.6. per gallon. It was raised to Rs.1.9.0. in 1937, but with the entry of fresh imports through Western India, Burmah-Shell again brought down the price to Rs.1.6.0. per gallon. The result was, according to Western India Oil, "that not only did we lose most of the business we managed to secure in the brief interval but we were even burdened with fresh liabilities on account of such commitments as we had to make to secure such business, in the shape of plot rents etc." In Bombay the price of kerosene was put up to the old level in 1938 after Bombay Petroleum Company was driven out of the market through cut-throat competition. See Western India Oil Distributing Company, pp. 14–16, Burmah-Shell ("The Price of Petrol", May, 1933) and *Commercial Gazette*, Calcutta, 20.7.36 ("B.O.C. defends").

33. *Capital*, 16.1.1936 ("Petrol Rate War") 23.1.1936 ("Position in India Explained"); *Commercial Gazette*, 11.5.1936, ("Relief to Petrol Consumers"); *The Indian Economist*, 8.6.1936 ("Monopolies and Rate Wars").

34. P.T., 10.6.1939, p. 753.

35. Goa, Legislative Diploma, No. 975, 29.11.1927.

36. New Zealand, Parliamentary Debates, Third Session, 1933, (reprinted in *Western India Oil*, pp. 35–54).

37. *Statistical Abstract for British India*, 1927–28 to 1936–37, 1936–37 to 1940–41.

38. The rate of railway construction slowed down from 774 miles in 1929–30 to 68 miles in 1934–35. But the number of locomotives in use was not reduced. For cotton textile, production increased from 377,000,000 to 715,000,000 pounds between 1933–34 and 1937–38, See *Statistical Abstract for British India*, 1927–28 to 1936–37 to 1940–41.

39. *Ibid*, 1927–28 to 1936–37.

40. P.T. 23.12.1933, p. 741.

41. *Ibid*, 15.6.1935, p. 705.

42. *Ibid*, 11.6.1932, p. 651.

43. *Ibid*, 10.6.1939, p. 753.

44. In 1961, for example, the proportion of tax in the listed price varied from $36 \cdot 4\%$ in the case of kerosene to $58 \cdot 9\%$ in the case of gasoline in India. In the U.K. the proportion of taxes varied from 11% in the case of kerosene to $62 \cdot 3\%$ in the case of gasoline. In both cases the average was higher than 40%. See Frankel (3).

45. P.T., 10.6.1933, p. 599.

46. From Annual Reports of Burmah Oil, reprinted in *Petroleum Times*. See note 30.

47. P.T., 19.6.1937, p. 836; 12.2.1938, p. 210; 16.1.1940, p. 17.

48. *Ibid*, 12.6.1937, p. 779.

49. E.W., 20.3.1947, p. 510.

50. P.P.S., May, 1946, p. 86.

51. P.P.S., March, 1942, p. 35.

52. *Ibid*, May, 1946, p. 86.

53. E.W., 24.4.1947, p. 686 and P.T., 15.5.1943, p. 228.

54. Indian Customs Tariff, 1939–1941.

55. P.P.S., September, 1941, p. 108.

56. *Ibid*, January, 1942, p. 8.

57. *Ibid*, April, 1942, p. 44.

58. *Ibid*, April, 1952, p. 132.

59. *Ibid*, February, 1943, p. 25.

60. *Ibid*, February, 1944, p. 35.

61. *Ibid*, May, 1946, p. 86.

62. *Records of the Geological Survey of India*, 1954.

63. Indian Customs Tariff, 1939–1945.

64. P.T., 9.1.1943, p. 5.

65. *Capital*, 23.6.1950, p. 1043; 7.9.1950, p. 1009.

66. According to a rough estimate, the territory now under Pakistan accounted for 20% of the oil consumption of undivided India. (See *Records of the Geological Survey of India*, 1947.)

67. The loss of Karachi, the fourth important port of undivided India which accounted for about 10% of total imports before the Second World War, caused some dislocation in the distribution system of oil to North west India.

68. Government of India (12), 1951–56, p. 191.

69. *Capital*, 18.3.1948, p. 499.

70. *Capital*, 17.2.1949, p. 255.

71. P.P.S., February, 1950, p. 38.

72. *Ibid*, July, 1950, p. 180.

73. *Capital*, 5.1.1950, p. 31.

74. From the year of devaluation up to 1955–56 (excepting in 1951) there were surpluses in current account of external trade. From 1956–57 onwards the current balance of trade shows deficits ranging from Rs.1,850,000,000 to Rs.5,010,000,000, See *Reserve Bank of India's Annual Report on Currency and Finance*, of relevant years.

75. Frankel and Newton (1) and (3).

76. E.W., 26.1.1951, p. 92.

77. India's large reserve of lowgrade coal with high ash content—with limited alternative uses—could be utilised as a raw material for the synthetic oil plant. The coal mining committee of 1937 in fact recommended such a use of coal. (See E.W., 11.12.1954, p. 1372, and E.E., 7.10.1955, p. 540.) Molasses, a by-product of the sugar industry, could be used as the raw material for the Power Alcohol industry. See Government of India (9).

78. See Government of India (12), 1951–56, p. 201; 1956–61, p. 332.

79. A number of oil-from-coal projects were prepared and a few of these were also approved by the Government. One of the companies interested in the plant was Henrich Koppers of West Germany. It was estimated that for the production of 0·25 million tons of petrol and 0·095 million tons of aviation spirit about Rs.600,000,000 to 800,000,000 would be needed. (See E.W., 11.12.1954, p. 1372, and also 1957–58 *Report of the Ministry of Steel, Mines and Fuel*, p. 53.) This was much higher than, for example, the initial estimated cost of building a 1·5 million ton refinery at Bombay by Burmah-Shell at Rs.22 crores. (See *Capital*, 20.12.1951, p. 759.)

80. Government of India (12), 1951–1956, p. 94.

81. *Capital*, March 21, 1950, p. 257.

82. Government of India (12), p. 94.

83. *Review of Trade of India*, 1947–1951.

84. *Capital*, 3.5.1951, p. 771.

85. The very fact that the international companies could effectively block the

entry of National Iranian Oil into the world market ultimately led to their victory over Mossadeque, then Prime Minister of Iran.

86. P.T., 3.4.1953, p. 359.

87. This they in fact did after a number of years when, very recently, National Iranian agreed to supply Madras Refinery its crude at a price far below world parity. See Chapter Eight.

88. See *Capital*, 2.3.1950, p. 357; E.E., 23.3.1951, p. 478; P.T., 11.7.1952, p. 588; 3.4.1953, p. 359; P.P.S., October, 1953, p. 366.

89. *Petroleum Times*, July 11, 1952, p. 588.

90. *Petroleum Press Service*, October, 1953, p. 366.

91. *Petroleum Times*, April 3, 1953, p. 359.

92. *Indian Petroleum Handbook*, 1964, pp. 6–8.

93. *Ibid*, pp. 8–9.

94. *Ibid*, pp. 15–20.

95. *Ibid*, pp. 24–25.

96. *Capital*, 21.5.1959, p. 713.

97. Government of India (7), p. 1.

98. P.I.W., 10.5.1965. The ban was initially for six months, but as yet it has not been withdrawn. A recent contract made by I.O.C. with the U.S.S.R. for importing 20,000 barrels per day for five years implies that the ban is expected to continue for a long time to come. See also P.I.W., 24.1.1966.

99. *Indian Petroleum Handbook*, 1964, p. 24.

100. Government of India (7), p. 3.

101. *Capital*, 30.5.1957, p. 762.

102. *Capital*, 15.12.1955, p. 790. To quote a bulletin of the Geological Survey of India, (*Mineral Wealth in India*, 1942, p. 19.);

"The search for oil in India, because of the expense in drilling operations, has been largely conducted by the big oil companies, who have their own geologists. Of late there has grown up a feeling that the search for oil in India has not been as extensive as the importance of this substance warrants and the possibilities of its occurrence justify."

Or, to quote the Joint-Secretary of the Ministry of Oil (*Capital*, 26,5,1960, p. 796):

"Oil venture needs the greatest of boldness and imagination and funds for its development programmes. Profit considerations may have to be sacrificed. Therefore, the Government or a Government undertaking alone would be in a position to take an overall view and explore extensively without restricting itself to proved or very promising areas alone." This was in effect a reply to Mr. Black's (World Bank) plea for non-involvement by the Government in exploratory activities.

103. See Chapter Nine.

104. *Capital*, 27.9.1962, p. 479; 24.1.1963, p. 114; E.W., 16.2.1963, p. 317.

105. See Chapter Seven.

106. P.P.S., October, 1967, p. 373.

107. Government of India (7), pp. 21–23 and *Commerce*, 14.1.1961, p. 47.

108. *Capital*, 16.11.1961, p. 725; 23.11.1961, p. 749. See also Chapter Seven.

119. Government of India (7), p. 22.

110. *Capital*. 13.8.1964, p. 253; E.E., 3.1.1964, p. 19.

CHAPTER 4

THE SYSTEM OF PRICING OIL PRODUCTS IN INDIA BEFORE 1945

WORLD PARITY PRICES

The historical review of the Indian oil market given in Chapters Two and Three clearly shows the international character of the oil companies operating in India. As will be shown below, their pricing decisions in India depended largely on the system of pricing adopted by their parent companies in the Eastern Hemisphere.

From 1905 onwards, conditions in the Indian market were stabilised and the leadership of the Burmah Oil-Asiatic group was accepted by Standard and the smaller companies. There was a definite arrangement about price-fixing between them. Every time there was any price change, the Burmah-Oil Asiatic group informed the office of Standard at Calcutta about this in advance. Sufficient time was given to the local office of Standard to cable its New York headquarters and ask for their permission to put the price up or down.[1] When Caltex entered the picture it agreed to follow Burmah Shell's price leadership.[2]

We now know very little about the system of pricing before the First World War. But it is known that a condition of the agreements of 1905 and 1906 between the oil companies was that in the event of a drop in supply from any company, others were not entitled, according to the rules of the game, to increase their market shares at the cost of the former, and all of them were supposed to increase their price quotations. The price war of 1909, as we have noted already, was fought by Asiatic against Standard because of the latter's alleged breach of this condition.[3]

Gradually a system of pricing, known generally as the "world parity price system" or "U.S. parity price system", was evolved by the major companies to cover India as well as other markets of the Eastern Hemisphere. In India, this system was adopted by the Kerosene Pool and, afterwards, by Burmah Shell, which took over the price leadership from the former in 1928. This was a kind of basing point system with the U.S. Gulf as the basing point for pricing both crude oil and oil products. As an example of the actual way of computing prices according to this system, the following table shows the components of the wholesale prices of superior grade kerosene ex-seaport installations at Bombay during 1928:[4]

f.o.b. U.S. Gulf price per unit of 8 gallons (= 65 cents for 10 American gallons)	= Rs.1.12.7
Freight from U.S. Gulf to Bombay	= Rs.1.3.0
Leakage and insurance	= Rs.0.0.6
Profit 10% on c.i.f. price	= Rs.0.4.10
Import duty and other charges	= Rs.1.8.6
Total ex-seaport installation price of kerosene of superior grade of 8 gallons	= Rs.4.13.5

An extra charge was made for inland transport and distribution costs when the products were sold in the interior of the country.[5]

This system of pricing applied to oil supplied from all sources including those from nearer sources such as Burma, Persia, the Far East, or Russia. In those cases, although the actual freight to India was less, for the purpose of fixing prices the oil was supposed to have come from the U.S. Gulf.[6]

THE ECONOMIC SIGNIFICANCE OF THE U.S. GULF PARITY PRICE

The fact that the U.S. Gulf was adopted as the basing point for pricing products and crude oil before 1945 needs some explanation. It was claimed that since U.S. oil accounted for more than 70% of the world export trade in oil, almost no oil-consuming country was in a position to do without importing a part of it. Since there could not be two or more prices for an identical commodity in the same market, the price of U.S. imports, the marginal supply, determined the price level in each market.[7]

Now, in the case of an internationally traded commodity, under competitive conditions, the following two conditions are fulfilled:

(1) The f.o.b. price is the same at a particular production point, no matter to which consuming centre it is exported.
(2) The c.i.f. price is the same in a consumption centre, no matter from which production point it has been imported.

Any departure from these two conditions is corrected under the pressure of demand and supply conditions in a competitive market. Furthermore, the system of f.o.b. and c.i.f. prices in different countries would be such as to make the aggregate world demand equal to aggregate world supply at those prices.

The U.S. Gulf parity system would conform to these conditions only if the f.o.b. prices of nearer sources of supply to a consumption centre were so high compared to the f.o.b. U.S. Gulf price as to offset their freight advantages over U.S. products. F.o.b. price of a nearer source could be higher if, among other things, the marginal cost of oil production was higher.

There is no easy way of testing this assumption in view of the absence of a free market in oil in the Eastern Hemisphere, where almost the entire crude oil production, but for Russian and a part of Rumanian crude, was under the control of the major oil companies. Even as late as 1949 the seven majors controlled 96% of the crude production and 79% of the refining capacity outside the communist bloc in the Eastern Hemisphere.[8] The independent refineries were only nominally independent since they received their crude supplies from the majors. Furthermore, the products of the refineries were sold by the vertically integrated oil companies through their marketing affiliates in different countries.

We know of a number of cartel arrangements among the international majors, on a world scale, starting with the Achnacurry Agreement (which is also known as the "as is" agreement) of September 17, 1928, following the Indian price war of 1927–28.[9] Under this agreement, the participants agreed to respect the current volume of business of each of them and to extend business with increases in demand only proportionately to their current market share. This agreement also formally accepted the U.S. Gulf as the basing point for pricing.[10] The other international agreements such as the "Memorandum for European Markets" (January 20, 1930),[11] "Heads of Agreement for Distribution" (1932),[12] and "Draft Memorandum on Principles" (1934)[13] also affirmed those main points of the "as is" agreement. Any company violating the provisions of these agreements was liable to pay fines. There were, however, some exceptions, such as Rumanian or Russian producers, who remained outside these agreements. The former was difficult to control through any agreement among producers because the producers numbered more than thirty and had diverse, often conflicting, interests.[14] But attempts were made on a number of occasions by the major oil companies to bring Rumania under international control and an agreement in Paris was signed with Rumanian producers in 1932 which stipulated, "Rumanian oil should be directed with the greatest promptness towards the controlled distributing organisations who agreed to adhere to the convention for quotas and prices in consuming countries."[15] It should also be noted that Standard Oil of New Jersey and Royal Dutch Shell were the two largest producers of Rumania and Rumanian prices f.o.b. Constanza were not entirely independent of U.S. Gulf prices because of their leading role in the market.[16] Russian production was, on the other hand, under state monopoly. But even in the case of this production centre, attempts were made to bring it under international control and a number of meetings were held with the U.S.S.R. Government for this purpose.[17] In fact, most of the Russian exports were sold through the major oil companies.

It is interesting to note that despite these attempts to control Russian and Rumanian production, a part of it was sold through various independent companies at much lower than U.S. Gulf parity prices.[18] The major companies claimed that these prices did not properly reflect world conditions since the amounts involved were small and these sales amounted to "dumping". However, it cannot be denied that these were the only sources outside the control of the major companies, with separate f.o.b. prices, and their prices were lower than those determined under the U.S. Gulf parity system. Furthermore, the average cost of production of crude in the Persian Gulf was appreciably lower than the average cost in the U.S. Gulf, as it still is now, which implies that the marginal cost was also possibly lower in the Persian Gulf than in the U.S.[19]

One possible explanation behind the U.S. Gulf parity system can be found in the oligopolistic structure of the world market for oil, assuming the desire of the oligopolists to maximise profit, subject to the usual oligopolistic restraints. In a market controlled by seven very large international, vertically integrated firms, with enormous resources, each participant was compelled to take account of reactions to its own policy decisions on other sellers. Any price war, resulting from mere suspicion by one of another's motives, or from a desire on the part of one to expand its market share at the cost of others, was virtually certain to assume an international character, thereby causing heavy financial damage to almost all the sellers. None was relatively strong enough to earn any decisive victory over others, but a market-sharing arrangement was meaningless without an agreement on prices. In view of the mutual distrust of the oligopolists, a simple, easily understood price formula was needed which would on the one hand reduce mistrust and rivalry and, on the other hand, allow a secure profit. A basing point system with U.S. Gulf as the base satisfied these conditions. The fact that a large part of the world export trade in oil originated in the U.S. Gulf surely strengthened its claim. The nearer sources, not controlled by the U.S. companies, had no reason to complain so long their supply was not large enough to allow them larger profits through lower prices. It was during the period of falling demand and increasing production during the late 1920s and 1930s, that this system came under pressure. So, formal cartel arrangements covering the whole world had to be made in order to maintain a rigid price formula.

It is quite possible to argue that had it not been for the dominance of a small number of firms in the Indian market, who also controlled the nearer sources of oil, the supply of oil from nearer sources might have increased at a lower price. We have already seen that the suppliers of oil from the Far East and Persia were not satisfied with their small share in the Indian market, but were still unable to increase it at lower prices because of their international links and adherence to the world parity price system. Other factors remaining constant, the demand for an oil product was fixed at a certain level by the world parity price and the amount supplied by each company to the market was determined by the market-sharing arrangements between them. The market-sharing arrangement was unfavourable to the expanding production of the Far East and Persia during the 1920s and 1930s, which caused their dissatisfaction. The discontent of Royal Dutch found expression through a number of price wars which failed to snatch away any part of Standard's market. Any price war would spread quickly to many parts of the world and no decisive victory could be earned in the Indian market without adversely affecting Royal Dutch interests in other markets. Again, price wars, resulting from high world parity prices, would reduce the economic rent of Burmah Oil, an ally of both Royal Dutch and Anglo Persian, in the Indian market. For these reasons it was difficult for the producers of the Far East and Persia to make their geographical advantage and low cost over Standard's American oil clear through price wars.

But although Burmah Oil, Anglo Persian and Royal Dutch Shell presented a united front against Standard during the price wars, the question of the respective share of the constituents within the alliance also gave rise to disagreements between themselves from time to time. As we noted in Chapter Two, it took ten years before the kerosene oil of Anglo Persian was allowed to make an effective entry into the Indian market. It was stated with reference to its entry to the Indian market in the 1928 Annual Report of Anglo Persian:[20]

"This has been made possible by a friendly understanding with other companies who were there before us, but who recognise that the contiguity of our producing fields to that market gives us, notwithstanding our late arrival, an indisputable claim to consideration.

"Hitherto, India as an outlet for our products has been virtually confined to Fuel Oil . . . We have now arranged to consign to the new company ('Burmah Shell') through the 'Burmah' a substantive share—and as the market grows, an increasing amount—of the import trade of that enterprise; and this, in respect not only of the heavier oils, but of all products, including kerosene and motor spirit.

G

"This development is one for which our thanks are due to the Burmah company, *but for whose good offices we might have had to consider a less satisfactory procedure* [author's italics]—even if we had not found ourselves faced with the necessity of establishing a fully equipped distributing organisation on our own responsibility."

This agreement with Burmah Oil and Royal Dutch Shell to secure a share in the import trade of Burmah Shell was preceded by Anglo Persian's undertaking to support Royal Dutch Shell against Standard in the price war of 1927–28.[21] At the same time, these companies agreed to form a joint marketing organisation in place of their separate distributing networks in Egypt.[22]

Within the alliance, Burmah Oil occupied a specially favoured position and was allowed to market its entire production in the Indian market through Burmah Shell. This arrangement, however, as we have noted before, proved unsatisfactory to its two important allies, during the depressing years of the 1930s, who were obliged to withdraw their supply from India because of competition from independents, and declining demand, in order to allow Burmah Oil to market its entire production.[23]

All these clearly show that the nearer sources were willing to supply a larger amount of oil to India, but were prevented from doing so by the oligopolistic world market structure of the 1920s and 1930s and the consequent rigid pricing system. A different and more competitive world market structure, with a flexible pricing system, might have enabled India to receive more oil at lower prices. The measure of price elasticity is valid only within a certain range and a drastic cut in price might have quickened the pace of substitution of petroleum for vegetable and animal oils during the 1920s and 1930s.[24]

THE KEROSENE POOL: ITS MECHANISM

While the world parity price system applied to all products,[25] it was partly modified to allow for the expansion of the trade in kerosene of inferior grade, almost the entire amount of which was exclusively supplied by Burma and India, as will be apparent from the following discussion of the mechanism of the Kerosene Pool of 1919–1928.

Superior kerosene oil was contributed to the Pool partly by the companies of India and Burma and partly by Asiatic. The latter was the sole agency for importing kerosene on behalf of the Pool from outside Burma. Most of Asiatic's import of kerosene came from the Far East, while a part also came from the Anglo Persian Oil Company. Each contributor was paid a "contribution price" for its products. The "contribution price" paid to Asiatic for imports was based on the U.S. Gulf parity price discussed above, but the superior grade kerosene of Burma and India, it was claimed, was contributed "at a price not above and generally below the price of imported oil".[26] The chairman of the Indian Tariff Board, however, refused to accept this statement and showed that the "contribution price" paid to the Indian and Burmese producers of superior grade was higher than the world parity price based on U.S. Gulf.[27]

Inferior kerosene was contributed in three ways.[28] First, a minimum of 195,000 tons of inferior kerosene was sold to the Pool by the producers of Burma and India at a fixed price of Rs.2.14.0. plus excise duty per unit of 8 gallons. 195,000 tons was the figure of Burma's trade in inferior kerosene in 1905, when the first agreement between Asiatic and Burmah Oil was signed. This amount was distributed among the producers of India and Burma in the following way: every company was allowed a free volume of 1,000 barrels per day, and contributed to the Pool the quantity produced in excess of that amount per day. If the amount obtained from different companies in this way did not make 195,000 tons, the companies made further contributions in proportion to the volume of their production.

For the rest of the inferior grade kerosene supplied by the companies of India and Burma, a "contribution price" was paid which was claimed to be "not above and generally far below the price of imported oil".

Inferior kerosene contributed by Asiatic from other countries received a price of Rs.0.4.0. less per unit of 8 gallons than the price for imported superior kerosene, which was based on world parity. This price-differential was based on the difference in price, prevailing between these two qualities of kerosene in the Far East market.

The actual ex-ocean installation prices of kerosenes were fixed on the basis of these "contribution prices" in the following way. Superiors from different sources were mixed before sale, as also inferiors. Kerosenes were then sold at prices which would cover the prices paid to the companies by the Pool, fixed for a period of six months. If there was any excess it was carried into the suspense account and the balance was taken into account in fixing the price for the next six months. The Pool did not make any profit and used to balance the estimated incomes and expenditures.

A difference was maintained between the prices of the same quality of kerosene, supplied in tin-containers or in bulk, equal to Rs.1.4.0. per unit of 8 gallons for most of the time. However, the price differential between superior and inferior kerosene was not fixed and fluctuated from Rs.0.8.0. to Rs.1.9.0. per unit of 8 gallons. It was never made clear on what basis this price differential was determined.

Immediately before the price war of 1927–28, the prices of two grades were Rs.5.12.0. and Rs.4.6.0., respectively, per unit of 8 gallons. By the middle of 1928 the price of inferior was increased by Rs.0.4.0. per unit while a price war in superior kerosene reduced its prices.[29]

As appears from the above account, the price of superior kerosene was more or less comparable to the world parity price, and sometimes higher, while inferior grade kerosene was sold at a price below world parity.

THE KEROSENE POOL: BENEFIT TO THE CONSUMERS

Almost two-thirds of the total demand for kerosene in India during the 1920s and 1930s was accounted for by kerosene of inferior grade.[30] As we have noted already, almost the entire amount of inferior grade kerosene was supplied from Burma but for a few parcels from the Far East through Asiatic. The latter, again, was said to be of much better quality than the inferior grade supplied by Burma.[31]

It was claimed by Burmah Oil that the operation of the Pool and the consequent lower price of inferior grade benefited the poor consumers of India, who otherwise would have had to purchase kerosene at a high import price.[32] This was a valid argument in the sense that the quality did not matter to the poor Indian consumers and if there had been no production in Burma, the consumers would have had to pay higher prices for kerosene. But to imply that Burmah Oil, in following this low price policy for inferior grades, was motivated by the spirit of charity and sacrificed its objective of profit-maximisation, would be wrong.

There are reasonable grounds for doubting that the difference in price between the two grades of kerosene was as big as their difference in quality. It was reported that the burning quality of this grade was very low, and it gave rise to a smoky flame; and that in other countries a part of this oil was transformed into petrol and superior kerosene, while most of it was sold as fuel oil or gas oil.[33] Since the price of fuel oil was Rs.0.3.0. to Rs.0.4.0. per gallon, which was less than half the price of inferior grade kerosene, during the 1920s,[34] it was more profitable on the part of the oil companies to sell this product as inferior kerosene at a much higher price.

The lower price of inferior grade kerosene was also necessitated by a number of other considerations. A high price for inferior kerosene would lead to its being substituted by vegetable and animal oils on the one hand, and superior kerosene on the other. It was admitted by Mr. Gray of Burmah Oil before the Indian Tariff Board, that the possibility of substitution by essential oils or superior grade was a factor taken into consideration when pricing inferior grade kerosene.[35]

Secondly, a higher price for inferior kerosene would have induced other competitors to develop an even more inferior quality of kerosene and introduce it to the Indian market, which would have destroyed Burmah-Shell's monopoly in the inferior kerosene trade.[36]

Lastly, this benefit of lower prices for inferior quality scarcely reached the ultimate consumer in full. Most of the middlemen used to mix kerosene of different qualities in different proportions before selling it and charged different prices. But the higher level of profit allowed on inferior grade kerosene to the middlemen by the Pool was probably an incentive given to them so that they would only sell the other products—particularly kerosene of superior grade—supplied exclusively by the members of the Pool. It was also reported that each middleman who got inferior grade kerosene from the Pool had to sell a certain minimum quantity of superior grade kerosene in the market in competition with Standard.[37]

NOTES

1. Indian Tariff Board (3), p. 87, oral evidence of Mr. Guthrie of the Standard Oil Company of New York.

2. See Chapter Three.

3. See Chapter Two.

4. Indian Tariff Board (1), p. 17.

5. On top of the seaport installation charges the companies added a post base charge and railway freight when sold to the interior. The post base charge included handling the oil, loss in transit, commission to selling agents, averaged for the whole of India. In 1928, for kerosene, the post base charge was Rs.0.7.0 per unit of 8 gallons. See Indian Tariff Board (2), pp. 52–54.

6. Indian Tariff Board (1), pp. 11–21.

7. *Ibid*, pp. 11–21.

8. U.S. (2), pp. 21–28.

9. *Ibid*, p. 199.

10. *Ibid*, p. 200.

11. *Ibid*, p. 230.

12. *Ibid*, p. 241.

13. *Ibid*, pp. 253–268.

14. Leeman, p. 91.

15. U.S. (2), pp. 236–239.

16. Issaui and Yeganeh, p. 25.

17. U.S. (2), pp. 239–240.

18. See Chapter Three.

19. U.S. (2), pp. 357–367.

20. 1928 *Annual Report* of the Anglo Persian Oil Company.

21. See Chapter Two.

22. 1928 *Annual Report* of the Anglo-Persian Oil Company.

23. See Chapter Three.

24. See Chapter Five.

25. *Burmah Shell: Commercial Gazette* (Calcutta), 20.7.36, "B.O.C. Defends", and Western Indian Oil Distributing Company, p. 3.

26. Indian Tariff Board (1), pp. 11–12.

27. *Ibid*, pp. 71–75.

28. The rest of the account about the mechanism of the Kerosene Pool is based on the Indian Tariff Board's three publications in 1928 mentioned in the bibliography.

29. *Review of Trade of India* of relevant years.

30. Indian Tariff Board (1), p. 18.

31. Evidence of Mr. Gray of Burmah Oil before the Tariff Board in 1928. See Indian Tariff Board (2), pp. 33–35.

32. Burmah Oil claimed that between 1919 and 1923 this saved Indian consumers £22,000,000. See Indian Tariff Board (3), p. 116.

33. Mr. Gray admitted that the inferior kerosene sold in India was not going to find any market outside India as a burning oil. See Indian Tariff Board (2), pp. 32–35 and Indian Tariff Board (3), p. 220.

34. Indian Tariff Board (2), p. 25.

35. *Ibid*, pp. 32–39.

36. *Ibid*, p. 96.

37. *Ibid*, p. 36.

CHAPTER 5

FACTORS AFFECTING CONSUMPTION OF OIL IN INDIA

DEMAND FOR ENERGY IN INDIA

The low level of consumption of oil in India is a reflection of the low level of demand for commercial energy in general. Various estimates made in recent years show that a large proportion of the total energy consumed in India is supplied by non-commercial fuels, such as woods, dry leaves, cow dung, etc. It is extremely difficult to indicate either the total amount of energy consumption or the proportion of non-commercial fuels in it, because the latter are not bought and sold in the market. However, most of the estimates give a figure between 68% and 78% of total energy consumption accounted for by the non-commercial sources.[1] The very non-commercial nature of the energy market, and also the dominance of cattle-dung (which accounts for three-fourths of total energy demand, according to most estimates) shows the degree of economic backwardness of India's economy. One of the studies on the world energy consumption undertaken by the United Nations has shown a very high positive correlation between *per capita* income and *per capita* commercial energy consumption in about fifty countries.[2] Given the very low *per capita* income in India compared to most countries of the world, the low level of consumption of commercial energy is not surprising. However, national income per head is not the only factor which affects energy demand, and much also depends on the country's economic structure. For example, a large transport industry accounts for a larger demand for energy. In any case, with economic progress, greater industrial activity, and expansion in transport network, in future the consumption of secondary energy will fall, particularly since more and more cattle-dung will be used as a fertiliser and a reduction of firewood supply will take place following the Government's efforts to prevent deforestation and soil erosion.

A recent estimate, prepared by the Energy Survey of India, shows that in 1960–61 about 22% of all energy came from coal, about 19% from oil, and about 4% from hydro-electricity, while the rest came from non-commercial sources. Total energy requirements are expected to be doubled by 1970–71 and increase 3·5 times by 1975–76, assuming a 7% rate of growth of national income. The share of commercial energy is expected to increase from 45% in 1960–61 to 58% in 1970–71 and then to 68% in 1975–76.[3] However, in view of the fact that the economy has grown at a far lower pace than planned during the sixties, these predicted percentages are likely to be over-estimations of the actual growth in commercial energy consumption.

The share of oil in the total energy consumption in the future will depend, on the one hand, on the rate of growth in demand for commercial energy, and, on the other, on the price and availability of other sources of commercial energy such as coal, electricity, gas, and nuclear energy.

SUBSTITUTES OF OIL

India possesses a large reserve of coal, an estimated 51,350,000,000 tons of proved reserve and 120,000,000,000 tons of potential reserve. The current rate of production is, however, very low as a proportion of this reserve. The production figure for 1965–66 was 70,000,000 tons, and it is expected to reach 106,000,000 tons in 1970–71. At this rate it will take about 500 years to exhaust the current proved reserve, without allowing for potential reserve and further exploration. Lignite reserves also account for another 2,160,000,000 tons. These figures indicate that there is enormous scope for expanding coal and lignite industries. There are two difficulties in the way of an increase in the use of coal: first, a large proportion of this coal is of inferior variety with limited uses, and secondly, being concentrated in the eastern sector of India, its use in the western part of India involves high transport costs and produces considerable strain on the railway network. On the other hand, being an indigenous raw material, its production involves relatively small foreign exchange cost. Coal and oil products can be substituted for one another for many purposes, such as for electricity generation, town gas or fertiliser production, or as locomotive fuel. Coal can also be used as a feedstock for producing oil. Both South Africa and China produce a substantial proportion of their oil from coal, and Germany did the same during the Second World War. In India schemes for producing oil from coal have been discussed many times in the past. One of the main arguments for such a scheme is that the large reserve of low grade coal with high ash content, which do not have many uses, can be used for producing oil. Such schemes have not been implemented so far because of their high costs, but further research in future might bring down the costs, thereby making "oil from coal" plants economically feasible.

There is also a great potential for a large electricity industry in India, based on the country's huge water resources. Over the past twenty years a good measure of development has taken place in electricity generation. Whereas the installed capacity of the electricity generation plants was only 2·3 million kilowatts in 1950–51, it is expected to reach a figure of 20,000,000 by 1970–71. But even this high percentage increase over the past twenty years looks insignificant in terms of India's needs. By the end of the Third Five Year Plan period in only about 8% of the villages was electricity accessible, and not many households in these so called "electrified villages" could afford to consume electricity.[4] As will be seen below, the growth of electricity as an illuminant does not necessarily reduce the consumption of kerosene in absolute terms, although it makes kerosene less significant as an illuminant and as an oil product in percentage terms. Furthermore, electricity is both a competitor and a consumer of oil. Its use as a locomotive fuel displaces diesel, as an illuminant and heating aid it replaces kerosene, as an industrial fuel it replaces diesel and furnace oil, and future research may even permit its use as motor fuel in place of petrol. On the other hand, the wide use of electricity is also expected to increase the demand for oil as feedstock for electricity generation. In the industrially developed countries the electricity supplying companies are among the most important consumers of oil.

In the developed countries of the world the consumption of gas closely competes with oil consumption because of the ease with which it can be used, and also because of its cheaper price. In the United States gas accounts for as much of commercial energy consumption as oil, and for the non-communist world as a whole its proportion is 18·8%, as against 29·8% for coal, 48·6% for oil, and 2·8% for hydro-electricity and nuclear power.[5] The natural gas industry of India is still in its infancy. The main sources of natural gas in India today are the associated gas deposits of Ankleswar and Nahorkatiya oilfields, and the non-associated gas deposits of Cambay. The gas seepages of Jwalamukhi (Punjab) have been known for many years, and recent drillings have confirmed the presence of gas. But the amount of gas discovered so far is not large, although in view of impressive gas discoveries in Pakistan, particularly in the western wing of that country, there are grounds for optimism. A difficult problem facing the producers of gas is the distance of the markets from the production centres. In the case of Nahorkatiya gas, most of the present production is flared, because of the absence of local demand. Only a small part of the total production is now consumed by the tea plantations and local industries. Namrup fertiliser plant, which was expected to be completed by late-1969 or early-1970, will be one of the main consumers of this gas.[6] Assam State Electricity Board, Assam Gas Company, and Assam Oil Company, are among the other important consumers of Nahorkatiya gas. In view of the smallness of the deposits, and the distance to be covered, the construction of a pipeline to Calcutta and its industrial suburbs is still economically unattractive. The gas deposits of Gujrat are nearer the markets. At present, gas from Ankleswar is carried through pipelines to Uttaran Thermal Power Station and State Fertiliser Corporation, and also to Baroda. Gas from Cambay goes through pipeline to Dhuwaran Thermal Power Station. However, natural gas is less important than liquified petroleum gas, a refinery product, as a fuel in India. Both the majors and Indian Oil are now marketing bottled l.p.g. in the urban centres of North India.[7]

In the following discussion on individual oil products, reference will be made to the inter-relationship between the demand for these products and the demand for other sources of commercial energy.

CONSUMPTION OF KEROSENE

Before the development of the automobile industry, particularly before the second decade of this century, kerosene was the most valuable oil product in the world, and during much of the last century, accounted for more than 60% of total oil consumption. Its main use was for lighting.[8] With the growth of the industry and technical progress, the demand for kerosene rapidly declined in the developed countries of the West. For example, in 1962, the share of kerosene in the total consumption in the U.S. was 7·41% while in the U.K., France, West Germany, Italy, and Australia the respective percentage figures were 5·25; 2·04; 0·73; 2·64; and 6·09.[9] The rapid growth of electricity in these countries has almost completely removed the need for kerosene as an illuminant, and its chief uses are now for heating, cooking and as aviation fuel. The market for kerosene as aviation fuel is increasing rapidly with the increase in the number of jet planes all over the world.

In contrast with the present status of kerosene in the developed countries of the world, kerosene continues in India to be the most important oil product, still accounting for more than 25% of the total consumption.[10] Again, its main use is still as an illuminant, and only a marginal amount of kerosene is used for cooking or heating purposes, or as jet fuel.[11] The predominance of kerosene can be explained, in general terms, by the low level of development of industries in India which alone can generate demand for other oil products such as diesel, motor spirit and fuel oil, and, in particular, by the fact that more than 80% of the total population of India still lives in the villages,[12] only a small number of which have so far been electrified.[13] In the villages, kerosene is the only oil product of any significance in demand, accounting for 1·65 million tons of oil consumption in villages in 1962, while other products, taken together, accounted for 0·65 million tons.[14]

In the following few pages we will trace, historically, the factors influencing the consumption of kerosene with time.

VEGETABLE OIL: A CLOSE SUBSTITUTE FOR KEROSENE

The price elasticity of demand for kerosene is generally accepted as negligible. But any measurement of elasticity is valid only within a certain price range and a drastic change in price may induce a correspondingly large response in demand whereas a small change in price produces no perceptible effect. Again, price elasticity of a commodity is a function of the price and availability of substitutes, and what makes a commodity a substitute for another depends on the consumers' tastes and preferences, which are changing with time. For example, vegetable oil is hardly accepted as a substitute for kerosene now in India. The only region where vegetable oil is still used as an illuminant is Uttar Pradesh–Madhya Pradesh region, but even there, it accounts for less than 1% of the total consumption of illuminants.[15] The only important substitute for kerosene now is electricity, and no consumer who is already used to using kerosene as an illuminant, thinks of switching over to vegetable oil so long as the former is available. But only thirty-five years ago, vegetable oil was considered as an important substitute for kerosene and the price of the former considerably influenced the pricing decisions of the oil companies with respect to the latter.

Before the entry of Russian oil into the Indian market, vegetable oil and animal oil were the only illuminants used in the country but for a few Europeans and wealthy Indians living in the towns, who consumed "American oil". The introduction of Russian oil hardly affected the level of consumption of American oil and expanded at the cost of vegetable and animal oils.[16] Consumption of kerosene increased from 37,000,000 gallons in 1889–90[17] to 1,167,000,000 gallons in 1903,[18] almost the entire amount of which was accounted for by the cheap kerosene of Russia and Burma, at a time when the general health of the Indian economy was not good and the country suffered from two of the worst famines of all times.

It is, however, impossible to be precise about the elasticity of substitution of oil for vegetable oil because of the very nature of the vegetable oil market. Part of the latter was sold in the market and exported to other countries. Since the last century India has had a large export trade in oil seeds.[19] But the part of the vegetable oil used as an illuminant seldom entered the market and was produced by the farmer himself in his gardens. In any case the demand for an illuminant was not very great because of illiteracy.[20]

One of the reasons for the continued use of vegetable oil, even after the entry of Russian oil into the market, was that vegetable oils had many uses besides being used as illuminants and were (and still are) indispensable as ointments and for the purpose of cooking in almost all households. But more important, probably, was its easy and free availability to the consumers. Even now the small number of consumers who still use vegetable oil as an illuminant, prefer it to kerosene mainly because the former is easy to get.[21] Two factors however encouraged the growth in demand for kerosene in Indian households. First, the introduction of cheap kerosene lamps and hurricanes which gave more clear light, were handy and more convenient than the small earthen lamps of vegetable oil. But even as late as 1930, there were many people who could not afford hurricane lamps and used to stick a piece of wick in an ordinary bottle after filling it with kerosene.[22] Secondly, the importance of the tin container which could be used for a number of other household purposes by the farmers. But the increase in the desire of the villagers for more kerosene was not always reflected in consumption figures, because of the non-availability of kerosene.

One of the chief obstacles in handling the expansion of the kerosene trade was the bad transport system, which prevented the extension of the trade further into the interior of the country. Roads were bad and unusuable during the rainy season, and it took a long time before the oil companies could set up their own retail-distribution network in the interior. The following passage gives an idea about the nature of the retail trade in kerosene during the early part of the twentieth century:

"(Kerosene used to) arrive in such ports as Calcutta, Bombay, and Madras in packed cargo lots which were sold outright to a few dealers; these dealers took their purchases out of the ships and sold them to lesser dealers, who in turn sold them to still lesser dealers, and so on until ultimately somebody put the oil into a lamp and burnt it. When the oil was used up, whether the lamp could be filled again depended entirely upon whether this array of dealers had adjusted their bargains with each other so that each was satisfied with the amount of profit he was going to make on the next lot of oil which might find its way to the lamp."[23]

There is evidence which shows that with the growth of transport and the availability of kerosene, the use of vegetable oil for the purpose of illumination was steadily declining. But the latter continued to be more important than kerosene as an item of consumer expenditure throughout the 1930s.[24] During the Second

World War, when the consumption of kerosene was restricted by the Government, a large number of consumers fell back on vegetable oil again.

ELECTRICITY AS A SUBSTITUTE FOR KEROSENE

Electricity, the most important substitute for kerosene as an illuminant, has so far, contrary to the general belief at the beginning of the 1950s,[25] failed to curtail the consumption of kerosene in India. Although the share of kerosene in total consumption has declined from about 50% before the war to 23% in 1967, and is expected to decline further to 14% by 1975, in absolute terms the consumption of this product has increased threefold between 1951 and 1967. The consumption is expected to increase from 3 million tons in 1967 to 4·5 million tons in 1975. This phenomenon is partly explained by the fact that until now, less than 8% of the total number of Indian villages have been electrified and even after 1975–76, more than 60% of the villages will continue to be without electricity.[26]

The most remarkable feature of the relationship between kerosene and electricity is that the consumption of kerosene does not fall with the increasing use of electricity. The *per capita* kerosene consumption in the cities is nowhere lower than the national average.[27] According to the National Sample Survey, the *per capita* consumption of kerosene in rural and urban areas is in the proportion of 34 : 66.[28] A survey of oil consumption in villages, undertaken by the National Council of Applied Economic Research, shows that there is hardly any difference in *per capita* consumption of kerosene between electrified and unelectrified villages.[29]

All this information suggests that the growth in electricity consumption is as yet producing no adverse effect on kerosene consumption, either in urban or in rural areas, and in most cases these two are positively correlated.

One of the explanations behind this phenomenon is the "demonstration effect" of electricity on the people's desire for light. It was observed in 1930 in India that, ". . . nothing so much promotes the desire for light as the possession of it, and where electric light comes into use for the first time, strangely enough, the demand for kerosene oil almost always increases."[30] With the electrification of an area those who cannot afford electricity try to increase their kerosene consumption.

A second explanation is the "income effect" of electricity on kerosene consumption. The growth of electricity consumption in an area, on the one hand, reflects the higher economic level of that area and, on the other hand, induces further economic progress.

Since the income elasticity of kerosene consumption is generally very high, we find a positive correlation between the consumption of kerosene and electricity.

A third probable explanation is that a large section of the urban population, as also most of the people living in electrified villages, use kerosene as an illuminant.[31] The installation cost of equipment for receiving electricity is very high compared to the average income of people living in urban areas.

Lastly, while the use of kerosene as an illuminant declines in an urban area with time, its total consumption does not fall because of the development of its other uses—particularly for heating and cooking. On average, 25% of the total kerosene consumption in urban areas is for lighting, while 75% is for other purposes.[32] It has been found that, but for soft coke, on the basis of the efficiency of utilisation, kerosene is the cheapest domestic fuel for heating purposes. Since the former is unclean and not handy, compared to kerosene, an increase in income of households is also accompanied by increased kerosene consumption for heating purposes in place of soft coke. It is only after the household has attained a considerably high level of income that the convenience of electricity consumption for heating purposes outweighs the cheapness of kerosene.

INCOME ELASTICITY OF KEROSENE

A number of cross section studies on energy demand in India, prepared by the National Council of Applied Economic Research of New Delhi and National Sample Survey in recent years, show, among other things, the impact of income on kerosene consumption in urban and rural households all over the country.[33] These studies confirm high income elasticity of demand for kerosene up to a certain income level. Both the time series data and the cross section data indicate three stages in the growth of demand for kerosene. In the first stage, below a certain income level, kerosene is a *luxury*, and most of the demand for illuminants is satisfied from vegetable oils. With the increase in income, vegetable oil is replaced gradually by kerosene as an illuminant. Ultimately, after a certain income level is attained, vegetable oil is considered only as a remote substitute for kerosene, and the latter becomes a *necessary* commodity. At a still higher level of income, consumption of kerosene as an illuminant declines because of the competition of electricity, but the development of its other uses first increases, then maintains at a constant level, the total consumption of kerosene. It is only after a very high level of income has been reached that the consumption of kerosene declines with increases in income. At this stage kerosene becomes an *inferior* commodity. India is passing through the second stage at the macro-level, as is the case with the overwhelming majority of the households. The number of households in the first stage is extremely small at present, likewise those in the third stage.

As time goes by, the rate of growth of demand for kerosene as an illuminant will reduce. Its use for heating purposes in urban households is likely to grow in future, since electricity is expensive, and, but for a few cities, gas is not available.

FACTORS AFFECTING THE CONSUMPTION OF LIGHT DISTILLATES

Demand for motor spirit is derived from the petrol-consuming motor vehicles and their effective utilisation. In a poor country like India, private motor transport in large numbers is out of the question. However, the large inequality of income and the existence of a small group of people with a very high level of income,[34] has made possible at least a certain demand for private motor transport. But the latter accounts for only 30% of the total consumption of motor spirit, commercial vehicles accounting for the remaining 70%.[35]

Motor spirit consumption figures show a remarkable degree of fluctuation in India. (See Table 5.) Before the beginning of the First World War, motor spirit consumption was insignificant. Between the two world wars, consumption rose from 4,000,000 gallons in 1914–15 to 119,000,000 gallons in 1937–38, with the huge increase in the number of motor vehicles in use in India,[36] and with the expansion in the number of retail pump outlets after 1930. During the Second World War, consumption reached a peak because of military needs and the high priority accorded to it by the Government. Despite a fivefold increase in consumption over five years, which reached its zenith in 1943–44 with a record 558,000,000 gallon figure, rigorous rationing had to be used and also other means adopted for curtailing motor spirit consumption. But in the years following the Second World War there was a drastic cut in motor spirit consumption, which was brought down to the pre-war level. From 1951 to 1961 the consumption of motor spirit was at a standstill and in fact slightly declined in absolute terms. Since 1961, and more particularly since 1963, consumption of motor spirit is again growing, with an increase in military activity as a result of conflicts with China and Pakistan.

The foremost cause of the low level of demand for motor spirit is the increased dieselisation of motor vehicles in India[37] since the end of the war. At the beginning, the Government took the initiative to encourage the substitution of petrol by diesel and maintained a differential tax system in favour of diesel against motor spirit.[38] This Government policy was a reaction to the wartime and postwar shortage in motor spirit supply. But very soon the technical advantages of using high speed diesel, particularly in vehicles with a capacity of more than 5 tons,[39] became clear to the consumers of motor fuel, and despite the increase in diesel taxes in later years, the number of diesel-driven vehicles is increasing rapidly compared to the number of petrol-driven vehicles. In addition to the technical and economic advantages of diesel as a motor fuel it still receives favoured treatment from the state Governments, as is evident from the comparative sales tax rates on petrol and diesel in different states.[40]

The second important factor is the Government policy towards the automobile industry after independence. Because of the foreign exchange shortage the Government placed numerous restrictions on imports of motor cars and assigned it a low priority in foreign exchange allocation. At the end of 1949, the Government decided to give protection to the domestic automobile industry, which was still in its embryonic form.[41] At present, imports of automobiles, particularly the petrol-using smaller vehicles, are small, while the domestic car production is still inadequate to generate a sufficient amount of demand for motor spirit.[42]

A third important factor is the multiplicity of taxes on motor vehicles. At present, motor vehicles are subject to excise duty, sales tax, and, in some cities, wheel tax. Tyres and rubbers bear, in addition to import duty, excise duty and sales tax on their raw materials. There is also an additional excise duty on batteries. In some cases the vehicles are taxed according to the number of passengers or the volume or weight of goods carried. The rate of tax, again, varies from one part of the country to another and sometimes inter-state transport services need to pay double-taxation.[43] This complex, uncertain and decentralised tax-structure is one of the major factors discouraging the growth of road transport as well as the demand for motor spirit in India.

Another form of taxation of motor vehicles is the lack of good roads, and the percentage of revenue spent on roads by the Government, according to the Motor Vehicles Taxation Enquiry Committee of 1950, was much lower than in the advanced countries.[44] A subject of constant complaint since the 1930s is the relative preference shown to railways as against road transport and the consequent neglect of the need for constructing feeder roads.[45]

PRODUCT IMBALANCE IN LIGHT DISTILLATES

A consequence of this low demand for motor spirit has been the creation of a large surplus of light distillates, which represents the difference between the total amount of light fraction produced and its total use as motor spirit, and as a solvent in the manufacture of paint and varnish. The part of light distillates which is not further processed for use as motor fuel is called naphtha, and is sold at a price far below that of motor spirit. Until recently, there was virtually no market for naphtha in India, and most of the production had to be sold abroad through the major international oil companies. As will be seen in the next chapter, the prospect for exporting this surplus light distillates was getting thinner in the world market. The rapid growth of the petrochemical and fertiliser industries in recent years, both in India and in the world market, has transformed the situation by creating a market for naphtha as feedstock for these industries. The long run prospect is now for a shortage of naphtha in India, unless the production techniques in the Indian refineries are changed to produce more of this product. The two industries mentioned above would account for about 5·6 million tons of light distillates (3·9 million tons for fertiliser units, and 1·7 million tons for the petrochemical units) out of a total light distillates demand of 7·5 million tons in 1975, if all the units so far approved by the Government are brought into being according to schedule.

The growth of the fertiliser industry, from a 0·2 million tons annual capacity in 1960–61 to an expected 2,000,000 tons in 1971, has raised the question about the proper feedstock for this industry. Naphtha competes with coal, lignite, and gas, as well as liquid ammonia, as a raw material for fertiliser production. A number of fertiliser units, including Sindri fertiliser, are based on low grade coal, and the units of Durgapore and Neyveli use coke and lignite, respectively. The fertiliser plant of Gujrat depends on natural gas as a raw material. But the units located near oil refineries—like those of Bombay, Madras, Barauni, and Cochin, are being based on naphtha in order to dispose of the surplus amount of this product. The present policy is to produce 70% of fertiliser from naphtha, subject to the total maximum of naphtha surplus.

The case for liquid ammonia is based on the following grounds. Firstly, it is available at a cheap price from the Middle East. Secondly, by dispensing with the stage of ammonia production, it simplifies the production process. Thirdly, since the long run prospect is for a shortage of naphtha in India, emphasis should be placed on alternative feedstocks. All these points, although valid, are argued from the point of view of an individual industry, isolated from the rest of the economy. The use of liquid ammonia, although cheaper, would involve foreign exchange cost, whereas naphtha is available from domestic refineries. Secondly, the import of liquid ammonia also implies that the production of fertiliser is carried out in two parts, and the first part of it is carried out in another country, with the consequent loss of benefits in terms of employment and industrial development.

H

Thirdly, since the conditions in the world market for oil products are changing frequently, as discussed in the next chapter, the prospect for finding market for surplus naphtha outside India is uncertain. On the other hand, the expected future shortages in naphtha in Indian can be bridged by changing the techniques of refinery production (see the next chapter) without making the country dependent on a foreign source of raw material. And even if the gap between the demand for and supply of naphtha remains, the case for using coal, lignite, or coke, in preference to liquid ammonia deserves serious consideration because of their domestic origin.

FACTORS AFFECTING THE CONSUMPTION OF HIGH SPEED DIESEL

While the importance of motor spirit among oil products is declining secularly—a trend which is unlikely to be reversed so long as the low priority given to private transport in national plans is not changed—high speed diesel shows a very high rate of growth, the highest among oil products. Consumption of h.s.d. increased from 65,000 tons in 1948 to about 3,000,000 tons in 1965. According to some estimates, by 1976 it will account for more than half the total oil consumption.[46] Of the total consumption of h.s.d., between two-thirds and three-quarters are accounted for by road transport.[47] There are a number of factors working in favour of the use of h.s.d. in larger amounts.

An important factor in the growth of the demand for h.s.d. as motor fuel is its higher efficiency, in addition to the tax advantage it enjoys over motor spirit. Its use is best suited to cars with a capacity exceeding 5 tons and the proportion of dieselised trucks and buses is rapidly growing.[48] A contributory factor to its growth will be the growth of long-distance road traffic over this period. Before 1956 the entire amount of long-distance traffic load was carried by railways alone. But by 1975–76, road transport is expected to account for 27·5% of such traffic.[49] The chief cause behind this change in the pattern of long-distance haulage is the desire of the Government to restrict the already over-loaded railway transport to heavy materials—such as coal, iron, etc.—and to allow the road transport to get a gradually increasing proportion of the haulage of finished goods. This is in line with the trend in the developed countries such as Britain and is the outcome of the relatively higher speed of road transport on the one hand and the relative fuel economy of the latter, on the other.[50]

A second factor in the growth of h.s.d. consumption will be the dieselisation of railway locomotives, which was started in the 1930s[51] but did not reach its momentum until very recently. Diesel locomotives are far superior to steam locomotives in efficiency, particularly on those sections which suffer from a shortage of water.

Despite the higher cost of maintenance of diesel driven locomotives, the service availability of the latter is higher because it is free from any wastage of time for watering, fire cleaning and other boiler requirements.[52] It is estimated that by 1975–76 one-fifth of the total capacity of railways will be converted to diesel traction[53] and the consumption of h.s.d. for railways will increase from 0·16 million tons in 1960–61 to 0·20 million tons in 1965–66 and 0·48 and 0·96 million tons in 1970–71 and 1975–76, respectively, according to present estimates.[54]

There is also a small demand for h.s.d. in power generation, but its share in the latter is declining because of the high price of diesel compared to the low grade coal needed for electricity generation.[55] But h.s.d. is also used for irrigation pumps and in small scale industries. It is now replacing light diesel oil in those fields, due to its higher efficiency and the introduction of more compact h.s.d. stationary engines.[56]

It is extremely difficult, however, to be precise about the scale of consumption of h.s.d. in future years. Given the present rate of growth of its consumption, its proportion is significantly high and necessitates huge imports in future years, involving large foreign exchange costs. Since most of its demand follows from the fuel policy, rail-road policy, and also the tax policy of the Government, much will depend on how far and to what extent, if at all, the Government will modify these policies with respect to diesel under the pressure of the foreign exchange crisis. Despite the lower efficiency of steam locomotives, the Government may prefer those to diesel imported from outside. Again, a discriminatory tax policy against diesel and in favour of motor spirit might slide the scale in favour of the latter.

FACTORS AFFECTING THE CONSUMPTION OF FURNACE OIL

Historically, the demand for furnace oil[57] in India was closely correlated with the progress of the cotton textile industry of Bombay which used it for firing the boilers under the stills; the rest of the demand derived from other industries, bunkers, and a small part of it was also used by the Digboi refinery.[58] That the effect of the 1930s depression was not severe on the cotton textile industry explains why the level of demand for fuel oil could be maintained in what were the worst years of the Indian economy.[59]

At present, approximately 28% of the consumption of furnace oil is for bunkers, while the rest is for industries. There is a very high correlation of 0·86 between the industrial index and furnace oil consumption between 1948 and 1962.[60] There are certain industries like glass, ceramics and certain chemical industries where the use of furnace oil is considered superior to the use of coal for technical reasons.[61] These industries account for about 14% of the furnace oil consumption.[62] But, for the bulk of its consumption, furnace oil acts as a substitute for coal.

However, the Indian economy is still coal-oriented and even in 1965 furnace oil is estimated to account for $4 \cdot 162$ million tons of coal equivalent of energy, which is less than 11% of the coal consumption of $39 \cdot 02$ estimated for 1965. The proportion of furnace oil is expected to increase with time, and, according to one estimate, will exceed 15% of coal consumption by industry by 1975.[63] The high proportion of coal in total energy consumption by industry follows from its two advantages. First, India possesses about 51,000,000,000 tons of coal reserve, which is much higher than the approximately 200,000,000 tons of crude oil reserve so far proved in India even after allowing for higher thermal efficiency of oil. In view of import restrictions on oil, this large coal reserve will be more fully exploited in future years. In fact the production of coal is increasing over time. A second advantage of coal is its cheapness, as is evident from the following figures:

TABLE 13

PRICES OF COAL AND FURNACE OIL (RUPEES PER TON)
Source: "Demand for Energy" (N.C.A.E.R.)

State	Coal	Furnace Oil
West Bengal	$21 \cdot 9$	224
Bombay	$35 \cdot 5$	176
Madras	$35 \cdot 3$	196
Punjab	$32 \cdot 4$	336

However, the price differential is not as big as it appears from the above figures since the coal of India is of an inferior quality and the efficiency of furnace oil is about 50% higher. Again, the price differential is not so high in Madras or Bombay which are situated more than 700 miles away from the coalfields of India, most which are located in Eastern India. Furthermore, the coal industry, despite a higher level of production, will still be unable to satisfy the needs of a large part of western India because of the shortage of railway wagons required for this purpose. It seems from all accounts that this chronic shortage of wagons will continue for a long time to come, while the demand for energy in industries will be increasing with industrial progress.[64] A number of industries are unwilling to depend on the irregular supply of coal and have, in recent years, switched over to furnace oil.[65] Further substitution will depend on a number of factors such as the relative price and availability of the two fuels.

CONSUMPTION OF OTHER PRODUCTS

Light diesel oil (a mixture of 90% inferior kerosene and 10% furnace oil) is an important oil product for small producers, particularly valuable in agriculture and small industries. Before the Second World War its importance was slight because of the small number of oil engines and tractors in use.[66] Between 1939 and 1949 there was a large growth in its consumption, from 9,391 tons to 346,000 tons.[67] Since then its growth has been negligible, and the smallest among major oil products, mainly on account of the growing use of h.s.d. by stationary engines.[68] However, renewed emphasis on agriculture in recent years and the consequent need for mechanisation of agriculture is likely to increase the rate of growth of l.d.o. consumption in future years. The number of diesel oil engines is expected to grow from 170,000 in 1960–61 to 400,000 in 1975–76 and the number of tractors may increase from 21,000 in 1956 to 1,000,000 in 1970–71,[69] resulting in a consequent increase in l.d.o. consumption from 580,000 in 1961 to about 1·7 million tons in 1975–76 in agriculture alone.[70] However, much will depend also on the extension of rural electrification by that time, which will restrict the growth of l.d.o. consumption.

Lubricating oil, the most highly priced oil product,[71] also suffered from the competition of vegetable oil until the end of the First World War. The latter restricted the consumption of lubricants[72] which only doubled between the two world wars, while fuel oil consumption increased fourfold and motor spirit consumption tenfold. But in recent years its consumption is increasing at a high rate (from less than 0·2 million tons in 1950 to an estimated 0·8 million tons by 1971) with industrial growth and progress in road transport,[73] although as a proportion of total oil consumption its consumption is declining. Because of a close correlation between industrial production index and the consumption of lubricants,[74] the growth in the latter in future years will bear a very close proportional relationship to the former.

Bitumen is mainly used in road-making, while 20% of its consumption is also accounted for by hydraulic engineering works, in waterproof roofing materials industry and also for making airport runways. Before the beginning of the first Five Year Plan in 1951, its consumption was limited, but the priority assigned to transport in the Indian plans has enhanced its importance. According to the twenty-year programme prepared by the chief engineers of all the states, the demand for bitumen for road purposes will be $1 \cdot 5$ million tons by 1981.[75]

ESTIMATES OF OIL CONSUMPTION

Recent years have witnessed a significant change in the pattern of consumption of oil products in India, along with increases in aggregate oil consumption. The consumption of oil has increased from less than 2,000,000 tons during the pre-Second-World-War days, and 4,000,000 tons in 1953, to 8,000,000 tons in 1960, and to 13,000,000 tons in 1967. At the same time the use of oil as an item of domestic consumption has yielded ground to its use as a factor of production in the industrial process. Whereas during the 1930s kerosene accounted for about half of the aggregate oil consumption, in 1967 its share was only 23%, and a substantial part of it was used for purposes other than as an illuminant. This trend of the diminishing importance of kerosene is associated with the increasing role of diesels among oil products. Although for a long time since Independence the share of light distillates in consumption was low, recent forecasts of increased consumption of this product in future, brings the pattern of oil consumption in India more in line with the pattern in the rest of the world. On the other hand, on a *per capita* basis, the present level of oil consumption in India is still exceedingly low, and reflects a poor level of industrial progress. The present per head consumption of oil in India—a quarter of a ton—is less than a fortieth of the figure for Japan, and less than one-hundredth of the figure for the United States.

The forecasting of the future consumption in India is a hazardous exercise. Both the demand and the supply conditions are to a great extent dependent on the Government policy towards oil. Given a certain national fuel policy, industrial policy, import policy, and tax policy, one set of data for oil consumption can be calculated, while, given another set of policy parameters, a different set of estimates for oil consumption would emerge. If a large amount of gas and oil deposits is discovered, either within India or outside under Indian ownership, their use may be encouraged through suitable changes in tax, price, and fuel policies. If, on the other hand, the prospect of such a discovery appears slim, and the pressure on dwindling foreign exchange reserve continues, its import—in the form of both crude oil and products—may be discouraged. The Energy Survey of India report, submitted to the Government in 1965, argued in favour of "allowing the relative prices of different fuels to reflect their scarcities or availabilities and encourage consumers to use those forms of energy which the Indian economy is best able to provide". The same report also predicted a small 10,000,000 tons domestic crude output per year by 1981, and, by implication, favoured the growth of other fuels such as coal, lignite, or hydro-electricity, which are available in large amounts from within the country. Such a policy would limit the growth of oil consumption.

The risk associated with the estimation of future oil consumption is clearly illustrated by the forecasts made at various points of time about the level of consumption towards the end of the Third Five Year Plan. The draft plan made an estimate of 9·96 million tons by 1965, which was revised during the early sixties to 11·7 million tons by the Oil Advisory Committee of the Government. In 1961 the estimate was modified to 14·14 million tons by 1966, and to more than 16,000,000 tons by 1966, in 1962. The actual consumption in 1966 was, however, only 12,000,000 tons, because of economic depression and rigorous rationing of kerosene. The present estimates of oil consumption by 1971 and 1975, are 22,000,000 and 32,000,000 tons respectively, which are far short of the estimates prepared in 1965 for those two years.

TABLE 14

REFINERY CAPACITY AND OWNERSHIP IN INDIA

Location	State	Company	Nature of the Co.	Date of Commence- ment	Capacity (Millions Tons)	Source of crude	Ownership
Digboi (Inland)	Assam	Assam Oil Company	Subsidiary of Burmah Oil	1899	0·4 0·5 (1975)*	Digboi (Assam)	Major International Co.
Trombay (Bombay) (Coastal)	Maharastra (previously known as Bombay)	Burmah Shell refineries	Equal Ownership of Shell and Burmah Oil	1955	3·50 (1963) 4·00 (1968) 5·20 (1975)*	Persian Gulf	Ditto
Trombay (Bombay) (Coastal)	Ditto	Esso (formerly Stan-vac refineries)	Subsidiary of Jersey Standard	1954	2·80 (1963)	Ditto	Ditto
Vizagapatnam (Coastal)	Andhra	Caltex Refineries	Subsidiary of Standard of California and Texas Oil	1957	1·10 (1963) 1·60 (1975)*	Persian Gulf and Indonesia	Ditto
Nunmati (Inland)	Assam	Indian Refineries	Central Govt. (85%) and State Govt (15%)	1962	0·75 (1962) 1·00 (1966)	Nahorkatiya and Moran (Assam)	State Owned
Barauni (Inland)	Bihar	Ditto	Ditto	1964	1·0 (1964) 2·0 (1965) 3·0 (1968) 4·5 (1975)*	Ditto	Ditto
Koyali (Inland)	Gujrat	Ditto	Ditto	1965	1·0 (1965) 3·0 (1967) 4·0 (1975)*	Gujrat	Ditto

TABLE 14 (*continued*)

Location	State	Company	Nature of the Co.	Date of Commence-ment	Capacity (Millions Tons)	Source of crude	Ownership
Cochin (Coastal)	Kerala	State (51%), Philips (25%), Indian Shareholders (24%)		1966	2·0 (1966) 3·5 (1975)*	Persian Gulf	Jointly owned by the Govt. and Independents
Madras (Coastal)	Madras	State (74%), National Iranian Oil Co. and American International Oil Company (26%)		1969	2·5 (1969)	Darius (Iran)	Ditto
Haldia (Coastal)	West Bengal	Indian Refineries		1971·	2·5 (1971)*	One-half through C.F.P. (from Iran) and the other half from open market	Government

*Estimated.

NOTES

1. N.C.A.E.R. (2), pp. 3–4; and *Oil Statistics*, July–September, 1965, pp. 23–27.
2. U.N. (3), pp. 1–29.
3. *Oil Statistics*, July–September, 1965, pp. 23–24.
4. *Third Five Year Plan* (Government of India), p. 404.
5. Petroleum Information Bureau, "Oil, World Statistics", p. 1.
6. *Economic and Political Weekly*, September, 1968, p. 1352.
7. Ministry of Petroleum and Chemicals, *Annual Report*, 1967–68.
8. Frankel (1), p. 62.
9. *Indian Petroleum Handbook*, 1964, p. 105.
10. Government of India (8), p. 35.
11. See *Eastern Economist*, September 20, 1960 (Oil Supplement).
12. The percentage of rural population is 82·2. See *The Census of India*, 1961.
13. Out of 559,665 villages only 41,784, that is less than 8% have so far been electrified. Again, not all the houses in these villages have got electricity since only a few of the villagers can afford to provide the necessary costs of installation of electrical equipment. (See N.C.A.E.R. (8), p. 96.) Again, "A significant factor of limitation on the spread of electricity for lighting in the villages is the type of housing construction in vogue." (See, *Eastern Economist*, September 20, 1960.)
14. N.C.A.E.R. (8), p. 47.
15. N.C.A.E.R. (8), pp. 30–31.
16. See Chapter Two, p. 30.
17. Watt (2), p. 811.
18. See Table 4.
19. *Kothari's Economic Guide and Investor's Handbook*, (1965), pp. 2207–9.
20. In 1921, for example, only 7% of the total population could write and read. See *Census of India* (1921), vol. I, Part A, p. 175.
21. 57·3% of the consumers of vegetable oil as an illuminant, according to a survey conducted by the National Council of Applied Economic Research of Delhi, prefer it because it is "easily and freely available". See N.C.A.E.R. (8), p. 93.
22. P.T., November 15, 1930, p. 773.
23. *Petroleum Times*, September 6, 1930, p. 395.
24. Desai (1), pp. 278–79.
25. Government of India (12), 1951–56.
26. *The Third Five Year Plan*, pp. 404–405.
27. Dhar, p. 11.
28. Dhar, p. 11.
29. N.C.A.E.R. (8), p. 73.
30. P.T., September 6, 1930, p. 395.
31. Even in Delhi as many as 55% of the households in the non-slum areas do not have electricity. See Dhar, p. 11.
32. N.C.A.E.R. (8), pp. 14–15.
33. N.C.A.E.R. (2), pp. 155, 181, 209.
34. Government of India (11).
35. Dhar, p. 6.
36. The number of cars imported increased from 3,352 in 1914–15 to 33,659 in 1929–30. Due to the depression in the following four years the import figures went down to 9,659 in 1932–33. From 1933–34 imports again increased and in 1937–38 32,000 cars were imported. See, *Review of Trade of India*, of relevant years.
37. The output of diesel-driven buses and trucks increased from 4,620 in 1955 to 24,146 in 1963, when the output of petrol-driven trucks declined from

4,428 to 4,235 and there has been no production of petrol-driven buses since 1960. See, *Indian Petroleum Handbook*, 1964, p. 89.

38. The differential tax rate gave diesel a Rs.1.32 per gallon price advantage over petrol. See Dhar, pp. 4–5.

39. Because of the high thermal efficiency of diesel, the cost per mile of a diesel-driven vehicle, including the cost of repairs is Rs.0.2.7 which is much less than Rs.0.5.9, the corresponding figure for petrol-driven cars. This cost advantage per mile of diesel compensates for its higher initial cost. See *Ibid*, and K. A. Mitter, "Thoughts on India's Automobile and Tractor Industry", in *Indian Industries*, (Engineering issue), 1958–59.

40. In most states sales tax on diesel is half the tax on diesel. The total central duty on diesel is Rs.484 per kilolitre, compared to Rs.547 on petrol. This is after recent increases in tax on diesel. See, *Indian Petroleum Handbook*, 1964, pp. 80–81.

41. *Capital*, 1.12.1949, p. 849.

42. In 1963 the output of automobiles was 52,197, of which 24,146 were diesel-driven. See *Indian Petroleum Handbook*, 1964, p. 89.

43. *Economic Weekly*, 16.1.1960, p. 71; *Commerce*, 16.3.1963, p. 438.

44. *Capital*, 4.1.1951, p. 2.

45. P.T., 20.1.1931, p. 845; P.P.S., December, 1956, p. 437.

46. *Eastern Economist*, 2.9.1960.

47. *Ibid*, also Dhar, p. 21.

48. It is estimated that out of a total number of 843,200 trucks in operation in 1975–76, about 480,600 would be driven by high speed diesel. See N.C.A.E.R. (4), p. 75.

49. N.C.A.E.R. (4), p. 72.

50. In terms of coal equivalent, for carrying 1,000 ton miles of cargo the respective consumption of fuel by rail (steam) and road (petrol) and road (diesel) are $0 \cdot 20$, $0 \cdot 107$ and $0 \cdot 091$. In the case of passenger traffic the comparative efficiency of diesel is still higher, See N.C.A.E.R. (4), p. 64.

51. P.P.S., March 20, 1936, p. 91.

52. Government of India (4), p. 149.

53. Government of India (5), p. 91.

54. N.C.A.E.R. (4), pp. 68–69.

55. It declined from 3% in 1950 to $2 \cdot 2\%$ in 1955, and less than 1% in 1960. *Ibid*, pp. 101–102.

56. N.C.A.E.R. (7), p. 32.

57. In the import trade statistics for the pre-Independence period, no separate classifications were made for h.s.d., light diesel oil and furnace oil, and all were lumped together under fuel oil.

58. P.P.S., 20.3.1936, p. 91; P.T., 20.6.1931, p. 845.

59. See Chapter Three, p. 94.

60. Calculated from data given in Table 11.

61. *Eastern Economist*, 2.9.1960.

62. Dhar, p. 25.

63. N.C.A.E.R. (4), pp. 86–89.

64. Hansen, pp. 221–222 and Singh.

65. Furnace oil needs less storage capacity. In addition, since 1962 (July) the Government has reduced by half the railway freight of furnace oil in many areas. See *Capital*, 28.6.1962, p. 1030, 25.1.1962, p. 158.

66. The number of oil engines was 4,274 in 1927–28 and 5,318 and 6,305 in the following two years, respectively. But then the number fell and, until 1946–47, never exceeded 3,535. See *Statistical Abstract for British India*, 1927–28 to 1936–37, 1936–37 to 1940–41 and *Statistical Abstract of India*, 1950.

67. *Eastern Economist*, 2.9.1960; *Capital*, 24.3.1948, p. 538.

68. Between 1950 and 1961 consumption increased from 329,000 to 555,000 tons. See *Eastern Economist*, 2.9.1960.

69. N.C.A.E.R. (4), pp. 93–96.

70. Consumption of oil for tractors, at a rate of 500 gallons per tractor, will equal 1·06 million tons, while that for oil engines, assuming about 1·15 tons per engine per year, will equal 460,000 tons. Adding a miscellaneous 10% for the use of L.D.O. in other agricultural implements, a total of roughly 1·7 million tons of L.D.O. is reached for agricultural pruposes by 1975–76.

71. See Tables 12 and 13.

72. P.P.S., March 20, 1936, p. 91.

73. Consumption increased from 139,000 tons in 1950 to 270,000 tons in 1961. See *Eastern Economist*, 2.9.1960.

74. In the U.K. the consumption of lubricants increased by 23% between 1938 and 1950, which exactly equalled the percentage increase in industrial output over those years. See, Government of U.K., *Sources and Nature of the Statistics of the United Kingdom*, vol. II, p. 213.

75. Dhar, pp. 26–27.

CHAPTER 6

DOMESTIC REFINING INDUSTRY

DOMESTIC REFINING INDUSTRY VERSUS PRODUCT IMPORTS
Before the Second World War the practice prevalent in the world oil industry was to locate refineries near the centres of crude oil production. In 1939, approximately 70% of the refineries of the non-communist world were resource-orientated, and only 30% were situated near the markets.[1] Such a policy was usually justified on three accounts: firstly, it allowed the oil companies to build very large refineries, which reduced their unit costs of installation and operation. The cost index of installation goes up from 100 for a 5,000,000 ton refinery, to 109 when the capacity is 4,000,000 tons, and then to 123, 144, and 190, when the capacity is further reduced to 3,000,000, 2,000,000, or 1,000,000 tons.[2] Cost of operation is also a decreasing function of output and the rate of increase in output. Secondly, it allowed for flexibility in the distribution of oil products for an international company, which was in a position to supply, from the resource-based refineries, its marketing affiliates in various countries, which had divergent patterns of relative demand for oil products. On the other hand, market-based refineries were likely to produce too much of some products and too few of some others, and were going to create marketing problems for the oil companies. Thirdly, refining being a weight-losing industry, there was scope for economising the cost of transport of that part of the crude which would be lost in the refining process, by building refineries near the crude source.

The present trend in the oil industry is, however, to locate the refineries nearer the consumption centres. In 1962, about 63% of the refineries of the non-communist world were market-orientated, and another 7% were intermediate refineries, whereas only 30% were resource-orientated.[3] The reasons are, from the point of view of the oil companies, partly political and partly economic. Economically, the advantages derived from the economics of scale of the large refineries are to be balanced against the high cost of distribution of oil products when these are supplied from refineries far away from the marketing centres. On almost every form of transport, the cost of transporting crude oil is cheaper than the cost of transporting oil products. Whereas crude is a single commodity, different oil products would involve separate costs for packaging and handling, and occupy more space. Even in the case of product pipelines, not all the products can be handled by the latter and, in particular, fuel oil would require to be transported by other means. The scope for reaping economies of scale in transportation is also much higher in the case of crude oil, in comparison with oil products.[4] The growth of large tankers has revolutionised the system of oil transportation, but the giant tankers of 100,000 or 200,000 d.w.t. with cheap unit cost can only be used for carrying crude.[5] Secondly, with the growth of oil consumption in the world it is now becoming increasingly possible to install large refineries even in the consumption centres far away from the crude source. It was estimated that about two refineries out of every five operating in 1965 had a capacity of between 2,000,000 and 5,000,000 tons, and almost all the cost estimates show that the scale advantages of large refineries drops sharply after the 2,000,000 ton mark. Furthermore, the research efforts of the oil industry have succeeded in reducing the cost gap between the large and the small refineries by suitable changes in the refinery design and crude intake capacity. A refinery with a crude distiller and platformer, using a single crude, is going to be far less costly than a refinery of the same capacity but capable of handling various kinds of crude and yielding varying proportions of oil products.[6]

But more than refinery technology and economics is involved in the present trend towards market-orientated refineries. It also reflects the desire of the oil companies to spread the risk of their investments geographically, rather than concentrating in the crude oil producing areas (mostly the Middle East and North Africa) both the producing and the refining activities. Since the Abadan crisis of 1951–53, when the oil industry was taken over by the Government of Iran, the international oil companies are under constant fear of nationalisation of their undertakings in the producing countries. The formation of O.P.E.C. (Organisation of Petroleum Exporting Countries) by the leading oil producers of the Middle East, and disputes with the latter on the question of royalty and tax payments have added to this fear. While the dependence of the oil companies on the oil producing countries of the Middle East and North Africa for the supply of crude oil is as yet unavoidable, the former are trying to diversify the sources of crude within this region, while at the same time arranging to keep as much of their business out of this region as possible. So long as the present huge shut-in capacity in the Western hemisphere continues to exist, any temporary shortage of crude oil in West Europe because of a crisis in the Middle East or North Africa can always be effectively met, although at a high cost to the companies. On the other hand, it would require at least eighteen to twenty-four months to build new refining capacity, and, hence, a loss of refining capacity resulting from any such crisis would produce a more severe effect that the loss of crude.

This trend is also an outcome of the pressure exerted by the governments of the oil consuming countries for building refineries within their territories in order to save a part of their foreign exchange costs. Some of the oil consuming countries, like Greece, or India, allow the import of oil products only to the extent that the consumption of oil exceeds the output of the domestic refineries. In those cases construction of refineries by the oil companies also entitles the latter to acquire a pre-emptive share in the market equal to its domestic refinery output. Even where the refineries are not allowed to market their products and are only paid processing fees, the installation of these refineries at least ensures a regular outlet for their crude. Many newcomers to the oil industry in the eastern hemisphere tend to view refinery construction as a price for buying the right to sell their crude on a long term basis to these refineries.

From the point of view of the oil importing countries like India, the establishment of a domestic refining industry ensures regularity of oil supply, makes it less dependent on the powerful international oil companies, makes a significant contribution to the industrial development of the country, and also saves a substantial amount of foreign exchange.

At least twice during the past twenty-five years Indian consumers suffered from a disruption in oil supply because of the absence of oil refineries within India. During the Second World War the Japanese army occupied South Burma and destroyed its refineries, which interrupted the supply of oil to India, although the crude producing regions of Burma were then still in the hands of the British. The impact of the Abadan crisis of 1951 was more severe because of the loss of the 25,000,000 tons refinery, which could not be made up within a short time. Again, the supply of oil products from abroad meant, during the pre-1954 days, an exclusive dependence on the international oil companies for this important raw material. The latter, because of their enormous economic strength and oligopolistic control over the world market, were always in a position to reduce the supply of oil to India if that were in accordance with their commercial objectives on a global basis. The establishment of a domestic refining industry, even when owned by the same international oil companies, makes the country less dependent on the whims of the oligopolists. Thirdly, although the number of jobs created by the refining industry is limited because of its capital-intensive nature, it acts as a nucleus of a large industrial complex which includes basic industries like petrochemical, gas, and fertiliser industries, which in their turn play a leading role in accelerating industrial progress. Last, but not least, it saves a substantial amount of foreign exchange, equal to the difference between the cost of importing oil products and the cost of importing crude for producing the same amounts of products, net of profit-remittance and other foreign exchange costs of a refinery. It has been estimated that, in the case of India, the net saving of foreign exchange amounts to about Rs.25 to Rs.35 per ton, even when the refinery operates under foreign ownership, which would imply, by 1975, an annual saving of at least Rs.800,000,000.

The construction of refineries also creates a number of economic problems. If the scale of oil consumption is not reasonably high, the size of the refinery becomes uneconomic, and the cost of domestic oil products compares unfavourably with that of imported oil products. It increases the cost of production of the industries using oil as their input, which offsets the advantage derived from saving foreign exchange by having a domestic refinery. Sometimes the governments of the oil consuming countries bear this additional cost for political reasons—but there is no ground for thinking that such an investment is wrong, simply because it is politically motivated and economically unsound. Refineries may be employed as symbols of national identity, particularly by the new nations of the poor world, an objective which is no less desirable than the maximisation of technical efficiency of a particular project. On the other hand, in response to the growing demand for smaller refineries in the countries of Africa, Asia, and Latin America, the oil industry has succeeded in developing refinery techniques and designs which minimise the cost disadvantage of the smaller units. In the case of India, of the eleven refineries so far built, or being constructed, or at the planning or talking stage, only three are below 2,000,000 ton capacity. Of these, Digboi, with less than half a million ton capacity, was built at a time when the average capacity of a refinery in the world was not very far from 1,000,000 tons. Being based on domestic crude, and located far away from the sea and the main consumption centres, there was little choice but to tailor the refinery capacity to the production of the oilfield. But the other two—Nunmati and Vizagapatnam—with less than 1,000,000 ton capacities, were products of faulty location policy, as would be seen in a subsequent section. As regards prices for the oil products of the domestic refineries, these are competitive with the prices of imported products, although the private oil refineries enjoyed tariff protection for several years under the refinery agreements of 1951–1953.[7]

A more serious problem which accompanies the establishment of a

domestic refining industry is the problem of product imbalance, which
is discussed below.

THE PROBLEM OF PRODUCT IMBALANCE

So long as a country is dependent on imports for the supply of
oil products, the only problem for its government or the oil companies
is to estimate the size of demand for each individual product at the
existing price, and to import accordingly. With the building of
refineries it becomes necessary to find a market for the whole range
of the oil products of the domestic refineries, either within the
country or abroad. Given a government policy of achieving and
maintaining self-sufficiency in refined oil products, the domestic
refineries are likely to produce surplus in some products and deficits
in others, unless the proportion of every product in the total demand
for oil exactly corresponds to its proportion in the refinery output,
and the overall supply of all oil products equals the overall demand.
No country is entirely free from this problem of product imbalance,
although some countries or regions face this problem in a more
acute form. With the shifts in relative demand over time, the nature
of imbalance also changes. Those products which are surplus at one
point of time, become short in supply at some other period. With
further research in refinery technology the oil industry succeeds in
adjusting production to the pattern of demand, and also in creating
new demand for products with few uses.

During the early days of the oil industry, the main use for oil was
as an illuminant, and kerosene was the most wanted product. From
the crude refining method the refiners then employed, about 70%
of the production was kerosene, but its production also necessitated
the production of motor spirit, which was volatile and inflammable,
and without much use. The latter was considered as an unwanted
dangerous substance, and was either flared or dumped secretly into
the river.[8] The invention of the internal combustion engine, and the
subsequent growth of the automobile industry opened up a new
world for the oil companies, while the competition from electricity
minimised the need for an illuminant. The invention of thermal and
catalytic cracking methods helped to increase the proportion of
motor spirit, while reducing the share of kerosene. At present
the refineries of the United States produce more than 40% of
motor spirit, and less than 7% of kerosene.[9] At the same time, kerosene has come to be increasingly used for purposes other than giving
light, such as heating, cooking, and also as a fuel for jet aircraft.

Recent years have also witnessed violent shifts in the pattern of the
relative demand for oil products, particularly in the demand for light
distillates. During the late 1950s and early 1960s the pattern of

I

consumption in the eastern hemisphere was favourable to middle distillates, and at a given production pattern of oil products, produced a surplus of light distillates, accompanied by a shortage of products like diesel or kerosene. In almost every market in Western Europe the petrol business came under pressure, and the relative price for that product had to be reduced, in order to dispose of what was produced when creating the necessary amount of middle distillates. This shift in the pattern of demand necessitated the introduction of hydrocracking methods which maximised the share of middle distallates in the output, while it also discouraged the use of catalytic cracking which increased the proportion of light distillates. Over the past two or three years, however, the trend is again clearly in favour of light distillates, thanks to the fantastic growth of the petrochemical and fertiliser industries, which use naphtha as feedstock. The growing use of naphtha in the town gas industry has also helped to boost the demand for the latter. The long run prospect is now for a shortage of naphtha, rather than a surplus, such as was feared only a few years ago.[10] This new shift in the demand pattern has again switched the emphasis in refining technology to producing a larger share of light distillates, to the employment of cracking methods, and to the use of lighter crudes.

Because of the joint production of petroleum products, refinery imbalance is unavoidable. The development of new uses—like the use of naphtha for town gas production, or the use of kerosene as jet fuel—is from time to time causing violent shifts in the pattern of the relative demand for oil products. The progress of refining technology, in response to these shifts in demand, is helping to restore the balance, but at the same time is also preparing the ground for new types of imbalance. It is interesting to analyse the factors which influence the choice of a particular production pattern from a set of production possibilities open to a refiner. These, together with the analysis of the factors influencing the pattern of consumption given in the previous chapter, will allow us to examine the phenomenon of product imbalance in depth.

PRODUCTION POSSIBILITIES OF THE REFINERIES

Technically, the production pattern of a refinery depends upon the nature of the crude oil used, specifications for various products and refinery design.

Crude oil varies widely in quality from one field to another. A crude oil of low gravity (measured in terms of higher A.P.I.) yields a relatively higher proportion of lighter fractions. The crudes of Libya or Algeria, with more than 40° A.P.I., are among the lightest, whereas some of the Venezuelan crudes, with less than

10° A.P.I., are very heavy and produce a huge proportion of heavy fuel oils. In the Middle East, Iranian crude is lighter than the crudes of Kuwait or Saudi Arabia. Indian crude, at 34° A.P.I., is considered to be of the lighter variety. The table below illustrates the relationship between the quality of crude and the product-mix of a refinery from a straight run distillation.

TABLE 15

PERCENTAGE YIELD OF DIFFERENT OIL PRODUCTS FROM DIFFERENT CRUDES

Source: *International oil prices (Shell International Petroleum Co.)*

Source of crude	Light distillates	Middle distillates	Heavy ends	Refinery loss
Bach Quero (Venezuela)	5	19	70	6
Kuwait	13	38	42	7
Qatar	19	50	24	7
Light Seria (Sarawak)	21	64	9	6

Crudes also differ in their sulphur content and waxy nature. High sulphur crudes are considered unsuitable for many industrial uses, and the fuel oil produced from such crude aggravates the problem of air pollution. Some of the cities of the United States, as well as countries like Japan, have passed legislation prohibiting the use of fuel oils with a sulphur content exceeding a given maximum level.[11] Because of the high sulphur content of most of the Middle East crudes, some of which contain as much as 3% or 4% sulphur, the present trend in the leading consuming countries of the world is to give preference to the low sulphur crudes of North Africa and the Far East. A costlier alternative is to process the crude through a desulphurisation unit. It has been estimated that the cost of reducing the percentage of sulphur from 2·25% to 0·5% is about 75¢ to $1·0 per barrel; but when the unit of operation is large and the cost of hydrogen is cheap, according to an alternative estimate the cost can be brought down to 25¢. A third alternative is to turn the heavier fractions into lighter products, by using hydrogenation processes, and this has been applied by the refinery of Kuwait National Petroleum Company and the U.K. refinery of Continental. But in both of these cases the cost of transforming high sulphur crude into low sulphur products has been found to be high.[12] The high cost of desulphurisation is, however, to a certain extent offset by the production of scarce sulphur, which can be sold at attractive prices.[13] There is as yet no law against the use of high sulphur fuel in India, and the crudes of domestic origin contain a low proportion of sulphur. The import of Darius crude, which contains a high percentage of sulphur, for the proposed Madras refinery, would require the installation of hydrotreating and hydro-sulphurising units in order to make the products suitable for industrial use.[14] Crudes of waxy nature, like the Indian crudes, on the other hand, require conditioning before transportaion through pipelines because of their tendency to solidify at low temperatures. Generally speaking, crudes of lighter variety with low sulphur content and low pour point, are considered to be desirable by the refiners. But the refiners also blend crudes of various quality in order to produce a required product-mix or products with desirable properties. The refiners of West Europe mix light Libyan crude with heavy Venezuelan crude, in order to obtain a higher proportion of middle distillates. The Esso refinery of India also uses a mixture of Arab Safaniya and Kuwait crude. High sulphur crude is also mixed with low sulphur crude in order to reduce the percentage of sulphur in the oil products.

The yield pattern also depends on the specifications laid down by the government for the various products. The refining process involves the breaking up of the crude oil into a number of oil products, all of which are hydrocarbons with varying arrangements of atoms of hydrogen and carbon. Molecules of hydrocarbon with up to four carbon atoms are available in gaseous form at normal temperatures and pressures, those with between five and 19 carbon atoms are liquids, and those with more than 19 carbon atoms are available in semi-solid or solid state. In other words, refinery products form a continuous array of hydrocarbons, with ethane gas at the one end, and solids like asphalt at the other. In a refinery the main part of the distillation unit is a fractionating tower, which is a tall and cylindrical column, though which the mixture of hot vapour and liquid crude is allowed to pass. The most volatile components—gas, motor spirit, and other light distillates—are collected at the top of the column, and the heavier components are pushed downwards. All the components, excluding the heaviest ones, form a mixture of vapours, which separate out by cooling to different temperatures—heavy ends first, then diesel, kerosene, and, last of all, the light distillates. Each fraction, thus separated, contains a number of compounds and boils within a given range of temperature, instead of boiling at a single point. As a result, the margin between any two consecutive fractions is blurred—for instance the light distillates contain some kerosene components, and the latter contains more volatile components of the motor spirit range. The specification of the boiling range for a particular fraction can never be very precise. It is always possible to increase the proportion of a particular fraction in the total production by extending the boiling range for that fraction, either by lowering the initial boiling point or by increasing its upward or final boiling point. But such changes cannot be effected without consequent changes in the quality of these products, and any significant expansion of the boiling range for a fraction makes some of the products unsuitable for use.

The proportion of various products in the aggregate refinery output depends largely on the refinery design. Various refinery techniques have been developed in the past for producing a desirable product-mix. "Distillation" refers to the process of initial separation of crude oil into various fractions, depending on their boiling ranges. "Platforming" improves the quality of the lighter fraction by reforming. "Cracking" involves a process by which the larger molecules of the heavier products are broken into smaller molecules, and the proportion of the lighter fractions is thereby increased. Among the two major cracking methods, "thermal cracking" depends on temperature, pressure, and time, whereas "catalytic cracking" employs a catalyst to break down larger molecules into smaller ones. "Viscosity breaking" or "Visbreaking" is an important application of thermal cracking to produce furnace oil of lower viscosity (which measures the resistance to flow of a liquid), while increasing the proportion of light products. "Hydrocracking" is catalytic cracking in the presence of a small amount of hydrogen introduced from the outside, which is used in order to increase the proportion of diesel oil, and also to improve the quality of motor spirit. "Propane Deasphalting" refers to the process by which bitumens (asphalts) are separated from lubricating oils.[15] There are other techniques available, which either vary the proportion of various fractions, or improve the quality of some fractions, or do both. As can be seen from the table below, the same quality of crude can be made to produce varying proportions of different refinery products, by subjecting it to the appropriate refinery techniques.

TABLE 16

PERCENTAGE YIELD OF VARIOUS OIL PRODUCTS FROM THE SAME KUWAIT CRUDE
BY APPLYING DIFFERENT REFINING TECHNIQUES

Source: *International oil prices (Shell International Petroleum Co.)*

Methods	Light distillates	Middle distillates	Heavy ends	Refinery loss
Distillation and Platforming	11	28	56	5
Plus Visbreaking	13	38	42	7
Plus Catalytic Cracking	21	36	35	8
Plus Propane Deasphalting	39	27	28	10
Plus Hydrocracking	15	53	21	11

RELATIVE COSTS AND PRICES AND PRODUCT-MIX

Faced with this wide range of choice of refining techniques and methods, the decisions of the oil companies on refinery design and crude intake would depend upon the alternative costs of various production patterns, and their relationship with the relative prices in the market.

An important aspect of refining economics is the joint cost nature of its production. What is important for the profitable operation of a refinery is the difference between the gross revenue from the sale of all products and the total cost of producing these products. Prices of individual products affect the profitability of a refinery insofar as these affect this difference. From the production side, a refinery is likely to be interested in producing more of the high-priced products and less of those products which would fetch a smaller price. The relevant prices would be expected long run prices, rather than immediate prices, since the measures taken to change the production pattern would require substantial investment and also a certain amount of time. A shift in the pattern of demand, and a consequent change in relative prices for oil products, would normally result after a time lag in the refining companies changing the production pattern. In many cases the shift in the demand pattern may be considerably neutralised by the relative price changes, because of the high degree of substitutability of the individual oil products in consumption among themselves. In the case of heavier road transport, a low market price for motor spirit would make its use more attractive than that of diesel. Cheap kerosene would replace diesel as a tractor fuel, and could even compete with motor spirit as automotive fuel. In such a case a lagged response by the refining companies to relative price changes might produce new imbalances in opposing directions unless the fact of the substitutability of various oil products in their uses is taken into account when planning the future production pattern.

Because of this joint cost nature of refinery operation, it is economically absurd to apportion the average cost of processing crude oil among various oil products. All the products are produced jointly, whether some of these are wanted or not. Even if the production of, for instance, furnace oil is considered undesirable by the refining company, the production of a certain amount of this product is unavoidable. In this case no cost has been incurred in order to produce furnace oil, since it was not desired by the refining company, and to attribute a part of the total cost of refining—equal to its proportion in the total volume of oil production, or to its proportion in the total sales—would be wrong.

It is, however, possible to compute the marginal cost of production of certain individual oil products. If, for example, it is intended to increase the proportion of light distillates from, say, 20% to 30%, by installing a catalytic cracking unit, the marginal cost of that increase in proportion is roughly equal to the sum of (a) the cost of installation (including the future discounted cost of maintenance) of the cracking unit, and (b) the discounted present value of the loss in earnings over the whole life of this cracking unit, because of a fall in the proportion of other oil products. This estimated marginal cost of increased motor spirit production plays an important role in the decision-making process. Unless the additional earnings over the whole life of the cracking unit, resulting from the increase in the proportion of motor spirit, net of item (b), and discounted, at least equals item (a), it would not be economically worthwhile for a private refining company to instal a cracking unit.

Cost considerations offset to the great extent the degree of flexibility in the output pattern achievable on a purely technological basis. A technologically feasible output pattern is not always economically justifiable. The more sophisticated and flexible the refinery, the costlier it becomes. A refinery with only a distiller and a platformer, using a single crude, would be very cheap to instal and run, but the introduction of a hydrosulphurier unit will increase the cost by 13%, and by 72% if a deasphalting unit and a catalytic cracking unit are also added to these.[16] To take another example, even when it is technically possible in India to achieve an output pattern which agrees with the pattern of consumption, by mixing Indian crude with Venezuelan crude, such a step may never be taken in view of the high cost of transporting crude oil from Venezuela. Another constraining factor is the foreign exchange cost of crude imports, which is compelling a number of countries to force the use of domestic crude by the refining companies operating in those countries, irrespective of their impact on the production pattern. In most cases the definition of "domestic crude" extends to crude produced abroad under the currency ownership of these countries. Examples are many, like the Khafji crude of the Neutral Zone owned by a Japanese company, the franc crude of Algeria, and the rupee crude of Iran, and in each of these cases the national crude—of both domestic and foreign origin—are accorded priority over foreign crude.

On the basis of the existing state of technical knowledge, there is a definite limit to the extent to which changes can be made in the production pattern under given conditions. This technical barrier can be broken through more intensive research work. For understandable reasons, the research promoted by the international oil companies is mainly applied, and is directed towards desired commercial ends. The estimated cost of research, relative to the estimated additional revenue which is expected if the research is successful, will be an important factor influencing the decisions of these companies about undertaking a research project. Over the past seventy years the main direction of their research in refining techniques was towards the production of a larger proportion of lighter distillates, because of the higher relative prices of the latter in the market. For some time during the 1950s and early 1960s a good deal of research was also done to produce a larger proportion of middle distillates, in response to a shift in demand in Western Europe towards the latter. But, under present demand conditions, no international oil company will spend money on research in order to increase the proportion of furnace oil at the cost of lighter fractions.

An important aspect of the research activity of the international oil companies is its centralised control. Because of their international character, these companies are likely to be less bothered by the divergence between the output and consumption of domestic refinery products, than those which are only regionally based. The former is able to skim off the surpluses of some markets, in order to bridge the deficits of others, for the same product, although it sometimes involves commercial loss due to transport costs. But so long as the cost of transport from one consumption centre to another, and also the cost of some wastage is low, relative to the cost of research, there would be no incentive for the international companies to undertake research for correcting the product imbalance of particular regions. Only when the regional imbalance also affects the demand and supply position on a global basis, and on a substantial scale, as it did during the 1950s and early 1960s because of a shift in demand towards the middle distillates in Western Europe, did the oil companies find it profitable to undertake research for correcting imbalance. In other words, a small market for the international oil companies like India is likely to receive little attention from the research division of an international oil company, even if the regional product imbalance is acute. On the other hand, because of the high cost of research—the research budget of the Royal Dutch Shell Group alone amounted to roughly Rs.800,000,000 in 1968[17]—it is virtually beyond the means of the government of small consuming countries like India.

PRODUCT IMBALANCE IN INDIA

The problem of product imbalance dominated the discussions on oil in India during the late 1950s and early 1960s. The refiners in India produced (and still produce) a surplus of light distillates, which accompanied an acute shortage of middle distillates, kerosene, and diesel. It necessitated the hard task of finding markets for surplus products in a competitive world, while continuing to import, in exchange for foreign currency, the deficit products. The long term prospect, it was feared at one time, was for this imbalance to grow. Over the past two or three years, on the other hand, the nature of the imbalance has begun changing—from a surplus to a deficit in light distillates—with the growth of the petrochemical and fertiliser industries. The long term prospect, based on present trends, is for this deficit in light distillates and surplus in middle distillates to grow. While only a few years ago the government was desperately trying to promote exports of unwanted naphtha, it has now succeeded in finding a domestic market for naphtha which is greater than the domestic output.

On the demand side, the problems arose because of faulty estimates of the consumption of various oil products. It was thought, immediately after Independence, that the consumption of kerosene would fall, whereas that of motor spirit would rise, as a proportion of total oil consumption. The high growth of motor spirit consumption during the 1940s strengthened this view, and the planned increase in electricity capacity was expected to reduce the need for kerosene as an illuminant. So when the refineries of the three international major companies were built during the 1950s, these were designed to produce, with the aid of catalytic cracking units, about 22% motor spirit, and only 33% middle distillates.[18] But the actual consumption of oil products did not conform to the expected pattern. The consumption of motor spirit levelled off after 1952, and its proportion in total oil consumption declined from about 20% in 1948, to 13% in 1961, and to 8% in 1966. On the other hand, the share of middle distillates very soon exceeded 50%. The refineries built in Barauni and Nunmati during the 1960s attempted to minimise the proportion of light distillates by not installing catalytic cracking units, but yet, because of the lighter nature of the domestic crude which these refineries used, the proportion of light distillates could not be reduced below 19%.[19] In order to avoid the production of a large surplus of motor spirit, the private sector refineries reduced its proportion; for instance Burmah Shell reduced it from 22% to 14·9% between 1955 and 1960.[20] The Government also took the step of amending the specifications of high speed diesel, by lowering the required initial boiling point from 150°F to 131°F, which increased the proportion of diesels at the cost of naphtha. But the overall effect of this change in the specifications was negligible.[21] In 1962, the proportion of light, middle, and heavy fractions in the total oil output for the whole country were 18%, 46%, and 36%, whereas their respective percentage shares in consumption were

12%, 52%, and 36%.[22] It was predicted that, given the policy of maintaining self-sufficiency in refined oil products, there would be a 1·6 million ton surplus of light distillates, with an accompanying 1,000,000 ton deficit in kerosene by 1966.[23]

For many reasons this problem was seriously viewed by the Government of India. The consumption pattern in India was then out of line with the pattern in almost any other country. Even in the countries of South East Asia at similar levels of development, the proportion of kerosene was not as high as it was in India (about 25%), and the proportion of motor spirit as low (about 8%)—the respective figures being 18% and 26% for that region.[24] There was hardly any incentive for the international oil industry to promote research for solving India's problem of imbalance in refining. On the other hand, the existing state of technological knowledge did not permit the refinery yields to conform to India's consumption pattern, by mixing various crudes and/or by applying various refinery techniques.

The only conceivable solution to this problem was to be found in foreign trade. So long as there was no public sector refinery, the problem was largely a matter of academic interest to the Government. But with the building of public sector refineries, the responsibility for marketing at least a part of the surplus devolved on the Government. Since the latter had no marketing apparatus of its own in other countries, this surplus could only be sold through trade agreements with other countries, or though international oil companies. The Government decided to accord priority to the products of the public sector refineries in the Indian market in order to force the international majors to export a larger share of the surplus. The foreign collaborators of the Government in Cochin and Madras were also asked to assume the responsibility for marketing the surpluses of these two refineries.[25] The Indian Oil Corporation itself also undertook to export to neighbouring countries a part of the surplus. Since the closure of the Suez Canal in June, 1967, the latter has succeeded in exporting light distillates to Burma, Thailand, Ceylon, and Japan, and these markets are likely to grow.[26] Two other alternatives which have not yet been tried by the Indian Government are as follows. Firstly, to invite two-way tenders from the oil interests, which combine offers to offtake surplus with offers to supply deficits. Countries like the U.A.R. and Syria have successfully implemented this alternative method of correcting domestic imbalance in the past.[27] Secondly, to combine deals for buying crude oil from abroad with undertakings from the seller of crude to buy surplus products. This method has also been successfully applied by a number of Latin American countries, and may be used by the refineries which are not tied to any particular source of crude.[28] However, all the alternatives discussed for getting rid of excess oil products were dependent for their success on the demand and supply conditions in the world market, and during the period discussed above the major markets in the eastern hemisphere were also suffering from a surplus of light distillates and a deficit of middle distillates.

More recent figures for domestic output and consumption also confirm the existence of imbalance. In 1967 there was a 500,000 ton deficit in kerosene, and a $0 \cdot 6$ million ton surplus in light distillates, but these figures were lower than those expected. The proportion of light distillates, at $10 \cdot 8\%$, was higher than the $7 \cdot 9\%$ predicted for 1966 in 1962, although the absolute consumption figure for 1967 roughly equalled the predicted consumption for 1966. The actual consumption of kerosene, on the other hand, was far below the $4 \cdot 1$ million tons predicted for a year earlier (see table 17).

The long term trend is for a shortage of light distillates, which by 1975 would amount to 2,000,000 tons, thanks to the planned growth of the petrochemical and fertiliser industries, which would account for $5 \cdot 6$ million tons of light distillates out of an aggregate consumption of that fraction of $7 \cdot 5$ million tons.[29] It is also estimated that by 1975 domestic refineries would produce surpluses of kerosene and heavy ends of 1 and $1 \cdot 3$ million tons respectively, given the current pattern of production.[30]

Between the two kinds of product imbalance discussed above, the more recent one can be handled more easily in terms of refinery technology. Whereas the lighter quality of domestic crude was considered to be a disadvantage in the past, its capacity to produce a larger proportion of lighter fraction would now be of great help. The use of lighter crudes of Sarawak or Minas of Indonesia, in preference to the heavier and high sulphur crudes of Kuwait or Saudi Arabia would now be necessary. Another alternative way of increasing the proportion of light distillates would be to raise the final boiling point of lighter distillates, but the effect of such a modification in the specification would be to increase the aromatic and sulphur contents of naphtha, which would make the latter less suitable for use in fertiliser production. Such a policy would also cause the qualities of diesel and petrol to deteriorate.[31] But, as is seen from the table above, there is still a vast scope for increasing the proportion of lighter distillates by installing catalytic and hydro-cracking units in the public sector refineries as also in the refineries which are partly owned by the Government.

It also needs to be stressed that consumption estimates given in the tables above are based on the assumption that all the fertiliser and petrochemical units so far planned and approved by the Government would reach their scheduled maximum capacities in time. If for some reason these industries are not established according to plan, the discrepancy between the anticipated and actual requirement for naphtha would also significantly alter the nature of balance or imbalance between the production and the consumption pattern of oil products. Furthermore, these estimates given above also assume no change in the pattern of relative consumer prices for these oil products. As observed in the previous chapter, many of the oil products can be substituted for one another in consumption, and changes in relative consumer prices would also significantly alter the balance of production and consumption. This point will be more elaborately discussed in Chapter Seven.

An important aspect of this problem of product imbalance is the shortage of lubricating oils, an expensive commodity. In 1964–65 it accounted for 15% of the total volume of oil imports and 28% of the total value of oil imports. The Government did not foresee the high rate of growth of consumption of this oil product, which is now expected to increase from less than $0 \cdot 2$ million tons during the early 1950s to $0 \cdot 8$ million tons in 1971. The private sector refineries established during the 1950s were not asked to set up lube plants, and the only sources of domestic production at present are the lube plants of Digboi and Barauni, with only 30,000 and 45,000 ton capacities respectively. If no further expansion takes place in lube output, the value of its imports will exceed the total value of imports of all other oil products taken together by 1971. Of the future capacities planned, the jointly owned plant of Esso and the Indian Government was expected to be on stream by 1969 (although the target date was 1966–67) with a 3,000 barrels per day capacity, and the Madras refinery, which is expected to be on stream by 1969 would also provide for another 3,800 barrels capacity per day. Another 4,500 barrels per day would be provided by the refinery of Haldia and the extension of Barauni. But all these would still leave about $0 \cdot 15$ million tons per year, or about 3,000 barrels per day uncovered by domestic output. Unless further capacities are built in the near future, lube oil will become the most important imported oil product.[32]

SIZE AND LOCATION OF THE REFINERIES

The refineries of India can be classified into three groups according to their location: firstly the inland refineries, situated near the sources of domestic crude. Examples of this group are the Digboi and Nunmati refineries of Assam, and the Koyali refinery of Gujrat. Secondly, the inland refineries based on domestic crude, but situated near consumption areas. The Barauni refinery of Bihar is the solitary example of such a refinery in the Indian context. Thirdly, coastal refineries, based on imported crude, such as the refineries of Bombay, Vizagapatnam, Madras, Cochin, and Haldia. There is no inland refinery in India which is based on imported crude oil, or any coastal refinery which draws a supply of crude from a domestic oilfield. There is also no refinery which depends for crude on both domestic and foreign sources. But there is a suggestion for a refinery to be located in the North West of India, which will depend on imported crude for the time being with the ultimate objective of switching over to domestic crude if more oil is discovered in that region.[33] Most of the coastal refineries mentioned above, as also the Koyali refinery, can be treated as market-orientated refineries.

When using foreign crude, the arguments for locating refineries near the sea ports are as follows: firstly, coastal refineries ensure flexibility of distribution, and avoid duplication of transport costs. The pattern of consumption is dissimilar in various parts of the country, the proportion of fuel oil consumption, for instance, is higher in Western India than in the East. A coastal refinery would be able to transport as much of a product to a particular inland region as it required, whereas the operation of a refinery in the inland area would involve firstly the transport of crude to that refinery and secondly the transport of surplus products from that area to other areas. It would involve unnecessary costs and an extra burden on the transport network. Secondly, since crude oil would arrive in large amounts from the foreign countries at the sea ports, it would be possible to build larger refineries at the coast, and thereby reap economies of scale. On the other hand, the same amount of crude, when transported into the interior for a number of refineries would be absorbed by units of smaller size. Thirdly, many of the sea ports are also important areas of consumption, and the location of refineries in those areas would also minimise the costs of distribution of oil products. In this case, coastal refineries would provide the advantages of both resource-orientated and market-orientated refineries up to the limit of consumption of that area. Fourthly, since a large component of the cost of refinery construction is the import of machinery, a coastal refinery is cheaper to construct, and also in most cases cheaper to operate—other factors remaining constant.

Most of these arguments are valid up to a point. So long as the inland consumption centres are small in size, the additional cost of building inland refineries is not generally justified, but the growth of inland consumption over time may justify the setting up of a refinery away from the coast, if the economy achieved in the cost of distribution of oil products, compensates for the additional construction costs, as well as the cost of the disposal of surplus oil products to other areas.

An important factor in the choice between coastal and inland refineries would be the development of various forms of transport. The growth of crude oil pipelines favours the installation of inland refineries, whereas a network of product pipelines would work in favour of large coastal refineries. The picture is complicated by the fact that not all products can be transported by product pipelines, particularly not fuel oil. So if the coastal refineries were required to transport a large amount of fuel oil to other areas, their operation would be less economic than those situated inland. Furthermore, whereas crude oil pipelines can be built with a large carrying capacity and made to cover a large distance, product pipelines, almost by definition, are smaller in size and length, and hence less economic to run. In the absence of extensive pipeline networks, capacity and freight structure of railways would be an important determinant in choosing the location for a refinery. Freights for products are normally higher because of additional handling and packing charges, and because of greater space requirements than those for crude. This again can be offset by policy decisions on the part of the railways, but so long as the higher freight for oil products exists, there remains the incentive for building refineries near consumption centres. Again, the carrying capacity of the railways in various regions would also be an important variable. The strain imposed on the railway system around Bombay was one of the factors which dictated the Government's policy against the expansion of refineries in that area for a period of time.

For the refineries using domestic crude, the case for a resource-orientated location policy is similar to that discussed at the beginning of this chapter. When these are situated inland, however, some of the points raised in this section against the inland refineries also apply, particularly the point about the higher cost of transport of equipment for building refineries inland. The cost of distribution of oil products can be excessive if such a refinery is situated at a long distance from the consumption centres. A further important argument against these refineries is the prospect of the oilfields, on which they are dependent for crude, drying out in the future, thus involving imports of crude from distant areas and the disposal of products to distant areas—both at high costs.

The question of size is related to the problem of location. The size of refineries based on domestic crude is largely a function of the capacity of the oilfields, when neither the capacity of the oilfields nor the level of consumption of the hinterland of the refineries is particularly high. For refineries based on foreign crude the decision concerning location should be based on the relative costs of transport of crude and products, as against the economics of scale. A giant refinery in Bombay, reaping enormous economies of scale, would also require to ship the major part of its products to other ports, at a coastal freight higher than the ocean freight on the crude from foreign sources. The development of large tankers of 200,000 cwt or more capacity, which are more economically used when the entire tanker load is discharged in a single port, favours large refineries, but their significance is not so great in India as in Europe because of the proximity of the Persian Gulf. In 1963, the ocean freight for carrying crude was about 8% of the c.i.f. price in India, whereas in the United Kingdom it was as much as the combined costs of refining, inland transporting, and marketing.[34] In addition, because the ports of India are situated in shallow water, they are unsuitable for receiving giant tankers, without incurring extra expenditure on deep sea discharging facilities. In view of the existence of a large number of small markets throughout this large sub-continent, the construction of a number of refineries, each geared to supply a particular region, seems to be a more prudent policy. The decisions on both the size and the location of the refineries must be linked with the inter-regional distribution of oil consumption, in order to mini-mise the transport of oil.

The choice of a particular site for the location of a refinery depends on various factors such as the provision of public utility services, port and transport facilities, and subsoil conditions. Not all the cities of India adequately provide for public utility services. The acute water shortage in Madras was a factor which delayed the erection of a refinery in that city for more than ten years.[35] The Cochin refinery needed to build a thermal power station in order to ensure the regularity of supply of electricity.[36] Port facilities are under-developed in some of the new ports like Kandla, Okha, or Haldia whereas the older ports like Calcutta are overloaded. The port of Madras is affected by monsoon for four months every year. While Bombay is the centre of coastal freight services, and also a large railway terminal, Assam and a number of other Indian states suffer from unsatisfactory communication facilities. The subsoil condition of Barauni has been found to be unsatisfactory, and additional costs had to be incurred in order to insure against possible damage from earthquakes.[37]

PRIVATE SECTOR REFINERIES

There was no dispute about the refinery location policy when, about seventy years ago, the first refinery of India was built in Digboi (Assam), near an oilfield. Its location was entirely in accord with the prevailing concept of constructing refineries near the source of crude. The production was small, a large buyer of oil was the tea plantations of Assam, and the nearest important consumption centre, Calcutta, was 800 miles away. Furthermore, oil was not an important subject for discussion in those days.

The size of Digboi, although small, was not uneconomic. The refinery process was simple, it handled only one kind of crude, and small refineries of this size were not uncommon in those days. A cracking plant was added to the refinery during the war and, since the discovery of oil in Nahorkatiya, it is also treating a part of this new crude.

The choice of Vizagapatnam and Bombay for the three private sector refineries was based on the report which a technical committee of the major oil companies supplied to the government in 1949.[38] Bombay was the nearest port in India to the Persian Gulf; the ocean freight for motor spirit from Iran in 1961 was Rs.8.45 per kilolitre to Bombay, but Rs.10.10 to Okha and Kandla in the West and Cochin in the South, and Rs.14.76 to the Eastern ports of Vizagapatnam, Madras, and Calcutta.[39] Its deep water port, its established bulk installations, its transport network with the rest of India, as well as its potential as a market for oil, were among other factors influencing the decision.[40] The choice of Vizagapatnam was also influenced by its proximity to Indonesia, from where the Caltex company receives a part of its crude requirement. Being located somewhat halfway between Madras and Calcutta on the East coast, its location was expected to help the supply of product to both of these two important consumption points.

The decision was, however, unrelated to the pattern of inter-regional consumption of oil in India. As a result, until 1962, when Nunmati refinery was built, more than four-fifths of the total refining capacity was concentrated in Bombay city alone, although the whole of Bombay region accounted for less than half the total oil consumption. For a considerable period of time, about 29% of the refinery output was distributed in the Calcutta area, 10% in Madras, 9% in Cochin, and 5% in Gujrat, although about 3·2 million tons out of 4 million tons of refining capacity were concentrated in Bombay.[41] This involved the distribution of about half the refinery output of Bombay to other parts of the country, at higher distribution costs. Even when the products were delivered by ship, the excess of coastal freight over the saving in ocean freight was substantial. To take an example, the coastal freight from Bombay to Madras was Rs.22.79 per ton, whereas the saving in ocean freight by installing the capacity in Bombay in preference to Madras was about Rs.4.63 per ton.[42] Furthermore, the capacity in Bombay was split into two parts, and no attempt was made to persuade the companies to build one bigger refinery under joint ownership.

The third refinery at Vizagapatnam, which came on stream in 1958 with a 0·675 million ton refinery, was not only unduly small, but the amount of oil consumption within its economic distribution area was even smaller than its capacity. A large part of the products of the refinery had to be sold outside the economic area defined by the world parity pricing system.[43]

PUBLIC SECTOR REFINERY AND POLITICAL CONTROVERSY

The question of refinery location became a subject of political controversy when the Government decided to erect a refinery under public ownership for processing crude oil from Nahorkatiya. Those who favoured Assam as the location of the new refinery advanced the familiar arguments of resource-orientated refineries. Those opposing Assam pointed out that the 0·3 million ton consumption need of Assam was adequately satisfied by Digboi, and another refinery in that state would create the problem of distribution of oil products. It was also stated that most of the machinery would require to be imported through Calcutta port, which is 800 miles away, and even personnel—both skilled and unskilled—would need to be hired from the other states. The difficult terrain, numerous rivers, and recurrence of floods, would make the transport bottleneck a serious one, it was argued.[44] The alternatives suggested were Bihar and West Bengal.

The Government appointed a committee in 1956, under the chairmanship of S. S. Vasist, adviser to the Railway Ministry, to recommend the best possible site for the refinery.[45] Two of the members of the Committee were oil experts from Rumania and France. The Committee were supposed to submit its report within two months, but because of the proximity of a general election, the report was not submitted until after the election, and even then it was not published on the grounds of "public interest".[46] However, it became known in due course that, on the basis of costs, the Committee unanimously recommended Budge-Budge near Calcutta as the site for the refinery.[47] The Government was too weak to accept the recommendation in the face of continued agitation in Assam against its oil being "stolen" by other states. It ordered a fresh enquiry "in order to appraise the economy of Assam and Bihar", both of which states offered to provide land free of cost, and power and water at reasonable rates for the proposed refinery, if it were installed within their borders.[48] After a long hesitation the Government decided to build two refineries, one at Nunmati (Assam), and the other at Barauni (Bihar), in order to satisfy the governments of both states. But

K

eventually both of the state governments concerned withdrew their offer of land and, instead, demanded a 15% share in the equity of their respective refineries, and this demand, surprisingly enough, was also fully met by the Central Government.

An immediate consequence of this dispute was a further delay in the development of the oilfields of Nahorkatiya, which remained unexploited from 1953 to 1962, firstly because of the dispute between the Government and the Burmah Oil Company, and then because of this location dispute. According to one estimate, the cost of this dispute was around Rs.250,000,000.[49] Furthermore, the additional cost of construction of these inland refineries over coastal refineries was considerable. It took Rs.407,000,000 to build the 2,000,000 ton Barauni, and Rs.180,000,000 for the 0·75 million ton Nunmati, both of which spent per unit of installed capacity much more than the Rs.170,000,000 required for the 2,000,000 ton Cochin. The small size of Nunmati was hardly in keeping with the world wide trend and, as in the case of the Caltex refinery at Vizagapatnam, the level of consumption in its economic area, as defined by the world parity pricing system, was very low, even for this small capacity.

The two refineries are connected with the oilfields through a pipeline for crude delivery. The pipeline is 720 miles long and covers a difficult terrain including ninety-two river crossings. At the present throughput of 2·75 million tons per year, the cost of pipeline transport is Rs.21.65 per ton compared with Rs.50.72 by railways, with the additional advantage that the pipeline ensures a regularity of supply.[50] The oil products of Nunmati are also piped to Siliguri, in West Bengal, which is also connected through a product pipeline with Barauni refinery and Kanpur, an important city in North India. The product pipeline is to be extended to connect Siliguri with Haldia refinery, when the latter is in operation.

No political controversy was provoked when the decision was made to build a refinery at Koyali in Gujrat, in order to process the crude oil of the Gujrat fields, which were discovered in 1960. Gujrat itself was a big market for oil, and there were proposals for building a refinery in Gujrat long before oilfields were discovered in that state.[51] All the nearest sea ports such as Kandla, Okha, or Bhavanagar, were also situated within that state, and there was hardly any scope for inter-state rivaly on this subject. Koyali, not being far from either the sea ports or the source of crude, was considered to be an ideal site. The proximity of Baroda, an important city (only ten miles away) with a large railway terminal strengthened its claim.

A situation similar to the one which arose in connection with the new Assam crude may arise in Gujrat if the success in exploration in various parts of the state makes crude production possible far in excess of consumption in that state, and a refinery outside this state is proposed for the use of a part of that crude.

The Koyali refinery is supplied with crude from Ankleswar through a pipeline, and its products are distributed through pipelines to Ahmedabad and Baroda, two important consumption centres. There are also several gas pipelines which join important consumption centres with the gas deposits of Ankleswar and Cambay.

Since Koyali, the Government has also decided on the location of three refineries based on imported crude, which are jointly owned by the latter with some independent international oil companies. All these refineries—at Cochin, Madras, and Haldia—are located on the coasts. Both Cochin and Madras are important sea ports and oil consumption areas. Haldia has been selected as proxy for Calcutta, whose port facilities are already over-used and where the water is not very deep. The former will supply the hinterland of the Calcutta port. Cochin has already begun its operation, and Madras will be completed by 1969. The construction of Haldia is going to start soon and it is expected to be on stream by 1971. As a result of these location decisions, all the coastal states excepting Orissa (which is neither an important consumption area nor equipped with any good port) have been awarded a refinery, and Maharastra has obtained two refineries. Refineries have become tools of state politics with which favours can be bought and sold.

DEMAND PATTERN AND REFINERY LOCATION

A satisfactory refinery location policy presupposes a detailed study of the distribution of the total oil consumption of the country over the various regions. For the earlier years a rough approximation of distribution can be obtained from the import trade statistics, since domestic output accounted for only 5% of the total consumption. For more recent years the figures of petroleum released by the Indian Institute are valuable. Table 18 gives the estimated throughput and consumption in 1971 and 1975 for various regions.

This table shows that if the programme of refinery expansion is fully implemented, there would only be minor surpluses and deficits in the regions listed, apart from more than a 1,000,000 ton surplus in the North and North East region, and an equal deficit in the Western region in 1975. The proposed North West refinery, with a 3,000,000 ton capacity would bridge the supply gap of the North West region. The latter's location has not yet been decided, although it has been tentatively suggested that preference should be given to the U.P.-Punjab area if crude oil is discovered in that region in the near future. If the exploration programme in that area fails, there would still be strong arguments in favour of locating a refinery in

TABLE 18

REFINERY THROUGHPUT AND CONSUMPTION FOR VARIOUS REGIONS: 1971 & 1975

Unit: Million tons per year

Region	Throughput 1971	Consumption 1971	Throughput 1975	Consumption 1975
North and North East	*6·9*	*5·6*	*9·5*	*8·1*
Barauni	3·0	—	4·5	—
Nunmati	1·0	—	1·0	—
Haldia	2·5	—	3·5	—
Digboi	0·4	—	0·5	—
North West	*3·0*	*4·5*	*7·0*	*6·6*
Koyali	3·0	—	4·0	—
(Another)	—	—	3·0	—
West	*6·7*	*6·2*	*7·9*	*9·1*
Burmah Shell	4·0	—	5·2	—
Esso	2·7	—	2·7	—
South West (Cochin)	*2·0*	*2·5*	*3·5*	*3·6*
South East (Madras)	*2·5*	*2·0*	*2·5*	*3·0*
East (Vizagapatnam)	*1·1*	*1·2*	*1·6*	*1·6*
Total	*22·2*	*22·0*	*32·0*	*32·0*

that region, or at least for undertaking a detailed cost study for such a project, in view of the expected substantial increase in consumption in that region by that period. So far all the refineries based on foreign crude have been built near the coast, but, as has been discussed earlier, the development of pipeline transport has now made inland refineries based on foreign crude an economically viable proposition, and has caused a major shift in the location pattern of the European refineries away from the coast.

There are three points worth noting at this stage: firstly, in view of the past failures of the Government in completing refinery programmes in time, there are grounds for suspecting that the planned expansion in refining capacity may not be attained, and even if the expansions are completed, the plants may still not be working at their full capacity. The refineries of Barauni and Nunmati have yet to reach their full capacity, and this can no longer be explained by the "teething troubles" experienced by new plants. If the programme is not properly implemented, the two regions to suffer most would be the North-and-North-East and North-West. Secondly, it needs to emphasised that the equalisation of aggregate consumption and supply of refinery products for each region would not by itself imply regional self sufficiency in each individual product. A programme of self sufficiency for each region, in order to minimise distribution costs, should also consider the problem of regional product imbalance. The furnace oil requirement of Bombay region exceeds its supply, although, until recently, it had a surplus of kerosene. The picture in the Vizagapatnam region is just the opposite, where a surplus of fuel oil accompanies a deficit in kerosene. Thirdly, the location policy of the Government need not be based solely on the criterion of maximum efficiency in the refining industry, in isolation from the rest of the economy. An accounting loss in the operation of the refining industry may be compatible with the national economic development programme. For example, for various economic and political reasons the development of Haldia or Okha is receiving priority in the national plan, and if the installation of refineries in these ports is expected to aid their development, an accounting loss in refinery operation can be justified as part of the cost for developing these ports. In the absence of a location policy and without public ownership, a refinery would be located in a place which allows it to maximise profit subject to institutional constraints. A well prepared location policy would consider the implications of such a policy on both the refineries and the economy as a whole, even if it involves subsidisation of refinery operations by the Government.

An interesting consequence of the location policy, given the present system of world parity pricing of individual oil products, is its effects on the profits of various refineries. This subject will be taken up in a subsequent chapter. (See Chapter Seven.)

GOVERNMENT POLICY TOWARDS REFINERIES

The 1948 industrial policy resolution of the Government of India placed the future development of the oil industry, along with six other basic and strategic industries, under the ownership of the Government. The only exception permitted under this resolution was "when, in the national interest, the state itself finds it necessary to secure the cooperation of private enterprise ... subject to such control or regulation as the Central Government may prescribe". It also kept open the question of acquisition by the Government of important industries, including oil, after ten years.

The terms and conditions incorporated in the Refinery Contracts of 1951–53 were far from the principles laid down by this policy resolution. Not only did these contracts allow foreign companies to set up plants under their exclusive ownership. but no control or regulation was imposed in keeping with the spirit of this resolution. Instead, the refineries were specifically exempted from the operation of the Industrial (Development and Regulation) Act of 1951, and assurances were given against nationalisation for thirty years. Although the foreign companies involved undertook to allow some private Indian participation, it was supposed to be confined to "preference shares", and even that promise has not yet been kept.

Moreover, these refinery contracts provided a number of concessions to the majors, which are not normally available to other industries of similar importance. The refineries were exempted from the payment of import duty on crude oil, and duty concessions on plant and machinery required for the refineries were granted. As will be seen in Chapter Nine, this concession on import duty contrasted with the sales tax on domestic crude which the public sector refineries had to pay for their feedstock. Furthermore, these refineries enjoyed tariff advantages for several years, although it was never clear against whom such protection was being sought.

The two main concessions provided in these contracts were the freedom of choice as to the source of supply of crude, and the agreement to sell their products at "import parity prices". Both of these will be discussed in detail in subsequent chapters. (See Chapters Seven and Eight.)

It is true that the majors might not agree to install refineries in India if the conditions relating to nationalisation or crude supply and product prices were not satisfied, but some other conditions—such as exemption from import duty and tariff protection—might be dropped if the Government bargaining team were stronger. In Australia, the Government refused to make the building of refineries by the majors conditional on tariff protection, but that "did not cause the companies to abandon or modify their Australian refinery plans".[52] What was not appreciated by the Government during that period was that the refineries were as essential to the majors as to India, for reasons outlined at the beginning of this chapter.

It is also clear that there were other alternatives to building refineries under the ownership of the major oil companies, which were not given enough attention at that time. It was possible to secure the help of the newly formed National Iranian Oil Company, which was struggling to find markets for its crude oil, since all its traditional supply areas were blocked by the majors, with the active support of the British and the U.S. Governments, after the nationalisation of 1951. As seen before, one or two proposals for such cooperation were floated during 1951–54, although the Government did not pay much attention to these.[53]

It was not until the mid-fifties that the idea of public ownership of refineries was translated into action. The Government, on the advice of Mr. K. D. Malviya, insisted on the exclusive ownership of the refineries which are based on domestic crude, and three refineries—Nunmati, Barauni, and Koyali—were constructed with the financial and technical help of the Rumanian and Russian

Governments. Both these aspects of the new refinery policy—
Government ownership and socialist help—came under severe
criticism. The Chairman of the Federation of Indian Chambers of
Commerce commented in 1959, "The Government's efforts at
present appear to be confined to mainly seeking assistance directly
from a certain group of countries. It is felt by the Federation that
the Government should not miss the opportunity of obtaining
similar assistance from other countries in the matter of exploration
as also of setting up refineries".[54] Fears were expressed by some that
these refineries would be used as "trojan horses" for communist
subversion.[55]

Leaving aside the political implications of these comments, it is
factually wrong to suggest that the Government sought socialist
help before exploring the possibilities of obtaining help from the
western countries. It was reported in January, 1958, that the Government was sounding the oil interests of a number of countries, including
the U.K., U.S.A., France, Italy, as well as Rumania and the Soviet
Union, for the supply of equipment on a deferred payment basis.[56]
It was also reported in September of that year that the oil companies
of the U.K. and U.S.A. who were approached declined to help,[57]
and that Soviet and Rumanian help was obtained on extremely
attractive terms—at low rates of interest and on condition of rupee
payment.

The arguments against public ownership in oil refining are similar
to those which are raised in connection with almost any other large
industry, such as fertiliser, steel, or heavy engineering. The costs are
heavy, and contain a substantial—about one-third—foreign exchange
component. If the foreign companies are allowed to undertake the
tasks of building and operating refineries, it is argued, the initial
costs—including foreign exchange costs—would be borne by them.
The latter would also have the advantage over the Government
management of their wider experience and technical expertise.[58]

It is not intended to go into the familiar arguments both in favour
and against government ownership. While admitting that foreign
ownership eases the burden on domestic foreign currency resources
in the short run, it may be pointed out that in the long run it involves
a much larger foreign exchange cost in terms of profit-remittances.
To take the example of the three foreign owned refineries built
during the fifties, the total investment on these amounted to approximately Rs.600,000,000, of which about one-third was in foreign
exchange; whereas between 1955 and 1961, in seven years, these
three companies earned a net profit of Rs.345,000,000 excluding
heavy depreciation, development rebates, and dividend taxes. A large
part of this net profit was remitted by 1961, and the rest was a

contingent liability on India's foreign exchange reserves. In other words, what the country gained in terms of foreign exchange by the foreign ownership of the refineries, has been outweighed by the outpayments in only seven years. This statement is further strengthened when one considers the inflated prices for imported crude which India has to pay in foreign exchange for these refineries. (See Chapter Eight.) On the other hand, the foreign exchange needed for the installation of refineries is obtainable from foreign companies and governments, without necessarily conferring equity ownership on them, as is seen from the experience of the state-owned refineries.

The argument about the wider experience of the major oil companies is undoubtedly valid. It is also a valid criticism that the performance of the state-owned refineries has not so far been particularly impressive. All three state refineries were completed behind schedule, and none of these has yet attained full capacity production. Like most other state-owned units, the public oil refineries have been mismanaged in the past and have faced heavy criticism. But this is due less to any basic weakness in public ownership itself than a reflection of the general inefficiency of the Indian Government in particular. Again, it needs to be noted that the units under public ownership are normally subject to more severe scrutiny—through parliamentary bodies—than those in the private sector. Whereas the inefficiencies of the public sector units are brought to light, the private sector units escape attention.

Again, the relative efficiency of the public and foreign private units cannot be measured accurately on the yardstick of the accounting losses and profits of these units alone. The public-owned units in India also show lower profit than those in the private sector for the following three reasons: first, the former are inland refineries, and so require a larger construction cost. Secondly, whereas imported crude did not pay until 1966 any import tariff, domestic crude had to pay sales tax. As a result, the public refineries paid more for their crude input than the private refineries. Thirdly, Nunmati refinery suffered from the phenomenon of "freight absorption", because of faulty location policy. (See Chapter Seven.) In other words, the lower profit is largely due to the policy decisions of the Government, and less to the performance of the units themselves.

Assuming that the foreign enterprises are relatively more efficient, there is another point to note on this question. Whereas such efficiency undoubtedly helps these organisations themselves, it is not clear what benefit, or how much benefit, the country derives from this efficiency. A particular example is the training of Indian engineers, which is virtually neglected by the major international oil companies. The Indian engineers have participated with the Soviet experts in the designing and construction of Koyali refinery, and have thereby gained the valuable experience which has been denied to them by the foreign companies. Although the cost of training and participation of the Indians in the decision making process inflates the costs of the construction and operation of the refineries in the immediate future, it brings in long term benefits to the whole economy, including the oil industry, and widens the scope of the scientific and technological progress of the country.

With the departure of Mr. Malviya from the Indian cabinet in 1963, the Government policy towards the refineries has moved towards more foreign private participation in ownership. Not only are the new coastal refineries of Cochin and Madras jointly owned by the Government and the foreign private oil companies, but the older private foreign refineries have been allowed to expand their capacities.

Burmah Shell and Esso refineries were initially licensed for 1·5 and 1 million tons capacities, respectively.[59] But the refineries were installed with 2·3 and 1·2 million tons respective capacities, and were very soon demanding further expansion.[60] Mr. Malviya opposed this on the grounds that such expansion would produce a surplus in the Bombay region, and require distribution to other parts of India, thereby putting enormous pressure on the already overburdened railway service from Bombay.[61] A further argument was that such expansion should be made conditional on the major companies agreeing to scrap the refinery agreements, particularly the provision relating to the source of crude. But despite Mr. Malviya's resistance to the proposal for expansion, such expansion was allowed, firstly during the final years of the Second Five Year Plan on the grounds of foreign exchange difficulties, then immediately after the Sino-Indian Border War of 1962 on the grounds of national security, and very recently on the familiar grounds of immediate foreign exchange needs. The present capacities of these two refineries, at 4·0 and 2·7 million tons, are far greater than those with which the refineries were originally installed, although because of increased consumption in the Bombay region the fear of regional surplus has vanished. (See Table 18.) However, this expansion has been carried out without any compensating change in the refinery agreements under which these refineries were originally installed. No advantage was taken of the fact that the majors can now increase their market share in India only through increasing refining capacity under their ownership.

There are grounds for suspicion that the World Bank put its weight as lender in favour of the major international oil companies and that the Government had to give way. The World Bank Mission of 1963 commented, "Likewise, in the refining and distribution of oil, development should, so far as possible, be left in private hands, except to the extent that Government intervention may be needed to ensure an adequate measure of competition. Private oil companies have already invested large sums in refining, storage, and distribution, and there is no reason to doubt that they will be able, as part of their normal business, to finance the additional facilities required to meet the growth of demand."[62] A more hard-hitting comment was made by Mr. Eugene Black, the Chairman of the World Bank, in 1961, "They cannot afford to waste scarce resources by putting prestige ahead of real need, by ignoring hard economic calculations, by refusing to accept productive capital, while they debate for years the respective roles of public and private enterprises."[63]

The refinery agreements on Cochin and Madras refineries provide for joint ownership with foreign oil companies, while the agreement for Haldia refinery provides for state ownership. In all these three cases the foreign collaborators finance the foreign exchange part of the construction cost, and provide crude oil on a long term basis. But whereas in the case of Cochin and Madras the foreign collaborators receive part ownership in equity (25% in the case of Cochin, and 26% in the case of Madras), and own exclusive rights to supply crude, in the case of Haldia the foreign collaborator supplies one-half of the crude and gets no part of equity ownership. One wonders why it was necessary to confer equity ownership on the foreign collaborators in the case of Cochin and Madras. If it was for the security of crude supply on a long term basis, such security was either not necessary or could be obtained without conferring equity ownership. (See Chapter Eight.) If it was for financing the construction of refineries, a number of companies were interested in lending foreign exchange for the purpose in exchange for long-term crude supply rights, as C.F.P. did in the case of Haldia. In any case, as will be seen in Chapter Eight, the contracts with independent oil companies did not confer any substantial differential advantage to the economy, although, as in the case of the refineries of Bombay and Vizagapatnam, they will involve a continuous drain on foreign exchange resources in the form of profit-remittances.

A major criticism of the Government refinery policy is that it has failed to revise the refinery agreements which were concluded under vastly different conditions. These were signed at a time when India imported 95% of her requirements of oil products from abroad, and the crude market in the Eastern hemisphere was under the virtual monopoly of the international majors. The international majors were immensely powerful in their bargaining strength. No less important, the Indian Government was ignorant of the intricacies of the oil business, while the major companies, who knew everything about it, were, for understandable reasons, reluctant to reveal the artificiality of oil prices and the vertically and horizontally integrated nature of their operations. The two parties at the bargaining table were equal neither in bargaining strength nor in knowledge. In the light of these facts, it may be asked how far these agreements are still legally or otherwise binding on the Indian Government.

There are historical precedents where governments have unilaterally revised the agreements concluded under vastly different economic and political conditions, and the major companies have subsequently accepted those revisions in their own interest. Such unilateral revision took place in a number of Middle East countries, the most recent example being in Libya. There is no reason why those major companies which have been persuaded or forced to accept unilateral revisions in the Middle East should not behave similarly in India in the event of unilateral revision of the refinery contracts. If, on the other hand, the Government adopts the policy of waiting for their consent, which is unlikely to come except in exchange for concessions in other spheres, the necessary reforms in the price structure would be delayed to the detriment of the economy.

TABLE 17

ESTIMATED AND ACTUAL PRODUCTION AND CONSUMPTION PATTERNS OF REFINERY PRODUCTS (IN MILLION TONS AND PERCENTAGES)

Products	Estimated output 1966	Estimated consumption 1966	Estimated surplus 1966	Actual output 1967	Actual consumption 1967	Actual surplus 1967
Light distillates	2·9(16·7)	1·3(7·9)	+1·6	2·0(15·5)	1·4(10·7)	+0·6
Kerosene	3·2(18·1)	4·2(24·9)	−1·0	2·5(19·4)	3·1(23·7)	−0·6
Diesel	4·4(25·4)	3·8(23·0)	+0·6	4·0(31·0)	3·7(28·2)	+0·3
Heavy End	6·9(39·8)	7·4(44·2)	−0·5	4·4(34·1)	4·9(37·4)	−0·5
Total	17·4(100)	16·7(100)	+0·7	12·9(100)	13·1(100)	−0·2

NOTES

1. Frankel and Newton (2).
2. *Ibid.*
3. *Ibid.* In a more recent paper Mr. Newton estimated that the proportion of resource-oriented refineries would reduce to 13·8% in 1968, and the corresponding figure for the market-based refineries would go up to 79·8%. Quoted from a paper submitted by W. L. Newton to a seminar at the School of Oriental and African Studies, University of London.
4. Frankel and Newton (2).
5. *Ibid.*
6. Hagemans and Ingall.
7. These agreements provided for two types of protection. Firstly, for diesel, furnace oil, and bitumen, the existing protective duties were to continue for ten years after the commencement of the refinery operations. Secondly, an additional protection of Rs.0.2.0 per gallon in excess of the excise duty on motor spirit was allowed for ten years. In 1956 Burmah Shell and Stanvac gave up their duty protection on motor spirit, and those on other products were surrendered respectively in 1959 and 1960. Caltex did not surrender protection until 1959, on the ground that its refinery was suffering from the phenomenon of "freight absorption", because of its location in an area distant from its main markets. It is inferred that the surrendering of the duties was related to the assurance given by the Government to the refineries about allowing expansion of their capacities. (See Government of India (1), p. 3, *Capital*, 4.6.1959, p. 787.) The degree of protection enjoyed by the majors in India was higher than that in most other countries. While the average protective duty was 2·3 pence per gallon in India, in Australia, France, Italy, Holland, and South Africa, the corresponding figures were 1·8, 1·9, 1·7, 1·3, and 0·5, respectively. (See Australia (1).) It was not clear why the majors needed protection, and who were the likely competitors against whom the protection was sought. The net effect of protection was to increase the price level in India.
8. Frankel (1).
9. *Indian Petroleum Handbook*, 1964.
10. *Petroleum Intelligence Weekly*, 18.11.1968; P.P.S., Dec., 1967, pp. 446–448.
11. P.P.S., Nov., 1967, pp. 421–422.
12. *Petroleum Intelligence Weekly*, 27.3.1967; *Oil and Gas International*, Feb., 1968, p. 47.
13. *Petroleum Intelligence Weekly*, 9.10.1967.
14. *Monthly Commentary on Indian Economic Affairs*, Feb., 1968, pp. 23–34.
15. Shell International Petroleum Company, *The Petroleum Handbook*, 1966.
16. Hagemans and Ingall.
17. Petroleum Information Bureau, *Oil Research*.
18. *Capital*, 29.6.1961, p. 939.
19. Government of India (8), pp. 7–10, *Eastern Economist*, 17.5.1963, p. 1023.
20. *Capital*, 24.12.1959, p. 892, 29.6.1961, p. 939.
21. *Ibid.*
22. Government of India (8), Appendix II.
23. Government of India (7), Appendix II.
24. Dhar, p. 32.
25. *Petroleum Times*, 31.6.1963, p. 268.
26. *Eastern Economist*, 28.7.1968, 19.1.1968.
27. *Petroleum Press Service*, April, 1965, pp. 134–135.
28. *Petroleum Intelligence Weekly*, 12.8.1968.

29. *Economic and Political Weekly*, 27.1.1968, pp. 235–236.

30. *Eastern Economist*, 8.3.1968, p. 402.

31. *Monthly Commentary on Indian Economic Affairs*, Feb., 1968, pp. 23–24.

32. *Eastern Economist*, Annual Number, 29.12.1967, p. 1257.

33. *Capital*, 24.1.1963, p. 114.

34. J. McB. Grant, pp. 257–258.

35. Another difficulty was related to the acquisition of land for this purpose. See *Capital*, 9.8.1962, p. 191.

36. *Eastern Economist*, 15.1.1965, p. 121.

37. Government of India (8), pp. 11–12.

38. *Capital*, supplement to 27.6.1957 number, p. 29.

39. Government of India (1).

40. *Capital*, supplement to 30.6.1955 number, p. 23.

41. Based on *Annual Statement of the Foreign Sea and Airborne Trade of India*, 1947–48 to 1956–57.

42. Saving in ocean freight equals the difference between the freight from the Persian Gulf to Bombay and the same to Madras, equal to Rs.6.31 per kilolitre (Rs.14.76 minus Rs.8.45), or Rs.4.63 per ton. For the coastal freight see *Capital* 3.8.1961, p. 175.

43. This created a problem of "freight absorption" and reduced the refinery profit under the existing system of pricing. See note 7, and also Chapter Seven.

44. See *Economic Weekly*, 8.9.1956, p. 1067; *Eastern Economist*, 5.5.1961, p. 1108, 16.11.1962, p. 904.

45. *Capital*, 4.10.1956, p. 473.

46. *Capital*, 20.12.1956, p. 865; 19.9.1957, p. 393.

47. *Eastern Economist*, 5.5.1961; Government of India (8), pp. 6–7.

48. Government of India (8), p. 22.

49. *Economic Weekly*, 24.8.1957, p. 1070.

50. Government of India (8), pp. 8–9.

51. In 1954 one Indian industrialist submitted a proposal, with the active encouragement of the Government of Saurastra, for building a refinery of 2,000,000 tons capacity at Bhavanagar, not very far from Koyali. A part of the total cost and the total foreign exchange cost were to be borne by the National Iranian Oil Company and a French firm. They sought the majority participation of the Government in its capital. The plan was in cold storage for two years, after which it was referred to the Vasist Committee. Since the refinery programme of the Government was at that time small, this proposal was rejected. Moreover, with the abolition of Saurastra as a separate state after the reorganisations of 1956, the plan was deprived of an influencial sponsor. See *Economic Weekly*, 7.7.1956, p. 790; 27.7.1956, p. 1,002.

52. Australia (1), p. 24.

53. See note 51 and p. 108.

54. *Capital*, 8.10.1959, p. 515.

55. *Capital*, 18.12.1958, p. 839.

56. *Capital*, 30.1.1958, p. 155.

57. *Capital*, 25.9.1958, p. 441, 18.12.1958, p. 839.

58. *Petroleum Times*, 9.3.1962, p. 163. A summary of W. J. Levy's paper on "Basic considerations for oil policies in developing countries".

59. *Reserve Bank of India, Annual Review*, 1951–52, p. 32.

60. See *Capital*, 4.6.1959, p. 787, 1.9.1960, p. 304, 7.4.1960, p. 515, 27.9.1962, p. 479, 17.8.1961, p. 257, 13.12.1962, p. 875.

61. Such an expansion was going to make the public sector refineries of Koyali and Cochin less profitable. See *Eastern Economist*, 7.6.1963, p. 1190 for K. D. Malviya's article on "Government Policy for Oil". The Defence

Department also raised objection to such concentration of refinery capacity in one area. See *Economic Weekly*, 15.12.1962, p. 1903.

62. *Capital*, 3.1.1963, p. 23.
63. *Commerce*, 6.5.1961, p. 893.

CHAPTER 7

THE SYSTEM OF PRICING OIL PRODUCTS
AFTER 1945

World Oil Prices: Crude and Products

Before 1945, all the major oil companies followed a common basing point system for the purpose of pricing both crude oil and oil products. As seen in Chapter Four, the choice of U.S. Gulf prices as a base for various products was thought to be justified on the grounds that supplies from the United States were essential for meeting at least a part of the consumption needs of almost all the consumption centres of the world. The fact that all the companies quoted identical prices in a market was interpreted as a reflection of the competitive market structure, since genuine competition also produces identical market prices. We have already examined the first argument about "marginal supplier" and have established that a consequence of adopting the "world parity pricing system" was to make the United States supplies competitive with supplies from nearer sources, and to deny to the latter the opportunity to translate their cost advantages (both in freight and in production) in terms of lower prices. In other words, the system of pricing which was adopted enabled the high cost U.S. crude to be sold to distant markets. On the other hand, the standardised prices, instead of reflecting the presence of competition, were a product of collusive price and market sharing arrangements among the principal traders of the world. We know of a series of written agreements among the major oil companies which were made during the 1930s in order to restrain competition and regulate production. The fact that some of the traders in oil from Rumania and the Soviet Union were outside these cartel arrangements explains the limited price wars which occasionally took place between the majors and the smaller companies in various markets. In subsequent years these major oil companies strengthened ties amongst themselves through joint participation in the concession agreements covering the major producing countries of the Middle East.

In 1945 Persian Gulf was adopted as the second basing point for the purpose of pricing. This meant that for markets nearer the Persian Gulf the price of a product was equal to the f.o.b. U.S. Gulf price plus the ocean freight from the Persian Gulf to that market, no matter from where the product was actually imported.

In other words, only the freight element was changed, while the f.o.b. element continued to be identical with the U.S. Gulf price, although the former implied a substantial saving in landed price for many markets.

An important factor behind this change was the radical transformation which the world trade in oil underwent over these years. The United States, which contributed about 70% of the world oil trade during the 1930s, was now reduced to insignificance as an exporting country and became a net importer as a result of phenomenal increases in domestic consumption. Its place was now taken by the Persian Gulf, which contained about 60% of the world's proved oil reserves, and now accounted for about 90% of the trade in crude oil in the Eastern Hemisphere. But that was not the sole explanation.

During the period following the outbreak of war in 1939, military activities in the Mediterranean and Western Europe cut down oil deliveries from the Middle East to these areas, and encouraged exports from the Middle East to East of Suez. But since the freight for delivering oil to these markets from the Persian Gulf was much smaller than the freight from the U.S. Gulf to those markets calculated under the parity system, this involved a large element of "phantom freight"—the positive difference between the calculated and actual freight.[1] This led the Auditor General of the United Kingdom to question the propriety of paying the freight from the U.S. Gulf to the consuming point when actually the bunker supplies were obtained from the Persian Gulf area.[2] Ultimately a compromise formula was worked out between the major oil companies and the Auditor General which adopted the Persian Gulf as the basing point for supplies from this source for the purpose of calculating freight. But the f.o.b. prices for bunker fuel remained identical in the U.S. Gulf and in the Persian Gulf.

The formula for pricing bunker fuel was extended to apply to other refined products and crude oil in 1945. The result of this new price formula was to equate the c.i.f. price of crude, as also of products, given the respective ocean transport costs, from the Persian Gulf and the U.S. Gulf to the consumption centres, at a point near South Italy. Accordingly, all markets to the East of that dividing point came under the Persian Gulf parity price while the markets to the West of it continued to follow the U.S. Gulf parity system.

TREND IN CRUDE PRICES

However, very soon two different trends developed in the methods of pricing oil products and crude oil. The f.o.b. Persian Gulf crude oil prices began drifting away from the f.o.b. U.S. Gulf prices.

L

The series of increases in the latter following the lifting of wartime control was not exactly followed by the Persian Gulf prices, and, by March, 1948, at an f.o.b. Persian Gulf price of $2.22 per barrel (for 36° A.P.I. crude), the delivered price of crude from these two regions at existing freight rates, was equal in London.

The f.o.b. price of the crude of the Persian Gulf was reduced further, in May, 1948, to $2.03 in order to equate the delivered prices of Persian Gulf and Caribbean crude in London. The f.o.b. Caribbean price was, since the pre-Second World War days, equal to the U.S. Gulf price for crude of similar quality, less the United States import duty of 10·5 cents per barrel. Since the distance of the Eastern seaboard of the United States was roughly the same from the U.S. Gulf and the Caribbean, this system of pricing made the delivered prices of crude from these two regions equal at the Eastern seaboard. But the Caribbean enjoyed a transport advantage of some $1.10 a ton over the U.S. on the basis of flat U.S.M.C. rates for shipments to Western Europe, until this price reduction in the Persian Gulf. There were further reductions in prices under the pressure of the European Cooperation Administration, which was interested in a lower price for crude shipments to Europe financed by it. By 1949 (July) the delivered price of crude from the Persian Gulf, at existing freight rates, became equal to the delivered price for the U.S. Gulf crude (and also that of the Caribbean) in New York and the f.o.b. price of Persian Gulf crude, consequently, was fixed at $1.75 for 36° A.P.I. In 1950, for the first time, Persian Gulf crude prices were formally posted.

It needs to be emphasised at this stage that the changes in the system of pricing, which have been discussed above, did not result from the pressure of competition between various sources of crude oil. Almost the entire amount of exports from the Caribbean, the U.S. Gulf, and the Persian Gulf was controlled by the seven major international companies. These companies, as seen before, were then, as now, linked with one another through their joint participation in producing and refining ventures in these areas, and quoted identical prices for their crudes and products of same quality. On the other hand, because of the vertically integrated nature of these international firms, most of these products and crudes were merely transferred to the marketing or refining affiliates in other countries of the same international corporation, and very little was sold to the outsider. The prices charged by one affiliate to another for these transfers were "internal book-keeping" prices, which, as will be shown below, were determined after taking into account the profit possibilities and tax minimising alternatives of all the activities of such a corporation, taken together.

It can be shown that, even ignoring the pressures exerted by the Auditor General or organisations like the European Cooperation Administration, the new system of crude pricing, with a lower f.o.b. price for the Persian Gulf supply area, was in harmony with the changing pattern of world oil trade, from the point of view of the international majors. With the spectacular increase in crude production, a large part of the crude of this area went to West Europe. But given the same f.o.b. price for both the U.S. Gulf and the Persian Gulf crude, the shipment of crude from both of these areas could be sold at the same c.i.f. price at a point South of Italy. The areas to the west of South Italy belonged to the U.S. Gulf supply zone, whereas those to the East of Italy belonged to the Persian Gulf zone, at the given ocean freight rates. As a result, the crudes of Persian Gulf origin, when sold to the markets west of Italy, received the same c.i.f. price as was being paid for the crudes from the U.S. Gulf. This gave rise to the phenomenon of "freight absorption", or the negative difference between the actual freight (between the Persian Gulf and the markets to the west of Italy) and the calculated freight (from the U.S. Gulf to that market) under the system of pricing in use. Given the same f.o.b. price of 100, and the ocean freights of 50 and 40, respectively, from the Persian Gulf and the U.S. Gulf, to, say, France, the crude producing affiliates were obtaining a c.i.f. price of 140, and only 90 as the "netback" or the price net of freight charge. In other words, the f.o.b. price of the Persian Gulf crude was already effectively reduced to a level below the U.S. Gulf price, when sold to markets nearer to the latter, even before the formalities of actually changing the f.o.b. prices of the Persian Gulf crude were undertaken, in 1949. The new reduced f.o.b. prices for the Persian Gulf crude were adopted to "simulate the conditions that would have applied in a freely competitive market, in order to assist the sensible allocation of resources between department of large international companies in conditions where such competition was largely lacking".[3] Table 20 on "World Crude Oil Movements" shows clearly the declining importance of the Caribbean as a supplier of crude, compared to the Persian Gulf, in Western Europe. It also shows that the supply of crude from the Persian Gulf to the United States exceeded the supply from the Caribbean to Western Europe, which largely explains why the delivered price of crude from the U.S. Gulf, Caribbean, and Persian Gulf was equalised in the Eastern seaboard of the United States in 1949 (July).

TREND IN PRODUCT PRICES

The f.o.b. prices of products in the Persian Gulf, in contrast to the crude prices, continued to be fixed at the same level as the f.o.b. U.S. Gulf prices, as quoted in "Platts Oilgram Press Service", a daily price-reporting bulletin published in the United States. Up to 1948 distinctions were made between different Eastern Hemisphere markets. For exports to China "High of Platts" was adopted, while for other markets east of Suez "Mean of Platts" was adopted. The markets west of Suez, however, were charged "Low of Platts" f.o.b. U.S. Gulf prices. This highly discriminatory price system, charging maximum, average, or minimum prices to different customers, was abandoned in 1948, and "Low of Platts" was adopted for all the markets supplied from the Persian Gulf. But it was not until 1957 that separate f.o.b. prices for oil products were posted in the Persian Gulf.

There were two reasons why the product prices in the Persian Gulf region continued to follow the U.S. Gulf prices until 1957, while the f.o.b. crude prices broke away from the latter as early as 1949. Firstly, while the Persian Gulf was emerging, throughout the 1940s and 1950s, as a leading supplier of crude oil, its refining industry failed to grow at the same pace. Most of the new refineries were located near the centres of consumption, in accordance with the current practice, and the Persian Gulf's oil was now transported in the form of crude to these refineries. Secondly, whatever small export of oil products was supplied by the Persian Gulf countries, a large proportion of this was sent to the markets East of Suez, including India, and the rest mainly to the countries of Europe which were situated near the Persian Gulf. In 1949, of the total Persian Gulf production of 540,000 barrels of products per day, 254,000 were sold to Europe, and 286,000 to other parts of the Western Hemisphere. There was no trade between the Persian Gulf and the Western Hemisphere in oil products. Since most of these markets were nearer the Persian Gulf than the U.S. Gulf, the phenomenon of "freight-absorption", the negative difference between the calculated and the actual freight, was absent in the case of oil products. The system came under pressure in the mid-fifties in Europe because the pattern of relative prices in the U.S. Gulf was no longer in harmony with the pattern of relative demand in Western Europe for different products. At the given prices there was a surplus of gasoline and a deficit in diesel in the market[4] and many of the independent refiners of Western Europe (who by then owned a significant portion of the refining industry of Western Europe—see Table 21) began selling gasoline at prices lower than those prescribed by the existing price formula.[5] In order to correct this product imbalance in Western Europe the majors began posting prices for refined products f.o.b. Persian Gulf from the middle of 1957. The latter took account of the slackening demand for gasoline and the increasing demand for middle distillates in the Western European market. (See Table 19.)

Under this new system of product pricing in the Eastern Hemisphere, all the markets to the east of Switzerland adopted Persian Gulf as the basing point, whereas for those to the west of Switzerland either U.S. Gulf or Caribbean was adopted.[6] As will be shown very soon, even this new system of pricing products in the Eastern Hemisphere could not be maintained after 1959 in most of the important consuming countries.

THE ECONOMIC SIGNIFICANCE OF THE PERSIAN GULF PRODUCT PRICES

We have already noted that a very small amount of the products produced by the refineries of the Persian Gulf are sold in an "arm's length deal" and the prices charged by the producing affiliate to the marketing affiliate of the same international parent are largely accounting prices. These prices are determined by the major companies on the basis of a number of considerations, such as the relative tax rates on incomes from crude and products in different countries in which these companies are operating, as also on a number of other economic and political factors.[7] The supply curve of the refining affiliate as well as the demand curve of the marketing affiliate for that product will be inelastic to changes in the posted prices of products in the Persian Gulf.

In actual practice, the posted prices are not so inelastic to changes in demand and supply as it may sound from the above discussion. The governments of the oil consuming countries are taking a growing interest in the prices paid by the affiliates of the major oil companies for imports because of their impact on the balance of payments. The governments are frequently putting pressure on the affiliates of the majors to reduce prices and, in some cases, are imposing quantitative restrictions on imports if the prices are too high in their judgement. In other words, the governments of the oil importing countries, in a number of cases in recent years, are taking over the role of buyers of imported products, either directly or indirectly, through their trade and import policies. The rapid decline in the posted prices (see Table 19) for products in recent years is also an outcome of this recent development.

From the point of view of the companies, however, these posted prices perform a number of useful economic functions. First, the posted prices help them to fix the respective level of profits of their different affiliates for the purpose of taxation.[8] Secondly, these posted prices, coupled with A.F.R.A. rates (discussed below) for ocean freight, provide a handy formula for use by the oligopolists without provoking any distrust from other oligopolists.

Thirdly, another significant use of the formula is made in the case of products produced by the consuming countries themselves from imported crude oil in refineries mostly owned by the major oil companies. There are a number of countries such as France, Italy, or the Netherlands which have been net exporters of refinery products for a long time, although the prices of products within those countries were fixed with reference to the f.o.b. prices in the Caribbean or in the Persian Gulf until recently.[9] Again, there are many countries which produce most of the refined products they need and import only a marginal amount. In view of the current trend all over the world to locate refineries near consumption centres, the importance of the import trade in oil products, as against crude oil, can be expected to decline more rapidly in future years.[10] It is significant that whereas the Middle East produced $27 \cdot 73 \%$ of the total crude oil produced in the world (including the U.S.A. and U.S.S.R.) in 1967, the percentage refining capacity of this region was only $5 \cdot 01 \%$ of the total. In the same year about $32 \cdot 7 \%$ of the world refining capacity was located in Europe and the Far East.[11] In other words, actual imports from the Persian Gulf are of limited significance in the region over which the Persian Gulf parity system is applied. Since most of the refining capacity in the eastern Hemisphere is still under the ownership of the major oil companies, (excluding the refineries controlled through crude supplies, indirectly),[12] a higher f.o.b. Persian Gulf price level of products produces a higher level of profits for the refiner-affiliates of the major oil companies. In other words, continuance of this pricing system by the affiliates in those countries, where imports from the Persian Gulf are either no longer required, or only marginally so, encourages the major oil companies to maintain Persian Gulf prices at a high level, other factors remaining constant.

However, a policy of high prices would fail to increase profits if the demand for the products is drastically reduced as a result. But there are reasons to believe that the price elasticity of demand for most of the major oil products is below unity, and the demand does not fall proportionately to increase in prices, unless the magnitude of price change is very large. Most of the major oil products have no near non-oil substitutes. The price of motor spirit constitutes only a small proportion of the total operating cost and depreciation of a motor car and the customer does not reduce its consumption with small variations in its prices.[13] Again, its substitute as motor fuel is high speed diesel, which is also an oil product. The same argument applies to the latter when used as automotive fuel. We have already examined in Chapter 5 the price inelasticity of demand for kerosene in India. The fact that furnace oil has some important close non-oil substitutes explains partly why it was kept outside the scope of the world parity system in a number of countries.[14] There is no price formula for minor products since many of these products are also produced by the chemical companies and/or are sold to large buyers at negotiated prices.[15]

Secondly, the price paid by the consumer differs greatly from the price received by the marketer because of the incidence of taxes. In most of the consuming countries of Europe and Asia, taxes and duties account for 45% to 65% of the prices paid by the consumers for diesel or motor spirit.[16] So, it will need a substantial price change by the marketer to produce any visible change in the selling price. Again, a reduction in the price by the marketer may be absorbed by the government in the form of taxes, as an increase may be neutralised by a tax concession declared by the government—as has been done in India on some occasions in the past.[17]

The forces operating against the working of this incentive to raise Persian Gulf product prices are those of the bargaining strength of the consuming countries *vis-à-vis* the major oil companies, the competition of the non-major sources of oil and also, sometimes, the conflicting interests of the majors themselves.[18]

RECENT DEVELOPMENTS IN THE WORLD PRODUCT MARKET

The basing point system—whatever be the base—which was more or less universal, with a few exceptions until 1959, in the eastern Hemisphere, has broken down because of the following reasons. First, the U.S.S.R. entered the oil product market for the first time since 1939, with a large volume of exports.[19] Furthermore, the U.S.S.R. (which is expected to exceed the crude production of the U.S.A. in the early 1970s[20]) began offering oil under highly attractive terms. The prices of products were up to 25% less than either the Persian Gulf or Caribbean f.o.b. prices,[21] while ocean freight was calculated from either the Black Sea or the Persian Gulf according to which one was nearer to the centre of consumption.[22] In addition, payments could be made in local currency and the Russians were willing to accept non-oil commodities in exchange which could not be exported otherwise.[23] A number of independent marketers in Western Europe as also in Japan[24] and India began importing Russian products to sell at less than world parity prices, while a large part was also purchased by state organisations in some countries.[25]

Secondly, there was a growing tendency among the oil consuming countries to build refineries in order to attain self-sufficiency in oil products which would economise on foreign exchange expenditures. A large part of this new capacity was either partly or wholly owned by the state organisations.

Thirdly, a number of non-major international oil companies also entered the scene as competitors. Some of these companies discovered crude oil in the Middle East and North Africa in large quantities and were willing to build and operate refineries in the consuming centres if that assured them an outlet for crude for a long period. Since in many countries domestic refinery products were given priority in the local market by the government, this provided an added incentive to these companies to build refineries for the consuming countries. Again, since these companies had no previous marketing organisation in those markets they could agree quickly to sell refinery products at lower than parity prices. The major companies, with developed marketing facilities in most countries, were reluctant to build refineries under this condition. They were also unwilling to work in a refinery project where the government had a majority-participation. All these favoured "independent" companies enormously. Notable among those were E.N.I., the state-owned international company of Italy, Philips, Continental, Standard of India, the U.S. independents, and Petrofina of Belgium. In recent years C.F.P., the state-controlled oil organisation of France, sometimes called the "eighth major" has also made a vigorous move to extend its markets East of Suez.[26]

The consequence of this intense competition has been to break down the downward inflexibility of petroleum prices in most markets.[27] As it now appears from the materials published in oil journals and government reports, the import-parity system subsists now only in two types of markets: in the first, the entire amount of oil products, but for marginal supplies, is sold by the affiliates of the majors and there is no government interference. In these markets, the "import-parity principle" is still maintained in more or less pure form, since no offer of discounts is necessary. This was the position of India before 1962 and also of most other countries before the 1960s. In the second, the government has imposed a schedule of prices in conformity with the import parity principle and has also introduced quota restrictions on imports. In these countries the marketers are virtually assured of a definite share of the market at the import parity prices and there is no incentive on their part to compete at less than parity prices. A classic example is Greece where the government purchases Soviet oil at low prices (25% below the Persian Gulf price for gasoline, 12%, 14%, and 19% below for kerosene, gas oil, and furnace oil, respectively) and sells it to the marketing companies, for distribution, at import parity prices, in order to supplement domestic refinery output.[28] It is interesting to note that more than three-quarters of the Greek market is still supplied by the international majors.[29] Because of the rigid adherence of the French government to the import parity principle until 1965, combined with quota restrictions, the French market was considered to be the most profitable market in Europe.[30]

In other markets the parity pricing system has come under severe pressure. These markets, again, can be divided into two groups: first where the pressure on the companies is being brought by the governments and, secondly, where the price-flexibility has resulted from competition of non-major companies, known as "independents", and the U.S.S.R.

In most of the countries where the governments are taking an active interest in oil prices, the latter have accepted "import parity" as a principle for the purpose of pricing, but are insisting on "discounts" off posted prices in the light of "competitive conditions" in the world market at present. In those markets the companies yield to pressure if the market is reasonably big and the government is strong. For example, India could secure discounts on Persian Gulf parity prices for products only after the state-owned distributing company, Indian Oil, survived a brief price war with the majors and stabilised its position in the market with Russian supplies.[31] In Ceylon, on the other hand, the majors refused to allow discounts, presumably because the market was too small to be given any concession.[32] But in view of the growing "oil consciousness" among the oil consuming countries, it is becoming increasingly difficult to offer discount to one country and deny it to others.[33]

But while a number of governments are willing to adopt a modified import parity system, subject to some discounts, there are others who have fixed a schedule of product prices without linking it to import parity. In Austria, for example, prices are negotiated between suppliers and the representatives of the consumers, with the government agencies sitting in as referees.[34] In a number of South American countries, such as Puerto Rico, Brazil, Venezuela, and Colombia, prices are fixed without any reference to the import parity system, on the basis of the costs of crude and refining and other considerations.[35] Most of these countries produce a large amount of the crude oil they need and have large state oil undertakings. There are still other countries where the governments pay lip service to the import parity principle by originally fixing product prices on that basis, but do not allow any change in the prices unless the fluctuations in the world market prices are very significant. A typical example is Portugal, where prices of products have not changed since 1961.[36]

However, a system of price control can be effective, under the present competitive world conditions, only if either the government has also imposed quota restrictions on imports and domestic refinery output, or the major companies supply almost the entire amount of oil needed for consumption in that market and can effectively bar the entry of newcomers. Neither of these two conditions has been fulfilled in the case of many of the countries of Europe and in Japan. In Italy, for example, maximum prices of products were fixed by an inter-ministerial committee (C.I.P.) on the basis of Persian Gulf parity until 1960. This was abandoned in May, 1960, and a new schedule of prices, based on average refinery prices was fixed.[37] But even these lower than Persian Gulf parity prices were higher than market prices reported from time to time.[38] This was because a large part of the refining capacity of Italy, about 49 % in 1964, was under the ownership of independents, while another 18 % was under the state-enterprises of Italy and France.[39] The vigorous competition of these refineries in the product market has brought down prices of gasoline, kerosene, and diesel considerably. A similar condition also prevails in Japan where the minimum "standard prices" fixed by the Ministry of International Trade and Industries (M.I.T.I.) on the basis of cost during the early 1960s bore no relation to the market prices, which were far below the "standard prices", and had to be abandoned in 1966. Here again, the presence of large "independent refiner-marketers", controlling a significant proportion of the market, has made the market competitive.[40]

In the markets of Switzerland, Sweden, and West Germany there are no government controls over prices, but the prices are far below the level of world parity prices, because of the competition of the Russians and independent refiners.[41] To give an example of the extent of competition in those markets, gasoline was selling in western Europe at 5¢ per gallon in the first half of 1964, which would require a posted price of 4¢ per gallon at the Caribbean if the import parity system were to be respected, but the actual posted price there was 8·9¢ per gallon. Again, the high price of diesel at that time at 6·375¢ in western Europe, would require a posted price of 5¢ in the Caribbean, when the actual posted price was 7·4¢ for 48–52 diesel index.[42]

This brief survey of the conditions for oil products in the world market shows that the import parity system or any other formula only indicates the absence of genuine competition in the market. "Only fools and affiliates pay posted prices."[43] That the import parity system or any other formula still subsists in any market in the eastern Hemisphere is either a reflection of the fact that the major companies are yet to experience serious competition in those markets, or because the governments of those countries are protecting these price formulae by restricting refinery output and imposing import quota restrictions.

OCEAN FREIGHT AND A.F.R.A.

Since ocean freight constitutes about 10% to 12% of the c.i.f. prices of products in India,[44] it is important to consider the basis on which it is calculated and also the ownership pattern of the world oil tanker fleet. Before the Second World War few tankers were in the hands of the private non-major shipowners.[45] The tanker freights were determined during the thirties by a tanker pool set up by the major companies.[46] After the Second World War the proportion of ownership of tanker capacity by the majors declined, and at present it is about 40% of the total.[47] But a large proportion of the independent tankers is tied to the major companies through long term contracts.

The A.F.R.A. (Average Freight Rate Assessment) is determined by a panel of six leading tanker brokers in London. This panel was established by Shell and Burmah Oil in 1949, in order to achieve stability in freight rates for determining oil prices.[48]

The assessment covers time charters, consecutive voyage charters as well as spot charters and provides a weighted average of these rates twice a year. From July, 1964, to October, 1968, A.F.R.A. was calculated for three groups of vessels separately; (a) general purpose tankers of 15,000 to 24,999 d.w.t.; (b) medium sized tankers of 25,000 to 44,999 d.w.t.; and (c) large tankers of 45,000 to 69,999 d.w.t.[49] In October, 1968, a fourth tier was added for the giant tankers of 80,000 to 159,999 d.w.t. size class, and the upper limit of the preceding class was raised to 79,999 d.w.t.[50]

The Damle committee on oil prices in India accepted A.F.R.A. for the purpose of calculating ocean freight, both for products and crude, and observed, "The adoption of spot charter rate is likely to introduce an element of uncertainty, which is not worth taking, particularly when the current low rates for spot charters are automatically reflected in the overall level of A.F.R.A."[51] It is indeed true that the spot rates have fluctuated from time to time over the past two decades, rising during the years of international crisis, and subsiding during the normal years. They reached their peak both during the Suez crisis of 1956 and after the closure of the canal in 1967, but during the intervening period they were extremely low. The A.F.R.A. rates do not generally rise as much as the spot rates during the years of crisis, but show a higher than spot rate during the normal years. On the other hand, it needs to be noted that world trade in many commodities—such as rubber, tin, or grain—is carried out on the spot market. A number of countries, such as

Brazil, have been purchasing oil for some years in the spot market.[52] Furthermore, the element of uncertainty inherent in the spot rate has been considerably reduced in recent years because of two developments. First, since the late 1950s oil tankers have been used more and more in the grain trade. Although the tonnage involved in this trade as a proportion of the total tanker tonnage has never been substantial, it sometimes accounted for about one-third of the spot market alone. In normal periods this opportunity for alternative employment of the tankers would provide the "floor" for the spot rates.[53] Second, the building time of a tanker has now been reduced to less than a year, and any shortage of tanker capacity in the world market is likely to be met within a relatively short time,[54] while in addition the tankers employed in the grain trade can be switched over to carrying oil within a short time. In other words, high spot rates as a result of an international crisis would be a temporary affair and would be brought down to normal levels in a short time through the installation of new capacities.

The importance of these two factors in dampening the fluctuations in spot rates has also been demonstrated by the recent figures. Whereas both during the Korean War and during the 1956 Suez crisis the spot rates rose to plus 300% Intascale,[55] during the tanker shortages following the 1967 closure of the Suez Canal these seldom exceeded plus 100% Intascale. Furthermore, the present indications are that the period of shortage will be over, and the rates will return back to their normal levels by the middle of 1969.[56] On the other hand, A.F.R.A. rates were consistently higher than the spot rates from 1957 to 1967, and during most of this period the difference between the two rates was as high as 60% in terms of Intascale rates.[57] To take a concrete example, in 1960 (March) the A.F.R.A. for the Netherlands–West Indies–London voyage was Intascale plus 6·8% and the spot rate was less than minus 40%, in money terms approximately 34 shillings and 13 shillings respectively.[58]

It is the opinion of a number of experts that the A.F.R.A., because of its method of weighting different rates, is not a true average of market rates.[59] It gives only 10% weightage to the spot rates, and 90% to time charters. Many of the time charter agreements of the present time were concluded during the Suez crisis when the tanker demand was at its peak, and, because of the far greater weight given to them in the A.F.R.A., the average figures show an upward bias. A large contributory factor in this upward bias is the practice of pricing company-owned tonnage, which constitutes about 40% of the total, at the same rate as the time charter rate, although these company-owned tankers are not usually rented in the open market,[60] and are used by the companies almost exclusively for their own requirements. In addition, the very fact that the panel which determines the A.F.R.A. has been sponsored by the major oil companies raises doubts about the fairness and impartiality of the panel.

By its adherence to the A.F.R.A. rates, the Indian Government has paid more for its imports of crude and products in the past than was necessary under world market conditions. The savings it made during the bad years of international crisis were much more than offset by the continuous high prices it was required to pay in foreign exchange under the A.F.R.A. rates. The future prospect is for the spot rates to show secular decline, and, consequently, for the A.F.R.A. to show higher prices because of its links with the time charters. The rapid growth of the giant tankers would take away a good proportion of the load of the smaller tankers, which are normally used in the spot market, and would depress its rates further, even if the Suez Canal remains closed.

Again, the A.F.R.A. is not the only alternative to spot rates. The Governments of France and a number of other countries have established freight formulae of their own, based on a combination of long term and short term charters.[61] The major companies are also willing to offer discounts off A.F.R.A., when carrying crude for the independent refineries under short term contracts, which are not normally available to the affiliates of the major oil companies. According to the reports published in the oil journals, the state organisations of the South American countries, as well as countries such as Pakistan, which purchase a part of their requirements from the world market, have succeeded in receiving excellent offers on c.i.f. prices, which presumably include discounts on both the f.o.b. prices and A.F.R.A. rates.

While the long-term solution is for the Government of India to build its own tanker fleet for carrying oil, a policy which is being followed by a number of other oil consuming countries such as Spain, the immediate need is to replace the present arrangements by freight schedules which are closely linked with the competitive spot market, or are at least in harmony with the discounts available on freights in deliveries to the refineries which are not tied to the major companies.

Oil Product Pricing in India

VALUED STOCK ACCOUNT AND DAMLE COMMITTEE

The price leadership of Burmah Shell and the world parity pricing system with the Persian Gulf as the basing point continued even after the independence of India. But from 1950 a formal change took place in the method of price fixing. The purchases made by the Government from Burmah Shell came to be governed by the "Valued Stock Account" formula, which was based on the import parity principle with Ras Tanura (Persian Gulf) as the basing point.[62] Burmah Shell charged other consumers the same price and other companies followed the prices fixed by Burmah Shell.[63]

This Valued Stock Account covered all major products excepting lubricants and greases and Burmah Shell maintained separate accounts for each product. To this account was debited the costs of the oil products sold, the revenue earned from sales on the basis of the agreed price formula was credited. Burmah Shell estimated the position of the V.S.A. from time to time and adjusted the selling prices to keep the account, as far as possible, in balance. The agreement was terminable at six months' notice.

The extent of Government control over the method of fixing the selling price was not very wide. Burmah Shell submitted to the Director General of Supplies and Disposals of the Government of India, "a certificate to the effect that the V.S.A. for the product concerned had been prepared on the basis of the agreed price formula and that all over/under recoveries were correctly accounted for." But the account was not subject to audit by the Government.

This V.S.A. agreement was terminated in May, 1958, at the instance of the Government, which now undertook an examination of the components of the wholesale selling price of the companies through the Chief Cost Accounts Officer of the Government. The companies, in anticipation of a likely suggestion for price reduction by the Chief Cost Accounts Officer, agreed to make *ad hoc* price reductions.

The report of the Cost Accounts Officer, submitted on March 28, 1959, was highly critical of the marketing expenses charged by the companies, and stated that there was scope for economy, to the extent of 20%, in administrative, installation, and distribution expenses. The report also commented on the extraordinary level of income of higher supervisory and managerial staff, which formed a very significant proportion of the total administrative expenses. The report singled out Burmah Shell for attack and observed, "presumably taking advantage of the position of price leader under the V.S.A. procedure, Burmah Shell might not have exercised proper control on cost." However, the report raised no question about the "import parity principle" or its application in India.[64]

The oil companies refused to accept the findings of the Chief Cost Accountant's report. However, they agreed with the Government on an *ad hoc* price arrangement, to continue up to March 31, 1961. The Price Adjustment Account for this purpose was similar to V.S.A. with the difference that it was not permitted to show a balance of more than 2,000,000 rupees. Meanwhile the Government appointed another enquiry committee on oil prices in August, 1960, under the chairmanship of K. R. Damle, then Secretary to the Ministry of Food and Agriculture. This committee, popularly known as the Damle Committee, submitted its report in July, 1961.[65]

This report declared a schedule of maximum prices for all major products excluding lubricating oil and greases. This schedule did not deny the "import parity" principle, but also took into account the fact of growing Soviet competition in the world market as also in India at prices 20% to 25% below those offered by the major companies. It also recommended the continuation of A.F.R.A. rates for calculating ocean freights. The most important result of this enquiry was the discounting of Persian Gulf f.o.b. prices on a fixed basis—10% for kerosene and high speed diesel, 5% for motor spirit, and 9·3% and 3% for light diesel oil and furnace oil respectively. The basis of these discount rates for products was the 8% discount then allowed by the major companies on the price of imported crude. This system applied equally to imports and the products of domestic refineries, and, as before, did not differentiate between nearer and distant sources of imports.

The companies were at first unwilling to accept the price-ceilings fixed by the Damle Committee on the ground that discounts on product prices were not available.[66] They conveyed their "final decision" to the Government and indirectly threatened the stoppage of product imports if the Damle prices were imposed on them.[67] However, their claim that discounts were not available on product prices was not well-founded, as reports about widespread price cuts, particularly in the markets of West Europe, had been appearing in the oil journals since 1959–60. Even in India, C.F.P. was selling to Western Indian Oil at discount rates long before 1962. They also attempted to create an impression that the suppliers of products were organisationally separate from the marketers in India, when in fact both the suppliers in the Middle East and their marketers in India were part of the same international parent organisation. Their apparent readiness to reduce crude prices combined with more stubborn opposition to lower oil product prices, can be explained in terms of the nature of their organisation and its relationship to the prices of crude and products. While the price at which crude oil is transferred from the crude producing affiliate to the refining affiliate of the same company is an internal accounting price, (see Chapter Eight), the prices at which the products are sold to the consumers are directly linked to the revenues obtained by such a company. The maintenance of the same prices, while allowing discounts on crude prices, could only mean larger revenue for the refiner-marketer affiliate, and a smaller revenue for the crude producing affiliate, while the total gross revenue of the entire international organisation would remain unchanged. On the other hand, discounts off posted product prices would result in loss of revenue, both to the marketing affiliate and to the international organisation as a whole. It was, accordingly, in the interests of the major oil companies operating in India to resist reductions in oil product prices as long as possible, and it took a year before these companies agreed to the Damle prices. This reduction in prices was not reflected in the consumer's prices since the difference was absorbed by the Government through taxes.

Another price enquiry committee was set up under J. N. Talukdar to recommend a price formula for a period of four years after 1965 (June), and this submitted its report in September, 1965. The report asked for a larger range of discounts, from 10% on furnace oil, 12% on motor spirit, kerosene and light diesel oil, to 15% on jet fuel, off Persian Gulf posted prices.[68]

As this brief survey of the pricing system in the post-war period indicates, the present system is nothing but an application of the Persian Gulf parity system subject to a fixed schedule of discounts for different products.

In the following few pages we will consider some of the important consequences of the present pricing system in India in the light of the following aspects of the oil economy of India:

(1) The government is firmly committed to the objective of self-sufficiency in refined products;

(2) No imports are allowed in excess of what is needed to supplement the domestic refinery output.

(3) Import trade in middle distillates, the deficit products, by the private oil companies has been prohibited from May, 1965. Since then the Indian Oil Corporation, the state-owned marketing company, has taken over exclusively the import trade in deficit products which it receives from the U.S.S.R. at low prices payable in local currency.

(4) These three aspects of the present oil policy of the government of India, mentioned above, are likely to continue for an indefinite period in the future in view of the spiralling foreign exchange difficulties.

In short, the present position is that the government imports no product from the Persian Gulf although the products in India, whether produced in India or abroad, are priced as if they had been purchased from the Persian Gulf at discounts fixed by the Government Committees.

UPWARD BIAS IN IMPORT PARITY PRICES

We have seen above the inherent upward bias of the Persian Gulf parity prices for oil products, as it boosts the revenues of the refineries, under the ownership of the major companies, situated in countries where such a parity system operates. In the absence of competition from the non-major oil companies, and given the inelasticity of oil products, such a policy of maintaining high posted prices for the products can be pursued without the risk of discouraging the demand for oil supplied by the major oil companies, within a given price range. For products which face stiff competition from non-oil substitutes, such as furnace oil (which can be substituted by coal) or chemical products, (which can also be supplied by the chemical companies), the parity system does not normally operate. Again, in markets where the major oil companies face the competition from oil companies not associated with their organisations, the parity system breaks down and is replaced by lower market prices. In cases where the major oil companies do not face serious competition, but the governments take an interest in oil prices and partly compensate for the absence of competition by putting pressure on these companies, the latter agree to adjust the parity prices to lower levels.

We have also seen that between 1945 and 1957 all the markets in the eastern Hemisphere paid U.S. Gulf f.o.b. prices, while the crude prices were allowed to drop to lower levels. The latter helped to swell the processing margin of the refineries under the ownership of the major companies, and while the markets of West Europe and Japan responded to the competition of the companies not associated with the majors from 1959 onwards, in markets such as India, where such an element of competition was absent, the prices were not lowered for another two or more years. In addition, adherence to the A.F.R.A. rates meant that between 1957 and 1967 India paid much more for ocean freight than would have been necessary if spot rates, which were more responsive to changing demand and supply conditions (unlike the company-owned or time charter rates), had been applied. But even assuming that the Persian Gulf prices are applicable to India, it can be shown that an Indian refinery (assuming equal refining cost per barrel in India and in the Middle East)[69] processing Iranian crude, will secure a higher refinery-margin than those in the Persian Gulf under this system, even if we overlook the reality of vertical integration. This results from the fact that ocean freight for products is higher than that for crude oil. But, because of the working of the

M

parity system, the Indian refineries are adding to their prices the ocean freight for products when what they are actually importing is crude. As a result, they are receiving the difference between the freights for crude and products over and above what is obtained as a refinery margin in the Persian Gulf. With the building of very large tankers, which are only capable of handling crude,[70] the difference in freight between crude and products will be greater (assuming, of course, that in future deep sea terminals will be installed for receiving delivery from such tankers), thereby swelling the refinery margin of the Indian affiliates of the major companies.

Again, assuming no difference in freight rates between products and crude, a rigid adherence to the Persian Gulf parity system implies that the difference between the price of products ex-refinery and the cost of crude must be identical in both the Persian Gulf and India. In other words, if the posted price of products produced from a barrel of crude is 100, and the posted price of a barrel of crude is 80, assuming an ocean freight of 25 for both crude and products, the c.i.f. prices would be 125 and 105 respectively, thereby yielding the same refinery margin of 20 as in the Persian Gulf. But there is no reason why this should necessarily be so. In view of the vertically integrated nature of the major oil companies, as discussed before, there is no special significance attached to the refinery margin in the Persian Gulf.

This upward bias in domestic prices affects the balance of payments situation of India because it involves a higher profit for the domestic refineries owned by the foreign oil companies.[71]

RELATIVE PRICES AND PRODUCT IMBALANCE

The problem of product imbalance has been discussed in detail in the previous chapter, mainly from the supply side, at a technical level. It has been found that the degree of flexibility attainable in the production pattern is circumscribed by the relative costs of alternative production techniques compared with their yields. Both the price obtained by the refiner (which is net of taxes and other payments) and the price paid by the consumer (which includes taxes and delivery costs) are relevant for an understanding of this problem.

Up to 1957, when f.o.b. U.S. Gulf product prices were adopted for the eastern hemisphere markets, the relative price structure for oil products net of taxes in the latter was not different from that in the former region. This provided a strong incentive for the refiners of the Eastern Hemisphere markets to try to adopt output patterns comparable to those in the United States and out of line with those in demand in the Eastern Hemisphere. Whereas the proportion of consumption of light distillates in the Eastern Hemisphere was relatively lower than that for the middle distillates, the refineries of that region produced more of the former, because relative prices favoured the production of light distillates. The changes which were introduced after 1957 in the system of pricing oil products made the new f.o.b. Persian Gulf prices comparable to the pattern of demand in West Europe, but failed to meet fully the problems of individual countries like India, whose pattern of consumption diverged from that of the markets of West Europe.

It was because the price of motor spirit f.o.b. Persian Gulf was higher than that of kerosene,[72] when the three refineries owned by the majors were constructed in India, that these were so designed as to yield a relatively larger proportion of motor spirit. Since each of these refineries forms part of an international group with many marketing affiliates all over the world, it is perfectly rational on their part to continue producing motor spirit in excess of its level of consumption in India at parity prices if these prices are high enough to offset the cost of exporting the surplus as naphtha at lower prices. The fact that these refineries reduced the proportion of light distillates between 1955 and 1960 was due, firstly, to the decline in the relative price of motor spirit in those years,[73] and secondly, to the appreciation of the fact that export opportunities were diminishing in the world.

It was, however, unfortunate that the adjustments made by the Damle report in the relative prices of products only aggravated this problem of product imbalance. As we have noted before, Damle prices allowed 10% discounts on h.s.d. and kerosene, while only 5% discount on motor spirit, for the purposes of calculating f.o.b. Persian Gulf prices. The result was that, although the f.o.b. posted price for h.s.d. was higher than that of motor spirit in the Persian Gulf because of these discounts, the latter had a higher computed f.o.b. price than h.s.d. in India. These discounts also reduced the relative f.o.b. price advantage of kerosene.[74] From the point of view of the refiner, therefore, the motor spirit trade was more attractive in India than selling h.s.d. and the kerosene trade was relatively not so profitable as it would have been otherwise without this schedule of discriminatory discount rates highly favourable to the motor spirit trade.

A second aspect of the system of relative prices in India is the method of taxation of oil products which, because of its high proportion in the wholesale price, affects differently the relative levels of demand for different products. Motor spirit, as in most other countries, is considered to be an attractive source of revenue by the government, while the rate of taxation of h.s.d. is low and that of kerosene is still lower. For example, in 1965, the central taxes and duties per kilolitre on wholesale prices of motor spirit, kerosene, and fuel oil in India were Rs.544, Rs.226 and Rs.484, respectively.[75] (See Table 22.)

Although this tax policy does not affect the prices per unit received by the refiners, it changes the pattern of relative prices from the point of view of the consumer. We have seen before that motor spirit has no non-oil substitute, but both h.s.d. and kerosene among other oil products can be used as automotive fuel. Again, although in the short run changes in the price of motor fuel hardly affect its demand, since the conversion of a car to diesel is not easy, in the long run the high price of motor spirit encourages dieselisation of motor vehicles. Furthermore, although h.s.d. possesses some technical advantages over motor spirit, there is no reason to suppose that the trend of dieselisation will continue despite price changes. The very high proportion of cars driven by motor spirit in the U.S.A., and the resulting higher demand for motor spirit in that country relative to Europe, is partly explained by the relatively lower price of motor spirit to consumers in the U.S.A.[76] In other words, a significantly lower consumers' price for motor spirit, relative to h.s.d., might generate considerable demand for it, despite low price elasticity within a small range of price changes.

It must be noted, on the other hand, that the government tax policy is not the only reason for the relatively higher price of motor spirit in India. In almost all the countries of western Europe the percentage of taxes and duties in consumer list prices on motor spirit is higher than it is in India.[77] But this has not prevented the market price from falling in Italy or Switzerland. And even with the present level of high taxes on motor spirit, h.s.d., and kerosene, expressed as percentages of consumers' prices, are 57·7, 47·9, and 7·4 respectively for imported goods and 53·2, nil, and 41·6 respectively for the domestic output,[78] in Japan the market prices of these three commodities were $4.92, $5.41, and $5.63 per barrel respectively in February, 1965.[79] Thus, despite relatively high tax rates for motor spirit the forces of competition and lower demand have been reflected in its relative price.

It is also interesting to note that in India the taxes on these three commodities in 1961 expressed as percentages of their wholesale prices, were 65·2, 62·2, and 38·4 respectively, for motor spirit, h.s.d., and kerosene, although the wholesale price of motor spirit (Rs.499.87) was considerably higher than those of h.s.d. (Rs.466.96) and kerosene (Rs.237.61) per kilolitre.[80] This was also despite the relative f.o.b. prices discussed before. One major reason for this higher price of motor spirit is its higher marketing cost. The latter, for the purpose of fixing Damle prices, was calculated as an average of the marketing costs of the companies in the past years, which, in the light of the Cost Accountants report, were gross over-estimations.[81]

INLAND PRICES, REFINERY LOCATION, AND PROFIT

An interesting aspect of the import parity system is its effect on the profits of refineries located in different parts of the country. The prices we have discussed so far are generally the wholesale prices at sea ports, to which are added the internal transport costs from the seaport to a consuming centre to derive under the formula the prices of oil products in that centre.

In short, for the purpose of determining the prices of oil products in an inland consumption centre, the nearest seaport is taken as the basing point.

It can be shown that this system of pricing products within the country, on the basis of the distance of a consuming centre from the sea coast, produces some arbitrary effects on the profitability of a refinery depending on its geographical location.

P	A	B	C	R	D	E	F	
100	110	120	130	140	150	160	170	200

The above diagram shows the prices of a product at different consumption points determined on the basis of the import parity formula with P as the seaport and R as the refinery. We can derive the following conclusions from the above diagram; assuming the cost of refining to be the same everywhere.

(1) The refinery will make maximum profit if it supplies oil only to the consumption point R, where the refinery is located. At this point the price of the product is 140 (c.i.f. price = 100 and computed inland transport cost = 40), while the actual transport cost is zero. The refinery makes an extra profit of 40, equal to the calculated transport cost from the seaport to the refinery, over an importer.

(2) At every point beyond R, the refinery will make the same extra profit of 40, since both the actual and the computed extra transport costs beyond R are identical.

(3) The extra profit of the refinery declines as its products move towards A, the seaport. For example, at C the price is 130 (c.i.f. = 100 and computed inland transport cost = 30), while the actual transport cost from the refinery to C is 10 which, together with c.i.f. prices, makes the delivery cost 110. The

refinery earns extra profit equal to 20 at C, which is less than the extra profit of 40 at R.

(4) At B, the midpoint between P and R, the extra profit disappears and the refinery is making as much profit as an importer could make from selling oil.

(5) At any point between P and B the refinery will obtain less profit than an importer; the extent of relative loss suffered by the refiner is equal to the difference between the transport costs from R and P to that consumption point. This is known as "freight-absorbtion" or "under-recovery of freight" because of the operation of the price formula.

To take a concrete example, the inland Nunmati refinery of Assam is the least profitable of all refineries in India, although Assam produces more than half of the domestic crude. There are various reasons for this, and one of these is the "under-recovery of freight", which amounted to Rs.5.6 million in 1963–64.[82] There are a number of consumption points, such as Siliguri in West Bengal, which are supplied exclusively by the Nunmati refinery, but their distance from Calcutta, the nearest seaport, is less than their distance from Nunmati. The result is that the Nunmati refinery is compelled to absorb a part of the inland transport cost and, consequently, yields a comparatively lower profit than other refineries. On our diagram, Siliguri may be located at, say, A, where the refiner makes a relative loss of 20. The Caltex refinery of Vizagapatnam also suffers from this phenomenon of "freight absorption".

It is interesting to note that if, instead of being located at A, nearer to the seaport, the consumption point were situated at a point, say, F, further away from the seaport but at the same distance from the refinery as A, our refiner could, instead of making a relative loss of 20, make an extra profit of 40. In other words, what matters really from the point of view of the profitability of the refinery is not the distance of the consumption points from the refinery, other factors remaining constant, but the geographical position of the consumption centre in relation to both the seaport and the refinery.

The main idea behind this formula for pricing products in different parts of India was to make the price of domestic product at any place equal to the price at which it could be imported to that place. This is probably realistic in an economy where free flow of imports and exports is allowed, since if the price of a domestic product is higher than the price of the imported product the former cannot be sold when the country is open to imports. But it is highly unrealistic to continue this assumption of free flow of imports when most of the consumption is satisfied by domestic refinery output and the imports are rigorously controlled, particularly when it makes the relative profitability of a refinery dependent "on the accident of geography rather than comparative costs".[83]

ALTERNATIVE PRICE POLICIES

We will now examine a number of alternative oil product price policies adopted by other consuming countries, not necessarily in any order of priority.

The very fact that an artificial price formula is maintained is the symptom of the imperfect nature of the oil market. One solution which suggests itself is to make the market more competitive by curtailing the dominance of the big international companies in the market and by encouraging the entry of new competitors. In recent years the government has taken a series of measures to diversify the ownership of refineries and to take away a larger part of the oil market from the hands of the major oil companies. But this has not necessarily led to competition or lower prices, as has happened in Western Europe or in Japan. The state-owned Indian Oil Corporation sells products at the maximum level of prices declared by the government. The major companies are not interested in price-competition so long as the import trade is rigorously controlled to allow only the minimum amount of import required to supplement the domestic output. Neither do we visualise the emergence of a new and strong competitor to the state-owned company or majors, since all the future refineries are, according to the present policy of the government, likely to be under the majority ownership of the government and their products would be sold through the state marketing company. In other words, under the present policy of the government, although the market share of the major companies will decrease, the market will not be "competitive" in the accepted sense of the term. The prices in the market, accordingly, will be the maximum prices determined by the government which the oil companies will follow. Prices will not automatically fluctuate according to changes in demand and supply conditions through the working of a competitive market mechanism.

The introduction of new competitors to the market is not possible without some relaxation in the import and refining policies of the government. A new competitor can enter the market with supplies from either foreign markets or from domestic refineries. Neither of these is possible unless the government allows imports in excess of the minimum needed to supplement domestic output or allows the establishment of refineries under the ownership of the independents with a total capacity exceeding the current level of consumption. But both of these steps would involve larger imports—either of products or of crude—thereby complicating the already precarious foreign exchange situation. It may be asked how this extra foreign exchange cost for the purpose of making the oil market more competitive would compare with alternative uses to which the same amount of foreign exchange could be put to the benefit of the country's economy.

Another alternative would be for Indian Oil to adopt an aggressive price policy as E.N.I. adopted in Italy. But here again, for various reasons, there are difficulties in following such a course of action. Firstly, since the imports are already under the monopoly of Indian Oil, Indian Oil is already assured of a share of the Indian market equal to the difference between total demand and the refinery output of the major oil companies in India. No price competition will increase its market share without involving additional imports at the cost of the domestic refinery output of the major oil companies. Secondly, in a market with such a small number of sellers there is very little real scope for the development of genuine competition between the sellers, on strictly economic grounds. This view is reinforced by the existing practice among the oil companies— including Indian Oil—to barter products.

We will now discuss a number of alternative price formulae which can form the basis of the oil price policy of the government and which can be implemented either through a schedule of maximum prices or though the pricing decisions of Indian Oil.

One alternative price formula is to adopt an import parity system, not necessarily connected with any single basing point. A number of countries, including Norway and two states of Australia, fix prices on the basis of the average import prices in a previous period.[84] An advantage of this system over the Persian Gulf parity system is that it takes into account c.i.f. prices of oil from a number of sources instead of mechanically following the prices of a particular source of products. But when the import is not free, and is controlled either exclusively by the major oil companies or by the government, the average price of imports does not necessarily reflect world conditions. For instance, in India, before the Indian Oil Corporation came to the market, the average import prices for products were identical to the prices posted in the Persian Gulf plus the ocean freight, ignoring the marginal imports by the Western Indian Oil from C.F.P. at discount prices. The pricing system for oil products announced in 1968, in France, linked the officially fixed prices to prices in all the three important oil centres, the Persian Gulf, Caribbean, and the U.S. Gulf, in prescribed proportions subject to upper and lower limits. But since the prices are posted in these three centres by the same group of major international oil companies, the weighted average of these prices would be higher than the prices prevailing in other markets of Western Europe, although it would probably be lower than the Caribbean parity prices France paid until 1965.

The government may also apply its subjective judgement in deciding the schedule of maximum prices on the basis of the current trends in the more competitive markets of the world. For instance, the import of gas oil, motor spirit, and fuel oil at discounts amounting to 19%, 23%, and 10%, respectively, below the c.i.f. Abadan prices, from Italy to Amin Oil of Pakistan, despite longer distance covered,[85] could be studied; and these prices, and not prices negotiated between the affiliates of the same international company, could form the basis of the prices declared by the government. One difficulty of properly estimating the current trend in oil prices would be, that in some cases, agreements on oil products form a part of a bigger deal between two governments, or between a government and a company, or between two companies. For example, the contract between the U.S.S.R. and Greece provides for the purchase by the latter of oil products in exchange for other commodities.[86] The U.S.S.R. has also entered into barter agreements with one or two Scandinavian companies.[87] In many cases product sales agreements are connected with crude purchase agreements.[88] In these agreements it is difficult to separate the price of one oil product from others, since all constitute parts of a barter deal which also covers, possibly, crude oil and a number of non-oil commodities.

Another, and perhaps the most acceptable, alternative way of fixing prices will be to make them dependent on the costs of crude oil and refining, with a reasonable addition for marketing expenses and profit. This price system is now being seriously discussed in Italy and France.[89] The Cochin refinery agreement with Philips, which stipulates a certain refinery margin over crude prices,[90] is also a kind of cost-plus arrangement subject to the maximum of official prices. The components of such a pricing system may be fixed at arbitrary levels. Like the Persian Gulf parity system, the wholesale prices of individual products will not be automatically responsive to the pressures of demand and supply but, unlike the Persian Gulf parity system, the government will be in a position to make suitable changes in the relative and absolute prices on the basis of changes in the market conditions of India.

One of the difficulties of the cost-plus system will be the problem of devising a relative price structure which, on the one hand ensures a sufficient profit-margin over the costs, and, on the other hand, corresponds to the pattern of consumption of oil products in India. But given the fact of joint cost we may only suggest that the prices of all products taken together should cover costs and reasonable profit, and that the relative prices of products should be determined on the basis of an assessment of the consumer's preference and broader economic policies. It remains open to a government to fix the price of a product at any level it likes, subject to the constraint mentioned above. The government may take into account a number of factors. The price of automotive diesel may be fixed at a relatively high level in order to encourage its substitution by motor spirit. The government may charge discriminatory prices to different users of diesel oil in order to discourage its less important consumption without curtailing its use in the essential sectors of the economy. Again, the government may adopt a lower price for kerosene which is still used by most villagers, while fixing a high price for furnace oil to discourage competition against coal. The pricing of oil products may be made in accordance with general economic programmes and order of priority.

A second difficulty may arise in relation to the problem of product imbalance. Under almost any pattern of refinery output and relative consumption of oil products, surpluses in some products and deficits in others, are bound to arise, although a properly thought out oil policy would endeavour to reduce these surpluses and deficits to a minimum. This raises the question of the prices at which the deficits can be bought and surpluses can be sold in the world market and also their effect on relative prices in India. One solution is to operate a separate export–import account under the guidance of the government. Small surpluses or deficits in either the external or the internal balance of the account may be adjusted through a tax-subsidy scheme by the government. But large variations in those balances would require suitable adjustments in internal prices, refinery capacity, and pattern of output. The problem of external balance would be minimised if both the purchases of deficits and sales of surpluses formed part of a bigger deal, covering crude and/or other commodities, with a government or a company.

An important factor of this cost plus system would be the price of crude—both domestic and imported. The price of imported crude has already been discussed and in the following chapter we will take into account the factors affecting the price of domestic crude oil.

TABLE 19

POSTED PRICES OF OIL PRODUCTS IN THE MIDDLE EAST AND VENEZUELA: 1955–1965.

Unit: U.S. Cents per American Gallon

Sources: Platts Oil Price Oilmanac, Petroleum Press Service

	Motor Venezuela*	Gasoline 79R Middle East†	Regular Venezuela*	Kerosene Middle East†	48–52 Index Venezuela*	Diesel Middle East†
31.12.1955	9.75	—	9.00	—	8.875	—
31.12.1956	9.625	—	9.75	9.60	9.50	—
30.6.1957	10.125	9.50	9.25	9.20	9.75	9.30
31.12.1957	9.625	9.30	9.25	9.40	9.25	9.10
31.12.1958	9.125	9.30	9.875	9.30	9.375	9.10
31.12.1959	9.375	9.00	9.75	8.80	8.625	8.50
31.12.1960	9.125	8.80	9.25	9.20	8.375	7.90
31.12.1961	8.00	7.60	9.70	9.60	8.60	7.90
31.12.1962	7.70	7.40	9.50	9.20	8.20	7.90
31.12.1963	7.30	6.60	9.20	9.20	8.00	7.70
31.12.1964	6.60	6.60	8.70	8.40	7.30	7.10
30.6.1965	6.60	6.80	8.70	8.60	6.60	6.80

*Ex-Curacao posted by Shell.
†Ex-Abadan Posted by B.P.

TABLE 20

WORLD CRUDE OIL MOVEMENTS

Unit: Million Metric Tons

Sources: (1) "World Energy Supplies"
(2) Levy (1), p. 127

Imports to	Year	Exports From						Total	Year
		United States	Caribbean Countries	Other Western Hemisphere	Middle East	Far East	Others		
United States	1930	—	4·85	3·85	—	—	—	8·70	1930
	1938	—	3·30	0·30	—	—	—	3·60	1938
	1949	—	14·45	2·30	5·20	—	—	21·95	1949
	1959	—	25·90	4·64	16·24	3·12	—	49·90	1959
	1963	—	27·80	12·60	15·60	2·60	0·05	58·65	1963
Other Western Hemisphere	1930	2·70	0·60	1·40	—	—	—	4·70	1930
	1938	3·75	0·35	2·90	—	—	—	7·00	1938
	1949	4·40	5·85	2·00	2·90	—	—	15·15	1949
	1959	—	66·67	1·52	8·96	0·06	0·58	77·79	1959
	1963	—	71·65	0·48	16·23	—	4·94	93·90	1963
Western Europe	1930	0·15	0·30	0·40	1·45	—	—	2·30	1930
	1938	3·65	1·95	1·55	4·15	—	—	11·30	1938
	1949	0·15	3·05	0·65	21·40	—	—	25·25	1949
	1959	0·13	16·37	0·25	119·70	0·78	7·67	144·90	1959
	1963	—	23·20	0·24	180·90	0·06	41·60	246·00	1963

TABLE 20 (*continued*)

Imports to	Year	Exports from						Total	Year
		United States	Caribbean Countries	Other Western Hemisphere	Middle East	Far East	Others		
Other Eastern Hemisphere	1930	0·40	—	—	0·10	1·05	—	1·55	1930
	1938	3·05	0·10	—	0·55	0·05	—	3·75	1938
	1949	—	0·10	—	2·05	0·35	—	2·50	1949
	1959	0·21	0·29	0·01	44·16	13·28	8·24	66·19	1959
	1963	—	0·43	0·17	98·46	15·23	15·30	129·59	1963
Total	1930	3·25	5·75	5·65	1·55	1·05	—	17·25	1930
	1938	10·45	5·70	4·75	4·70	0·05	—	25·65	1938
	1949	4·55	23·45	4·95	31·55	0·35	—	64·85	1949
	1959	0·34	109·23	6·42	189·06	17·24	16·49	338·78	1959
	1963	—	123·08	13·49	311·19	17·89	61·89	527·54	1963

TABLE 21

OWNERSHIP OF WORLD REFINERY CAPACITY (EXCLUDING NORTH AMERICA AND SOCIALIST COUNTRIES), 1958, 1964, 1967

Unit: Million Barrels per Stream Day

(Percentages Given in Parentheses)

Sources: 1. Oil and Gas Journal, ("World Oil Report" of each year)
2. Skinner's World Petroleum Handbook
3. Petroleum Press Service.

	Government owned			U.S. Independents			Other Independents			Majors			Total		
	1958	1964	1967 (esti-mated)	1958	1964	1967 (esti-mated)	1958	1964	1967 (esti-mated)	1958	1964	1967 (esti-mated)	1958	1964	1967 (esti-mated)
Total Europe	361 (10·0)	910 (12·2)	1,317 (12·4)	78 (2·2)	165 (2·2)	435 (4·1)	1,005 (27·9)	2,096 (28·1)	2,942 (27·8)	2,162 (59·9)	4,289 (57·5)	5,909 (55·7)	3,606 (100)	7,460 (100)	10,603 (100)
Italy	102 (14·2)	300 (18·0)	312 (13·6)	59 (8·2)	65 (3·9)	117 (5·1)	347 (48·0)	747 (44·8)	1,068 (46·6)	214 (29·6)	556 (33·3)	794 (34·7)	722 (100)	668 (100)	2,291 (100)
West Germany	28 (7·0)	133 (9·0)	215 (10·6)	—	51 (3·4)	104 (5·1)	181 (44·5)	506 (34·0)	646 (31·9)	197 (48·5)	796 (53·6)	1,060 (52·4)	406 (100)	1,486 (100)	2,025 (100)
U.K.	—	—	70 (3·2)	—	10 (0·7)	126 (5·8)	10 (1·1)	22 (1·6)	92 (4·2)	908 (98·9)	1,373 (97·7)	1,895 (86·8)	918 (100)	1,405 (100)	2,183 (100)
France	83 (11·6)	171 (13·1)	244 (15·3)	—	—	—	266 (37·3)	530 (40·5)	638 (39·9)	364 (51·1)	607 (46·4)	717 (44·8)	713 (100)	1,308 (100)	1,599 (100)
Central and Latin America	805 (28·6)	1,288 (32·8)	1,618 (36·7)	104 (3·7)	199 (5·2)	210 (4·7)	58 (2·1)	25 (0·6)	38 (0·9)	1,845 (65·6)	2,409 (61·4)	2,549 (57·7)	2,812 (100)	3,921 (100)	4,415 (100)

TABLE 21 (continued)

	Government owned			U.S. Independents			Other Independents			Majors			Total		
	1958	1964	1967 (estimated)	1958	1964	1967 (estimated)	1958	1964	1967 (estimated)	1958	1964	1967 (estimated)	1958	1964	1967 (estimated)
Asia and Australia	3 (0·2)	135 (4·3)	132 (8·3)	31 (2·5)	130 (4·2)	225 (5·6)	409 (33·4)	1,425 (45·6)	1,679 (41·7)	782 (63·9)	1,433 (45·9)	1,786 (44·4)	1,225 (100)	3,123 (100)	4,022 (100)
Middle East	65 (4·5)	124 (6·9)	352 (16·8)	105 (7·3)	184 (10·2)	184 (8·8)	114 (8·0)	146 (8·1)	211 (10·0)	1,149 (80·2)	1,353 (74·8)	1,353 (64·4)	1,433 (100)	1,807 (100)	2,100 (100)
Africa	75 (76·4)	186 (37·0)	315 (41·3)	—	5 (1·1)	5 (0·7)	2 (2·1)	69 (13·8)	101 (13·2)	21 (21·5)	242 (48·1)	343 (44·8)	98 (100)	502 (100)	764 (100)
Total	1,309 (14·3)	2,643 (15·7)	3,934 (18·0)	318 (3·5)	683 (4·1)	1,059 (4·8)	1,588 (17·3)	3,761 (22·4)	4,971 (22·7)	5,959 (64·9)	9,726 (57·8)	11,940 (54·5)	9,174 (100)	16,813 (100)	21,904 (100)

TABLE 22

CONSTITUENTS OF THE BASIC CEILING SELLING PRICE AT BOMBAY OF DIFFERENT PRODUCTS, 1961

Unit: Rupees per Kilolitre

Source: Government of India (1)

	Motor Spirit 79 Oct.	%	High Speed Diesel	%	Kerosene	%	Light Diesel Oil	%	Furnace Oil*	%
F.o.b. Posted	96·59	19·3	101·03	21·6	111·86	47·1	91·14	38·9	52·00	39·1
Less Discount	4·83	—	10·10	—	11·19	—	8·76	—	1·56	—
Net f.o.b.	91·76	18·4	90·93	19·5	100·67	42·4	82·38	35·1	50·44	37·9
C.i.f. including ocean loss	100·61	20·1	101·23	21·7	110·42	46·5	93·14	39·7	62·61	47·1
Marketing Margin including profit	63·03	12·6	51·30	11·0	33·18	14·0	28·13	12·0	14·34	10·8
Company's Basic Retail Outlet and Other Landing Charges	10·19	2·1	6·25	1·3	2·77	1·1	6·54	2·9	7·47	5·6
Government Duties	326·04	65·2	308·18	66·0	91·24	38·4	106·63	45·4	48·63	36·5
Ex-Company Storage Point	499·87	—	466·96	—	237·61	—	234·44	—	133·05	—

*Rupees per metric ton

NOTES

1. For example, the actual freight from Ras Tanura (Saudi Arabia) to Bombay under U.S.M.C. flat rate, was $2.40 per ton, while the calculated freight from U.S. Gulf to Bombay was $15.90 per ton. See Levy (1) p. 128.
2. U.S. Maritime Commission tanker rates from U.S. Gulf, Caribbean, and Persian Gulf to the United Kingdom were $7.65, $6.55, and $10.90 per ton, respectively. See Levy (1), p. 128.
3. Hartshorn, p. 142.
4. U.N. (2), p. 28.
5. Hartshorn, pp. 147–148.
6. P.O.P., 18.1.1960; 24.2.1961.
7. Penrose (1) see also Chapter Eight.
8. Penrose (1).
9. France, Italy, and the Netherlands together exported (net of imports) $6 \cdot 7$, $13 \cdot 7$, and $10 \cdot 8$ million tons of products in 1951, 1955, and 1957 respectively. See *World Energy Supplies* (United Nations), 1951, 1955, 1957.
10. Frankel and Newton (3).
11. *Indian Petroleum Handbook*, 1964, pp. 99–102.
12. See Table 17.
13. Frankel (1), pp. 51–54 and Hartshorn, pp. 121–124.
14. For example, in Australia. See Australia (3), p. 9.
15. Government of India (1), p. 35.
16. Frankel (3), Table 1.
17. Government of India (1), pp. 13–15.
18. Before the effective entry of the "independents" and Russians in the world market, and except during periods of price war, the competition among majors took the form of secret rebates and commissions in f.o.b. price or ocean freight. (See P.O.P., 3.2.1959.) The competition of non-major companies in recent years disrupted the market-sharing arrangements between the majors in the markets of Europe and compelled them to resort to vigorous price-cutting in order to protect their share of the market. But examples of direct price competition between the majors are most clearly seen in cases of bids for contracts of supply and purchase of crude and products in South America, and some countries of the Middle East and Africa. See P.O.P. of the last four years.
19. See Lubell (2), for a detailed discussion on the Soviet offensive.
20. Ashton (Table on "World Petroleum Consumption and Production by Areas").
21. See P.O.P. of recent years.
22. For example, in Western Europe oil is sold f.o.b. the Black Sea, while for markets east of Suez the Persian Gulf is adopted as the basing point for calculating freight. See *Ibid*.
23. For example, Greece sells tobacco, citrus fruit, cotton, etc. in exchange for oil. (See P.O.P., 24.1.1961.) The U.S.S.R. Government has also entered into barter agreements with some Western companies, as in Sweden. (See P.O.P., 25.1.1961.)
24. For example, Idemitau, Daikyo, and Asia Oil of Japan. See P.O.P., 30.12.1959; 23.1.1959; 14.6.1960.
25. Hindustan Organisers, an associate of Western India Oil, were negotiating a contract for importing oil products from the U.S.S.R., immediately prior to the formation of Indian Oil, which afterwards monopolised trade in U.S.S.R. oil products in India. See Government of India (7), pp. 13–18.
26. In India C.F.P. was selling to Western India Oil at discount rates oil products long before other companies did. (*See Government of India* (1),

N

pp. 130–32.) For a discussion on C.F.P.'s programmes for the expansion of its foreign activities, see P.I.W., 1.2.1965; 8.2.1965. It is called the "eighth major" because of its large share, 23·75%, of the Iraq Petroleum Company, and of 6% of the Iranian Consortium, jointly with major companies. It owns crude also in Algeria. 35% of its equity is held by the French Government. (See *Skinner's Oil and Petroleum* Yearbook, 1965.)

27. By prices we mean wholesale market prices. Under the import parity system the wholesale market price of a product consists of: (a) c.i.f. import price of that product; (b) tax and other government charges; (c) marketing expenses and commission, including the cost of internal transport from the seaport to the consumption centre. No distinction is made between the prices of domestic output and imports, even if the latter is insignificant and non-existant.

28. P.O.P., 24.1.1961; 17.8.1965.

29. *Ibid*, 11.8.1965.

30. *Ibid*, 27.3.1964.

31. See Chapter Three, pp. 118–120.

32. This is partly because the governments of the oil consuming countries, because of their foreign exchange difficulties, are now more aware of the happenings of the world oil market, and also partly because of the competition among the affiliates (who are eager to maintain a good relationship with the governments of the countries in which they are operating) to extract better terms from their parents.

33. P.O.P., 18.1.1960.

34. *Ibid*, 18.1.1960.

35. *Ibid*, 23.8.1965.

36. *Ibid*, 20.8.1965. Also, for example, Austrian prices, see *Ibid*, 18.1.1960.

37. *Ibid*, 23.2.1961.

38. *Ibid*, 30.4.1965; 16.8.1965.

39. See Table 17.

40. Nearly half of the Japanese oil market is supplied by the independents. See *Economic Journal* (Japan), 18.5.1965.

41. Independents control 20% of the West German market. See P.I.W., 4.1.1965 and P.O.P., 12.8.1964.

42. P.O.P., 1.7.1964.

43. Adelman (1).

44. Government of India (1), p. 35.

45. During the thirties the majors owned outright, or controlled under long term contracts, almost all the vessels in which their oil would normally be shipped. Even in 1949 the majors controlled about two-thirds of the total privately-owned tanker fleet. See U.S. (2), pp. 26–27, and 205.

46. *Ibid*.

47. Newton (1), pp. 216–217.

48. *Ibid*, pp. 218–219.

49. Newton (2), p. 2.

50. P.I.W., 21.10.1968.

51. Government of India (1), pp. 38–39.

52. P.O.P., 1.12.1961.

53. Newton (1), pp. 219–220.

54. *Ibid*.

55. Intascale rates, calculated on a port to port basis by the International Tanker Nominal Freight Scale Association, which operates under the general supervision of the London Tanker Brokers' Panel, are used almost universally in the eastern Hemisphere for freight fixation. See Newton (3).

56. P.I.W., 5.8.1968.

57. Newton (1), p. 219.
58. P.O.P., 18.3.1960.
59. Newton (1).
60. *Ibid.*
61. *Ibid*, p. 218.
62. The components of the formula for a product were: (1) f.o.b. price Persian Gulf, (2) freight from Ras Tanura to the Indian port, (3) wharfage, landing charges, insurance, etc. (4) importer's profit, calculated as a percentage of c.i.f. prices, (5) Government taxes and duties; to this ex-seaport installation price were added, (6) internal transport cost, (7) marketing expenses and commissions, and (8) sales taxes imposed by state legislatures, to determine the wholesale marketing price at any consumption centre in India. See Government of India (1).
63. See *Ibid*, pp. 13–15 for the following account of the U.S.A.
64. A summary of the report was published in *Capital*, 3.9.1959, p. 333.
65. Government of India (1).
66. *Eastern Economist*, 7.11.1961, p. 919.
67. *Capital*, 16.11.1961, p. 725; 23.11.1961, p. 749.
68. Government of India (2).
69. The cost of refining in the Middle East, despite the larger capacity of the units, is not very different from that of other regions, because of higher costs of importing equipment and social overheads. See Issawi and Yaganeh, pp. 99–100.
70. Frankel (2), pp. 173–176.
71. It is important to note that the rate of profit-remittance of the oil companies is higher than that of other foreign manufacturers. During 1956–60 the oil companies remitted Rs.80,000,000 per year, which was significantly higher than the average of Rs.30,000,000 for other foreign manufacturing firms in India.
72. See Table 19.
73. *Ibid.*
74. Whereas the f.o.b. prices of 79 octane motor spirit, high speed diesel, and superior kerosene were Rs.96.59, Rs.101.03, and Rs.111.86 respectively, the computed f.o.b. prices were Rs.91.76, Rs.90.93, and Rs.100.67 respectively, per kilolitre, in 1961, in India. See Government of India (1), pp. 102–104.
75. *Indian Petroleum Handbook*, 1964, p. 30.
76. Adelman (2), pp. 84–85.
77. Frankel (3).
78. *Ibid.*
79. P.I.W., 5.4.1965. In 1964 the difference between the market prices of motor spirit and middle distillates was greater, when the market price of gasoline was about half the "minimum standard price". See P.O.P., 20.5.1964.
80. See Table 22.
81. *Capital*, 3.9.1959, p. 333.
82. Oil Statistics, January–March, 1965, pp. 16–17 and Government of India (8), pp. 6–7.
83. U.N. (2), p. 27.
84. P.I.W., 8.4.1968.
85. *Ibid*, 10.5.1965.
86. P.O.P., 24.1.1961.
87. *Ibid*, 25.1.1961.
88. P.I.W., 5.4.1965.
89. *Ibid*, 21.6.1965; P.O.P., 23.2.1961; 2.12.1963; 16.8.1965.
90. See Chapter Eight.

CHAPTER 8

THE SUPPLY AND PRICE OF IMPORTED
CRUDE OIL TO INDIA

CRUDE SUPPLY ARRANGEMENTS

With the growth in recent years of the refining industry in India, the question of the price of crude oil is becoming increasingly important. Since India produces only a small part of her total crude oil requirements, her refining industry is heavily dependent on imports. Out of an estimated 14·4 million tons of crude consumption in India in 1967, only about 5·7 million tons were supplied by the domestic oilfields. Of the nine refineries operating in 1969, four are dependent on domestic oilfields, while the rest draw supplies from foreign sources.

Except for Digboi, which was built a long time ago, and the refineries under exclusive Government ownership—like Koyali, Barauni, and Nunmati, which are based on domestic crude—the oil refineries were set up under refinery contracts between the Government and the foreign oil companies, each of which contained provisions concerning the supply and the price of imported crude. The 1951 contracts with Burmah Shell and Standard Vacuum (the predecessor of Esso in India), and the 1953 contract with Caltex gave the companies freedom of choice as to the source of supply of crude oil, and exempted crude oil from import duties.[1] There was no reference to price, although the crude was expected to originate in the Persian Gulf, and by implication, was expected to be based on the prices posted at the Persian Gulf.[2] The Cochin refinery contract with Philips Petroleum, a U.S. international independent, which owns 49% of the ownership with the Government and private Indian interests owning the rest, granted the foreign collaborator the right to import crude oil. The latter was free to choose any source of crude.[3] The Madras refinery contract with the American International Oil Company (a subsidiary of Standard Oil of Indiana, an independent international company of U.S. origin) and the National Iranian Oil Company (the state-owned oil enterprise of Iran) also stipulates that the foreign collaborators, who together own 26% of the equity with the Government owning the rest, should be the sole supplier of crude. The crude would be supplied from the Darius oilfield of Iran, which is jointly owned by the two foreign collaborators, at a price of $1.35 per barrel.[4] The most recent contract with C.F.P. of France, and the Rumanian state oil organisation, for the construction of the Haldia refinery under exclusive state ownership, also provides that the C.F.P. should supply one-half of the total crude requirement, presumably from its Middle East sources, while the other half should be supplied by the Government from other sources.[5] All the agreements give priority to the domestic crude, and the contract for Madras refinery also provides for the priority of "rupee crude" produced abroad.

As will be seen from this account, each of the refineries, excepting Haldia for half of the requirement, is tied to a supplier or a number of suppliers, and there is no option for the purchase of crude from the world market at competitive prices. Since the crude supplying companies themselves are producers of crude in large amounts in the nearby Persian Gulf area, these arrangements are likely to continue for a long period, at least until the expiry of the period of refinery contracts—thirty years in the case of the majors, and fifteen years in the case of the other companies.

THE PRICE OF CRUDE OIL: MAJORS

Until 1960 (June), the price of crude oil to India was calculated on the basis of the import parity formula, with the Persian Gulf as its base. The price structure was similar to that for oil products described in the last chapter, with the A.F.R.A. ocean freight and other incidental charges being added to the Persian Gulf posted price. No discount was allowed on the price.[6]

In early 1960, the Government concluded an agreement with the U.S.S.R., to import 3·5 million tons of crude oil at a reported discount of 20% to 25% on the price at the Persian Gulf for crude of similar quality.[7] This offer was made all the more attractive by a subsidiary stipulation that this purchase could be paid for in inconvertible rupees. Thus, besides saving a good deal of foreign exchange because of lower prices, the Government could make a further saving in foreign exchange to the extent that the U.S.S.R. purchased commodities with rupees which would not otherwise have been exported. Since the Government had no refinery of its own, it asked the refineries under the ownership of the major international companies to process imported Soviet crude in place of the crude oil supplied by their parent companies from the Middle East. The companies at first undertook to examine it, and then refused to refine it on the ground that they had long standing agreements with their suppliers of crude, which could not be easily set aside.

This, however, was not a true statement, since the suppliers of crude were no different from their own affiliates in the Middle East, and there was no written agreement about the supply of crude which governed their relationship. Their opposition to Soviet crude was based on commercial ground, their reluctance to sacrifice an outlet for their Middle East crude in India, and their long standing fear of Soviet competition in the world market. These very same companies also took a similar stand against Soviet crude or oil products in many other markets of the world, in order to retain their grip on the world oil supply. Politics of the cold war also played its role, as could be seen from various statements made by business or political interests on this issue.

The Government, however, did not nationalise the refineries because of their straight-forward refusal to conform their activities to India's interests, as was done by Fidel Castro's Government in Cuba in a similar situation. Neither was it strong enough to force the oil companies to accept the Soviet crude, as was done by a small country like Finland. Instead, it decided to step down and break off the agreement to purchase crude from the U.S.S.R.

The companies, on the other hand, were quick to realise the necessity of making some adjustment in view of the Soviet competition. Accordingly, they agreed to allow a 15¢ discount off posted crude price in the Middle East.[8] The amount of discount was increased in the following year, and the companies paid $1.57 per barrel, compared to a posted price of $1.78 per barrel f.o.b. Bandar Masur of light Iranian oil, between 1962 and 1964. From the beginning of 1965, the companies made a further cut of 2¢ per barrel in response to a request made by the Government to the oil companies in view of the precarious foreign exchange position of the country.[9]

In July, 1965, the price was further reduced under Government pressure, and the prices of crude oil from different sources became as follows:[10]

Source of Crude	Posted Price $	F.o.b. Price to India $	Discount per Barrel $
Iranian Light	1·78	1·48	0·30
Kuwait	1·59	1·34	0·25
Saudi Arabia (Safaniya)	1·47	1·31	0·16
Minas (Indonesia)	2·10	2·10	0·00
Mixed Crude	Not known	1·40	Not known

The Talukdar Committee report on oil prices (1965) commented that the prices charged by the private oil companies on crude were "neither fully competitive nor most favourable in world markets".

It recommended a cut by 10¢ on the price of Light Iranian crude and 5¢ on the crude of Kuwait and suggested a cut in foreign exchange allocations to force the companies to yield to the Government's demand for lower prices. The Committee also asked the Government to enquire from Esso the exact proportion of different crudes used by the latter in order to determine the level of discount applicable to Esso's mixed crude.[11]

Towards the end of 1965, with the worsening of the balance of payments position of the country, the Government again began insisting on further cuts in oil prices, now being strengthened by the report of the Talukdar Committee. The companies yielded to the pressure at the beginning of 1966, the price of the light Iranian crude was brought down to $1.41 (39¢ discount), that of Kuwait to $1.31 (28¢ discount), while the price of Esso blend now became $1.36.[12]

There was a further 3¢ cut in the price of light Iranian crude in July, 1968, when the Government threatened to reduce foreign exchange allocation for imports by the foreign oil companies unless its instructions to bring prices of crude oil further down was complied with.[13]

A COMPARISON WITH WORLD CRUDE OIL PRICES

A comparison with the situation in the world market since 1959 will show that downward changes in the world market prices were always reflected in India after a certain time lag, and, as we have noted already, under pressure from the Government. Before 1959 there was generally no discount available on f.o.b. crude prices in the Middle East, although there was evidence of discounts allowed on c.i.f. prices, by way of reduced ocean freights, or allowances based on quantity purchased.[14] However, the U.S.S.R. was supplying a small independent refiner of Japan crude oil at discounted prices from 1958.[15] In January, 1959, for the first time in the world, Standard Vacuum allowed 10% discount on Persian Gulf posted prices to its Japanese affiliates in order to meet the Soviet challenge and also to secure a larger foreign exchange allocation—which was based on the f.o.b. prices—from the Government.[16] Throughout this year, most of the Japanese refiners were able to secure their crude at 20¢ below posted prices from the Middle East.[17] So, when in the middle of 1960 the major oil companies allowed discount on crude oil prices to India for the first time, it was reported in Platts Oilgram Press Service, "In Tokyo there is a general feeling that the recent announcement of crude price cuts to the Indian market merely brings in line (for the Indian buyers) the discounts that already have been offered to Japan."[18] It was also reported that every Japanese refiner was then securing at least a minimum of 18¢ discount on Iranian crude. (See Table 23.)

It is also significant that after the price reductions of 1965 (July) the Petroleum Intelligence Weekly reported that the major companies admitted that, "the move in India was designed to eliminate the 'differential' and keep prices (which they) charged their affiliates in India on a parity with other markets East of Suez."[19] Again, this reduction in prices failed to match the 42¢ discount offered in November, 1965, on a 50 : 50 mixture of 34° Agha Jari and 38° Abu Dhabi crude, to Pakistan, by an independent Pakistani importer-refiner, who received his supplies from C.F.P., through a Swiss intermediary.[20] It was also reported that Atlantic, an independent international company, offered to Daikyo, a Japanese independent, light Iranian crude at $1.31, which was 10¢ less than the price of the same crude in India during that period.[21]

The price concessions obtained by India during 1968 were also some way behind those secured by the independent refiners of a number of countries during that year. It was reported from Japan in September, 1968, that the independent refiners there, were buying light Iranian crude at prices ranging from $1.33 to $1.35 per barrel.[22] The price quoted for the same crude by Dawood Petroleum, a Pakistani independent, in an offer during the same period, was still lower, only $1.28.[23] Compared with the price at which the same crude was sold to India by the international majors, the prices quoted in Japan or Pakistan were between 3¢ and 10¢ cheaper. That these prices were not exceptional, and more or less reflected the trend in world prices, was confirmed by the list of offers for selling 2·5 million tons of crude oil annually to Pakistan, which were published towards the end of 1968.[24] Most of these offers were given in terms of c.i.f. prices, probably in order to hide the extent of concessions given on f.o.b. prices alone, but even allowing for a low transport cost of 26¢, the f.o.b. prices appear to be exceptionally low, ranging from $1.25 quoted by Dawood, to $1.27 quoted by Shell, and $1.28, $1.29, and $1.32, quoted by Burmah Oil, Esso, and Caltex, respectively.[25]

POSTED PRICES AND DISCOUNT

As in the case of the oil products, the prices posted for crude oil in the Middle East by the major oil companies, and published by the Platts Oilgram Press Service, are not subject to the freeplay of the forces of demand and supply, as the oil companies would like us to believe. In fact very little crude is "sold" at the posted prices. The major companies which own an overwhelming proportion of the crude oil produced in the Middle East, also possess wide networks of refineries, and more than 90% of the crude they produce is transferred to their refining affiliates in other countries at internal book-keeping prices.[26] When the amount of crude produced by a major is not equal to the amount required by its refineries, it needs to correct its imbalance between demand and supply by selling and buying from other organisations. Some majors like British Petroleum or Gulf possess surplus crude oil, whereas some others like Shell suffer from deficit. More often than not, the majors enter into long-term contracts between themselves in order to eliminate their imbalance, such as the contract between Gulf and Shell for selling the former's share of Kuwait crude to the latter. But the prices agreed in those contracts bear no relationship to the posted prices. Before 1959, the very few cases where crude oil was sold at posted prices involved independents who brought crude from majors for their refining operations. But even in those cases, the so called "independents" virtually functioned as appendages of the giant international corporations, and, in the absence of alternative sources of crude, they had little option but to accept crude from the latter at posted prices.

Until 1959 the posted prices were used as internal prices at which the producing affiliates of a major oil company transferred their crude oil to the refining affiliates. The amount of crude purchased by the refining affiliate from the crude-producing affiliate was not related to this transfer price; and whatever the posted price, the former was not allowed to purchase from any alternative source. The posted prices were linked to the overall profitability of the entire vertically-integrated organisation of an international major, but not with any particular stage of activity such as refining or crude-producing. The overall profit of such a company was measured by the difference between total receipts from the sale of products, and the total costs of the entire organisation, including the production, marketing, refining, and transporting stages. In the absence of Government intervention, it was possible for a major company to distribute the overall profit among its various activities in any way it wanted, by adjusting the internal book-keeping prices of the inputs and outputs of those activities. For a number of reasons, the major companies preferred to show higher profit at the crude production stage, and to attribute lower profit, even loss in some cases, to downstream activites, by manipulating the internal prices. Since the profit from crude production was shared equally by the companies and the Governments of the oil producing countries, a higher posted price meant that more was paid in taxes to the Governments of the producing countries, and less to the parent countries of the oil companies and also to the oil consuming countries.[27]

These higher payments to the oil producing countries were expected to work as an insurance against nationalisation or adverse Government policy in areas where the majors had invested on a large scale. Furthermore, this tax on profit paid to the oil producing countries could be offset against the tax liability of those companies in their countries of origin. In the case of the companies of U.S. domicile, the prospect of obtaining $23\frac{1}{2}\%$ "depletion allowance", on income earned from crude production, before taxation, provided the incentive to show as much profit as possible, at the crude production stage.[28] In other words, the high prices for crude helped to reduce the tax liability of a major, and also to improve relations with the oil producing countries.

All the majors used to declare identical prices for crudes of the same quality. A "gravity differential" of 2¢ per degree of A.P.I. was adopted. For instance, the 34° crude of Abadan was charged 4¢ higher than 32¢ crude f.o.b. the same port. The crudes of Kuwait fetched the lower prices because of their lower A.P.I. The price differences were also related to the freight-distance of a producing centre from Abadan. The further a production centre was from Abadan, the higher became the f.o.b. price of its crude, the difference being equal to the ocean freight or, in some cases, to the pipeline freight.

This system of pricing worked smoothly for the major oil companies so long as there were few competitors, and the oil consuming countries were indifferent to the question of crude prices. The appearance of the Soviet Union as an important crude oil supplier in 1959, particularly to Italy and Japan, caused a downward revision in the posted prices, for the first time since the posting began in the Persian Gulf in 1950, from $1.99 to $1.81 for 34° A.P.I. Iranian crude, and similar cuts in the prices of other crudes.[29] There was a further 8¢ to 10¢ cut in the posted prices in 1960, again in order to counter the Russian challenge in the world market.[30] But the discovery of crude oil in large amounts in Algeria and Libya (where independent French companies, as well as important U.S. independents such as Marathon, Philips, and Continental, played an important role) has made these reductions inadequate for meeting the competition of the newcomers. On the other hand, the Governments of the leading oil producing countries have joined together in opposition to any further decline in posted prices, which reduce their share per barrel. The organised opposition of the Organisation of the Petroleum Exporting Countries (O.P.E.C.) has ruled out any further reduction in posted prices, while the pressure of competition is compelling the majors to allow discounts off the posted prices.

As things stand now, the posted prices are not related to the prices at which the crude oil is sold in the world market, except as the basis for the calculation of discounts. They are still used as reference prices for the purpose of taxation by the Governments of the oil producing countries, subject to a fixed schedule of discounts. These discounts, which are used for the purpose of taxation, it must be emphasised, bear no relation to the actual discounts, and are declining every year on a fixed basis, and should be eliminated by 1972.[31]

Since the profit attributed to the crude oil production is shared between the Governments and the oil companies on the basis of the posted prices, subject to fixed discounts, any discount offered on posted prices in excess of these deductions would reduce the profit accruing to the crude-producing affiliates of an international oil company to that extent. In view of the tax benefits associated with crude production, a major company is naturally reluctant to allow discounts off posted prices to the refining affiliates, if it can be avoided. There are only three situations where the major oil companies agree to offer discounts. Firstly, where a refinery is jointly owned by a major with an independent company, and where the latter puts pressure on the former to reduce crude price and to increase the profit of the refining operation. A number of refineries of Japan and Pakistan belong to this category. Secondly, where the Government of the oil consuming country has forced the oil companies to reduce prices. Examples are many including India and Turkey. Thirdly, where the Government has taken account of the crude prices and the method of delivery of crude before awarding refinery contracts, and where at least a part of the crude oil is not tied to any particular source and is open to the lowest bidder. The examples are the countries of Latin America, as well as Pakistan and Greece.

The inverse relationship between the price of crude and the degree of competition in a particular market was also admitted by the representative of a major international oil company before the Australian Tariff Board in 1965. He explained the difference between the rates of discount prevailing in the markets East and West of Suez in terms of "market difference of competitive pressure".[32] Whereas in West Europe the majors face stiff competition from the independent crude oil producers of North Africa, this element of competition was virtually absent, until very recently, East of Suez. With the growth of the oil production of Libya and Algeria more of this crude is now being delivered in the European markets, where it is replacing the crude of the Middle East. A part of the displaced Middle East crude is now finding its way to the markets East of Suez. A number of U.S. independents, as well as C.F.P. of France, are playing an important role in pushing this crude to the markets of Japan and Pakistan. It is clear from the reports appearing in recent years in the oil journals, that the increased competition of the independents, coupled with the closure of the Suez Canal since 1967, has succeeded in wiping out the differential in discount between the markets East and West of Suez.[33]

The competition of the non-major crude suppliers, although an extremely important factor in reducing the price of crude oil, can be felt only in those markets where the refineries are independent and are responsive to changes in crude prices. In a captive market, where the entire refining capacity is owned by the major oil companies, the competition in the crude oil market is not exploited by the refineries, since the latter are supplied with crude by their own parent establishments at prices dictated by their central organisations. Even in Western Europe the average price paid for crude imports by different countries varies according to the relative share of the non-major oil companies in those markets. Countries like Holland, or the United Kingdom, where between 90% and 100% of the refining capacity is owned by the major oil companies, still pay very high prices for their crude, whereas Italy or West Germany, where the independents account for about half or two-thirds the total refining capacity, import crude at very low prices.[34] An important reason why the Japanese pay so low a price for their crude import (in 1967 the average price—including the high price paid by the affiliates of the major oil companies—was only $1.47, and the target for 1970 is $1.31[35]) is also the existence of a relatively high proportion of the refining capacity under the ownership of the Japanese independents.

Generally speaking, an independent refinery is expected to look for the cheapest source of crude, while affiliates are deprived of any freedom of choice as to the source of crude. A vigilant Government can force the affiliates of a major oil company to bring down the prices of imported crude, either by making lower price a condition for participation in the future refinery programme, or by cutting down foreign exchange allocations for relatively more expensive crudes, and by accruing priority to cheaper crude. The latter method is followed by Japan, which has encouraged even the affiliates of the major oil companies to deliver crude to Japan at relatively lower prices.[36]

In India, the ownership of all the refineries by the majors until 1962, meant that the pressure of competition, which worked in Japan, Germany, or Italy, did not operate here. Furthermore, the extent of control which could be exercised by the Government on crude prices is limited by the provisions of the refinery agreements which allowed freedom of choice of source of crude to the companies. The fact that in spite of these limitations the Government has succeeded in reducing crude oil prices can be explained by the following factors.

First, no company can function satisfactorily in a country, by provoking the active hostility of the public, Government, and press, whatever its legal standing. After the offer of Russian oil at cheap prices, the majors had to show that they were not taking unreasonable advantage of their monopolistic position in the Indian market and that they were no less concerned about the effect of high import prices on the balance of payments of the country.

Secondly, the majors were fully aware of the growing potential of a market of 500,000,000 consumers who, although now very poor, are aspiring for a higher standard of living within a short time. The open hostility of the Government, even if it does not lead to nationalisation, might seriously affect the future prospects of a company in this growing market. The companies are still hoping for a change in the Government oil policy towards refinery ownership and are obviously unwilling to carry the quarrel on crude prices too far.

Thirdly, probably the most important factor is that, although nationalisation of the refineries is ruled out for thirty years by the agreements with the majors, there is no such agreement covering the marketing organisations of these companies. In other words, nationalisation of marketing facilities cannot be ruled out if the positions of the companies and the Government became irreconcilable, and the companies are aware that the ownership of refining capacity in itself is of limited value without a market for selling products.[37]

In recent years the Government also threatened to cut the foreign exchange allocation for crude imports of these companies unless the prices were lowered.[38]

THE PRICE OF CRUDE OIL: INDEPENDENTS

When the refinery agreements with the major companies were negotiated there were few alternative sources of crude, and the world market was firmly under the control of the seven major international oil companies. The representatives of the Government were ignorant about the intricacies of the world oil business, and could not find any fault with the posted prices of the Persian Gulf crudes. The stipulation that the refineries were entitled to choose their own source of crude was accepted without reservation by the Government side as something normal and conforming to the established practices of the world oil industry. The extent of ignorance of the Indian officials about the state of affairs in the oil industry, its vertically and horizontally integrated nature, the relationship between an affiliate and its parent company, the significance of internal book keeping prices to the companies and the governments, and its other aspects, was also revealed by the report of the Damle Committee on prices (1961), in which the following paragraph appeared:

"In all cases, the procurement of crude oil is arranged by the oil companies through one or more intermediaries, to whom they pay no remuneration for the service rendered, except nominal charges paid in this regard by S.V.O.C. (Standard Vacuum Oil Company)... The oil companies do not have access to the invoices of the original producers/suppliers of crude oil and remittances of foreign exchange are settled by them on the basis of the invoices of their immediate consignors, who are not the original producers/suppliers of crude oil. In such a situation, it is difficult to know precisely what transpires between the original producers/suppliers and the immediate consignors and how their relations are governed in regard to remuneration on transactions passing through their hands."[39]

The above shows that the Damle Committee was unable to grasp that the refineries in India, their immediate consignors, and the suppliers, all were parts of one and the same corporate organisation, and the reason for maintaining so many intermediate organisations was to maintain secrecy about oil prices.

The recent agreements with the independents for building and operating the refineries of Cochin, Madras, and Haldia, were negotiated under vastly different conditions. The major oil companies were weakened in the world market because of the competition of the independents, many of whom possessed large amounts of crude not tied to buyers, and were looking for outlets. There were examples of other countries who adopted various alternative arrangements for securing their crude at the most advantageous terms. The years of secrecy about how the oil industry worked were gone, and there were volumes of information to which any research worker had access. For Cochin there was a vigorous contest between Philips, E.N.I., and Burmah Shell, each modifying its offers stage by stage, in order to make these attractive to India.[40] For Madras, fourteen parties submitted their bids, and Burmah Shell even went to the length of agreeing to the Government's majority share in the refinery and the distribution of oil products by Indian Oil, thereby discarding its previous firm stand on these two points.[41] A number of companies, including Gulf, C.F.P., Kuwait, Rumania, and a Japanese consortium applied for the Haldia refinery.[42] The area of choice was sufficiently large, and the bargaining strength of the Government considerable.

But despite the changed world situation, and the past experience of bitter quarrels with the majors over crude oil prices, it seems that the Government did not fully appreciate the risks of future conflict inherent in tying a refinery to a particular source of crude, when contracting for Cochin and Madras. The entry of Philips (Cochin) and American International and National Iranian (Madras), apart from taking the market further from the control previously exercised by the majors, has given little differential advantage to India in terms of prices. The crude for Cochin is obtained by Philips from Standard Oil of California, an international major and co-owner of Caltex, and is sold at the same price as that charged by the major companies for the same crude. The price of Darius crude for Madras will be supplied at $1.35, as against a posted price of $1.63 for this 34° gravity crude.[43] This price, although lower than the $1.78 quoted for light Iranian crude of the same gravity, does not explain the whole story. Because of the high sulphur content of this crude, it is not suitable for many uses and increases air pollution, which makes it unacceptable to many consumers in Western Europe and Japan. Very recently, this crude has been offered to Pakistan at $1.31.[44]

ALTERNATIVE SUPPLY ARRANGEMENTS

It is not known why alternative arrangements, which did not make a refinery fully dependent on a particular source of supply and enabled the latter to secure crude at cheaper prices, were not negotiated. First, the Government might make arrangements under which a large part of the total crude requirement would come from a source chosen by the Government, while the rest could be supplied by the foreign partners from their own sources. The Greek Government supplies one-quarter of the crude for Hellenic refinery, which is partly owned by Esso, and is at present insisting on the right to supply the entire crude need.[45] The arrangement with C.F.P. for supplying half of the crude requirement of Haldia refinery, while the other half would be secured by the Government,[46] follows the pattern set by the East Pakistan refinery, which has been built by the same French company.[47]

Secondly, instead of actually supplying one-half of the total crude requirements of the refinery, the Government might simply reserve the right to supply one-half of the crude at its option at any time, after giving notice to the foreign partner. The right might be exercised if and when the Government thought that the companies were importing crude at prices higher than could be obtained elsewhere. The very existence of this right in the hands of the Government might prove a sufficient deterrent against a high price. A variant of this system now applies to the Karachi refinery of Pakistan. There, in the event of the offer of crude from outsiders at lower prices, the major companies participating in the refinery are given an opportunity to match this offer. If they fail to reduce prices to the lower level the Government is entitled to ask the outsider to supply the oil.[48] It was, however, pointed out that the provision was not very effective, since the independent suppliers were loth to offer crude when they knew that this offer would only be used to force the major companies to lower prices.[49]

Thirdly, the Government might invite tenders for supplying crude for, say, three years. A number of South American state oil organisations, like Y.P.F. of Argentine, A.N.C.A.P. of Uruguay, and Petrobras of Brazil, have followed this system for several years, and have succeeded in generating competition between the oil companies in getting the contract. The major companies try to outbid one another, and in some cases have quoted prices lower than those of the Soviet Union, in order to secure these contracts.[51] As has been already observed, the Government of Pakistan has also followed this example of the South American with success, when inviting tenders for supplying Pakistan Refinery Ltd.[51]

Of the various alternatives suggested, the last system would seem preferable, in view of the condition of overproduction and declining prices in the world market. It is true that a long term contract, while tying a refinery to a particular source of crude, also ensures regularity of supply. But the future prospect for the oil industry is for the surplus in crude production to continue, and for the prices to continue their declining trend, down to about a dollar per barrel by the end of the 1970s.[52] In such a market fear for the uncertainty of supply is unfounded, and the price paid for a long-term contract is likely to be higher than the prevailing world price. On the other hand, the third alternative discussed above would ensure flexibility and would allow a consuming country to make the maximum possible use of the existing competitive situation.

NON PRICE CONSIDERATIONS IN CRUDE SUPPLY

It needs, however, to be stressed that, although the f.o.b. price of crude is the most important component of the landed price, what matters from the point of view of an oil consuming country is the latter, which includes, apart from the f.o.b. price, ocean freight. Many of the offers these days also include discounts on freight, and quote only c.i.f. prices. The offers also sometimes specify the type of ship which would carry the crude, and its nationality. The use of a giant tanker, as seen before, reduces the cost of transport even without discounts, whereas the employment of tankers bearing the flag of the consuming country would save foreign exchange cost otherwise needed for transport. In the case of India, the possibility of using giant tankers is limited because of the shallowness of the sea near the coast, and the domestic tanker fleet is small and confined to coastal trade. There is no reason why India should not also possess a tanker fleet for carrying crude from other countries, although because of the proximity of the supply areas in her case the saving resulting from using a national fleet would be comparatively less than would be the case with many other countries.[53] On the other hand, the Government has not yet explored the cost conditions of installing oil discharging terminals in deep sea and transferring the crude from the terminal to the mainland, compared with the savings to be gained by employing giant tankers.

Apart from the price of crude and the cost of ocean transport, the mode of payment for crude is also an important factor to be considered. Most offers include provisions about loans, at a specified rate of interest, for covering the cost of purchase. When the period covered by the crude supply contract is long enough, loans are offered covering the cost of building the refinery, and, in some cases, also the cost of allied projects, whether or not the supplier is going to own a part of the equity. The offers submitted by Mobil and C.F.P. for Haldia[54] are examples of this.

Payments made in foreign currency are more expensive than those made in local currency. The crude supply agreements with the Soviet Union normally include provisions for payment in local currency, or in terms of other domestic products. In some cases, the major oil companies have undertaken to secure an export market for the commodities of the consuming country, thereby enabling the latter to pay for a part of crude imports from these additional export receipts. An interesting example is provided by Petrobas, the state-owned company of Brazil, which, since 1964, has followed a policy of linking crude oil imports to the exports of Brazilian manufactured goods not traditionally exported. This policy stipulates that without the crude seller guaranteeing at least 20% of the value of imports as exports, the contract would not exceed 10,000,000 barrels and a twelve months period. The oil companies have found this condition to be a lesser evil compared with the prospect of the Brazilian market being captured by the Soviet Union. Shell has already accepted this policy, and others are also trying to meet this condition.[55]

An important corollary of almost all the recent crude supply offers is the accompanying offer to withdraw surplus products resulting from the use of supplier's crude at a mutually agreed price. During the early and middle 1960s, when most of the oil consuming

countries were faced with the problem of surplus naphtha, it was
thought that the ability of the major companies to dispose of these
surpluses more easily than others, because of their wider marketing
network, would make their offers more attractive to the consuming
countries, other factors remaining constant. This argument in
favour of the major oil companies as suppliers of crude is no longer
valid in view of the changed demand and supply conditions for
naphtha in the world market.

RUPEE CRUDE: PRODUCED AT HOME AND ABROAD

The long-term objective of the Government is to achieve self-
sufficiency in crude oil production, and to operate domestic refineries
independently of imports. As things stand now, this objective is not
likely to be achieved in the near future, and fresh discoveries of
oilfields would even be inadequate for meeting the needs for additional crude in view of the rate of growth of oil consumption in India.
Very recently the Government has made arrangements with C.F.P.
for supplying the Barauni refinery which is now solely based on
domestic crude with 500,000 tons of imported crude per year, when
its expansion programme is carried out.[56] It is still very much an
open question whether the proposed North-West refinery will be
based on domestic crude or on imported crude; the decision
depending on the prospect of crude discoveries in that region.
Future discoveries would encourage the establishment of new
refineries based on domestic crude, rather than forcing the refineries
at present based on imported crude to switch over to domestic
crude, except for a temporary period pending the construction of
new refineries, or the expansion of existing refineries.

The extent of the replacement of imported crude by domestic
supplies in future would only depend on the amount of crude oil
discovered in India, and the refinery agreements with the foreign oil
companies would not be affected. All the agreements stipulate that
the domestic crude, if and when available, would obtain priority
over crudes purchased from abroad.[57] In accordance with this
provision, the Bombay refineries of Esso and Burmah Shell processed
the crude of Ankleswar for a period until the completion of the
Koyali refinery.[58]

There is no corresponding provision in the refinery agreements,
relating to crudes produced abroad under Indian ownership except
that concluded on the Madras refinery. Until 1964, when for the
first time the Oil and Natural Gas Commission was granted concession rights for exploring a part of the rich offshore Iran,[59] in
collaboration with E.N.I. of Italy and Philips of the United States,
the possibility that India would venture outside was not taken into

consideration. The current Indian share of production from this oilfield is one million tons per year, but this figure is likely to increase in the near future. If the amount involved is not large, most of it might be absorbed without upsetting the existing crude oil importing arrangements. If, on the other hand, the amount is large and requires the replacement of crude imports from other souces, the major oil companies and Philips might refuse to process it in place of crude from their own sources. As we have noted earlier, one of the motives behind refinery construction by these companies was to secure an outlet for their crude output of the Middle East, and it is more or less certain that these companies would be unwilling to surrender this business without a fight, or without compensating concessions in other fields.[60] Both the amount and the price of such crude would be a matter for dispute. But whether or not it is incorporated into a written contract, the Government is always in a position to use the threat of a cut in allocation of foreign exchange for crude imports, unless a proportion of such crude were accepted. In France, the Government has compelled the refineries owned by the major oil companies to accept a part of the "franc crude" of Algeria at a price higher than that prevailing for that crude in the world market. The Government requires 55% of the crude needs of the country to be satisfied from "franc crude" produced abroad.[61] Similarly the Government of Japan requires the refineries operating in that country to accept "Yen crude" produced in the Middle East and Sumatra, at a negotiated price. In both cases the Governments had to face, and are still facing, enormous opposition from the foreign oil companies, but still succeeded in the end in forcing such crude on the latter under the cloak of "voluntary" agreements.[62] One can only hope that the Government of India would not be deterred by the accusations about the violation of refinery agreements to which a policy of replacing imported crude by "rupee" crude might give rise.

TABLE 23

Some Crude Imports from the Middle East by Japan at Discounted Prices, 1959–1962

Unit: Dollars per Barrel

Source: Platts Oilgram Press Service for Given Dates

Date	Crude	Selling Co.	Purchasing Co.	Nature of the Purchasing Co. / Affiliate	F.O.B. Offered	F.O.B. Posted	Discount
19.1.59	Arabian	Caltex	Nippon Petroleum Refining	Affiliate	N.K.	N.K.	0.10
22.12.59	Kuwait	N.K.	N.K.	N.K.	N.K.	N.K.	0.22
21.1.60	Iranian Light	N.K.	N.K.	Independent	1.43	1.86	0.43
21.1.60	Ditto	N.K.	N.K.	Ditto	1.36	1.86	0.50
18.2.60	Neutral Zone	Aminoil	Idemitsu	Ditto	N.K.	N.K.	0.43
1.3.60	Ditto	Getty	Mitsubishi	Associate of Tidewater	N.K.	N.K.	13%
14.3.60	Iranian Heavy	N.K.	Taiyo Oil	Independent	1.17	1.62	0.45
2.6.60	Iran	C.F.P.	Daikyo	Ditto	1.52	1.67	0.15
29.7.60	Kuwait	Stanvac	General Bussan	Affiliate	1.55	1.59	0.04
5.1.61	Iran	N.K.	N.K.	Indepdneent	1.34	1.63	0.29
11.1.61	Iran	N.K.	N.K.	Ditto	1.49	1.78	0.29
24.3.61	Neutral Zone	N.K.	Daikyo	Ditto	1.15	1.28	0.13
27.9.61	Kuwait	Gulf	Idemitsu	Ditto	1.43	1.59	0.16
27.9.61	Kuwait	Mobil	Nippon Mining	Ditto	1.46	1.59	0.13
27.9.61	Burgan	Aminoil	Idemitsu	Ditto	1.32	1.48	0.16
27.9.61	Iran	C.F.P.	Toa	Ditto	1.50	1.78	0.28
29.12.61	Arabian	Caltex	Nippon Oil/Koa	Affiliate	1.51	1.59	0.08
22.11.61	Qatar	Tidewater	Mitsubishi	Associate	1.67	1.95	0.28
22.11.61	Kuwait	Gulf	Various	Various	1.39	1.59	0.20
2.4.62	Kuwait	Gulf	Various	Various	1.41	1.59	0.18
19.12.62	Kuwait	Esso	Various	Various	1.41	1.59	0.18
19.12.62	Iran	Mobil	Various	Various	1.59	1.78	0.19

N.K. = Not Known

TABLE 24

CRUDE OFFERS FROM THE MIDDLE EAST AND AFRICA TO A.N.C.A.P. OF URUGUAY: 1961–1965

Unit: Dollars per Barrel

Source: Platts Oilgram Press Service for Given Dates

Crude	Date	Gravity	Offering Company	F.O.B. Price Offered	Posted Price	Discount	Freight	C.I.F.
Kuwait	7.8.61	35–35·9	BP	1.61	1.67	0.6	0.50	2.11
Ditto	21.1.65	31–31·9	BP	1.29	1.59	0.30	0.685	1.975
Ditto	21.1.65	31–31·9	Gulf	1.44	1.59	0.15	0.685	2.125
Ditto	21.1.65	31–31·9	Panama (Southern Marine Corporation)	1.43	1.59	0.16	0.78	2.21
Qatar	12.3.63	41–41·9	C.F.P.	1.525	1.95	0.425	N.K.	N.K.
Arabian (Light)	21.1.65	34–34·9	California Crude Sales	1.54	1.80	0.26	0.63	2.17
Arabian (Medium)	21.1.65	29–29·9	Texaco	1.39	1.55	0.16	0.58	1.97
Arabian (Heavy)	21.1.65	27–27·9	California Crude Sales	1.26	1.47	0.21	0.66	1.92
Iran	21.1.65	34–34·9	Shell	1.55	1.73	0.18	0.84	2.39
Ditto	21.1.65	34–34·9	Pan American	1.35	—	—	0.69	2.04
Iraq	21.1.65	35–35·9	C.F.P./Y.P.F.	1.31	1.72	0.41	0.92	2.23
Khafji	12.3.63	28–28·9	Arabian Oil	1.33	1.46	0.13	—	—
Algeria	16.7.64	42–42·9	S.A.F. R.E.P.	1.85	2.35	0.50	—	—
Ditto	16.7.64	40–	C.F.P.	1.825	2.35	0.525	—	—
Ditto	21.1.65	40–42	Sinclair	1.80	2.35	0.55	0.465	2.265
Libya	12.3.63	40–	Esso	1.80	2.23	0.43	0.47	2.27
Ditto	16.7.64	38–38·9	Texaco	1.75	2.19	0.44	0.46	2.21
Ditto	21.1.65	39–41	Sinclair	1.65	2.23	0.58	0.55	2.20
Nigeria	12.3.63	33–33·9	BP	1.85	—	—	0.45	2.30
Ditto	16.7.64	33–33·9	BP	1.85	—	—	0.42	2.27
Ditto	21.1.65	33–33·9	Gulf	1.84	—	—	0.49	2.33

TABLE 25

F.O.B. Prices of Crude Imports by Italy: 1964 (January) to 1965 (April)
(Adjusted for Gravity Differential)

Unit: Dollars per Barrel

Source: Platts Oilgram Press Service for Given Dates

Country	F.O.B. Port	1964 (Jan.)	1964 (April)	1964 (July)	1964 (Oct.)	1965 (Jan.)	1965 (April)	Posted Price
Algeria	Bougie	—	1.77	—	1.88	—	2.21	2.23
	La Skhirra	—	1.72	1.75	—	—	—	2.18
Saudi Arabia	Ras Tamura	1.50	1.51	1.45	1.54	1.60	1.43	1.80
	Sidon	2.14	2.06	2.18	2.19	2.15	2.07	2.17
Abu Dhabi	Jabal Dhena	—	1.64	1.60	1.68	—	—	1.78
U.A.R.	Ras Gharib	—	1.13	1.61	1.09	1.02	1.12	—
	Wadi Feiran	—	1.09	1.08	1.12	1.12	1.26	—
Iran	Bandar Masur	1.50	1.78	—	1.47	1.55	1.41	1.78
	Kharg Island	—	1.48	—	1.50	1.44	—	1.69
	Persian Gulf	—	—	1.31	1.48	1.48	—	—
Iraq	Banias	2.18	1.71	1.77	1.84	1.80	1.69	2.17
	Tripoli	2.12	1.93	2.01	2.06	2.00	1.90	2.17
	Fao	1.68	1.25	—	1.26	1.22	1.21	1.78
	Khor-Al-Amiya	1.69	—	—	—	—	1.20	1.74
Neutral Zone	Mina-Abdulla	1.35	1.12	1.11	1.11	1.08	1.19	1.70
	Mina Saud	—	1.17	1.25	1.18	1.14	1.16	1.70
Kuwait	Mina-Al-Ahmadi	1.46	1.45	1.43	1.42	1.40	1.39	1.65
Libya	Es Sider	1.61	1.58	1.54	1.62	1.57	1.57	2.11
	Brega	2.23	2.24	2.23	2.21	1.81	1.88	2.11
U.S.S.R.		1.25	1.26	1.27	1.29	1.25	1.35	—
Venezuela		1.55	1.89	1.72	1.42	1.29	1.97	—
Average		1.55	1.50	1.51	1.52	1.51	1.53	—
Platts Oilgram Dates		22.5.64	23.7.64	18.11.64	24.2.65	19.5.65	14.7.65	—

TABLE 26

CRUDE OIL IMPORTS TO INDIA: 1954-55 TO 1964-65

Units: Tonnes and Thousand Rupees

Values Given Within Parentheses

Sources: Monthly Statistics of Foreign Trade of India, Government of India

Year	Indonesia	Iran	Qatar, Trucial Coast, Oman	Saudi Arabia	Kuwait	Others	Total
1954-55	—	—	—	35,000 (14,642)	—	—	35,000 (14,642)
1955-56	—	—	—	1,272,000 (127,941)	—	—	1,272,000 (127,941)
1956-57	—	—	—	2,114,000 (178,953)	—	—	2,114,000 (178,953)
1957*	157,609 (14,828)	1,811,532 (161,036)	178,779 (16,468)	672,086 (59,082)	643,313 (46,043)	15,362 (1,447)	3,463,319 (297,457)
1958*	95,331 (8,944)	156,296 (14,675)	—	1,488,320 (128,390)	24,425 (1,930)	—	1,779,734 (155,386)
1959*	—	—	—	1,183,500 (93,314)	—	—	1,183,500 (93,314)
1960*	111,224 (9,293)	—	—	1,587,539 (118,685)	—	—	1,698,763 (127,978)
1960-61	288,001 (24,045)	964,740 (73,339)	178,313 (13,497)	1,270,119 (90,578)	—	5	2,701,178 (201,459)
1961-62	157,237 (12,888)	4,112,392 (278,280)	249,449 (18,694)	1,801,019 (113,785)	—	—	6,320,097 (423,645)
1962-63	124,598 (10,095)	3,194,497 (229,848)	—	1,007,985 (61,586)	—	2	4,327,082 (301,530)
1963-64	211,792 (16,226)	4,245,467 (282,241)	17,974 (1,311)	2,661,753 (161,927)	—	2	7,136,988 (461,706)
1964-65	335,130 (25,625)	2,082,516 (139,279)	—	1,811,089 (107,363)	—	—	4,228,735 (272,268)

*Calendar year

TABLE 27

POSTED CRUDE PRICES 1954–1968

Unit: Dollars per Barrel

Source: Petroleum Intelligence Weekly, August 30, 1965

Year	Iran (Abadan)	Iraq (Tripoli)	Kuwait (Mina-Ahmadi)	Qatar (Umm Said)	Saudi Arabia (Ras Tanura)	Venezuela (Puerto La Cruz)
	34°	36°	31°	40°	34°	35°
1954	1.86	2.39	1.72	2.08	1.97	2.88
1955	1.86	2.39	1.72	2.08	1.97	2.88
1956	1.86	2.46	1.72	2.08	1.93	2.80
1957	1.99	2.69	1.85	2.21	2.08	3.05
1958	1.99	2.49	1.85	2.21	2.08	3.05
1959	1.81	2.31	1.67	2.03	1.90	2.80
1960–1968	1.73	2.21	1.59	1.93	1.80	2.80

NOTES

1. See P.P.S., October, 1953, p. 366; *Capital*, 15.11.1951, p. 583.
2. Government of India (1), p. 16.
3. *Petroleum Times*, 31.5.1963, p. 263.
4. *Capital*, 12.11.1964, p. 691; *Eastern Economist*, 1.1.1965, p. 11.
5. Petroleum Intelligence Weekly, 10.7.1967.
6. Government of India (1), pp. 16–24.
7. *Capital*, 2.7.1960.
8. P.O.P., 29.7.1960.
9. P.O.P., 12.1.1965.
10. P.O.P., 14.7.1965, 28.7.1965.
11. P.I.W., 6.9.1965, 4.10.1965, 20.12.1965, and also Government of India (2), p. 29.
12. P.I.W., 3.1.1965; 10.1.1965.
13. P.I.W., 1.7.1968.
14. P.O.P., 3.2.1965.
15. P.O.P., 23.1.1959.
16. P.O.P., 29.1.1959; 30.1.1959.
17. P.O.P., 8.9.1959; 9.11.1959; 22.12.1959.
18. P.O.P., 29.7.1960.
19. P.I.W., 19.7.1965. In West European markets, notably in Italy, crude prices were lower still. For example, Iranian light crude was sold to Italy in October, 1964, more than six months before price reductions in India, at $1.47 per barrel. See, P.O.P., 27.1.1966.
20. Although it was denied by C.F.P., as well as by Amin Group, the Pakistani organisation involved in the deal, the participation of C.F.P. was widely rumoured. See P.I.W., 15.11.1965, 22.11.1965.
21. P.I.W., 1.11.1965.
22. P.I.W., 9.9.1968; 14.10.1968.
23. P.I.W., 20.5.1968.
24. P.I.W., 28.10.1968.
25. P.I.W., 20.5.1968.
26. See comment by A. F. Ansor, Chief of Fuels and Energy Division of the U.S. Department of States, in *Petroleum Intelligence Weekly*, 5.4.1965.
27. Penrose (3), pp. 203–213.
28. *Ibid.*
29. *Platts Oil Price Handbook* of relevant years for data.
30. *Platts Oilgram Press Service*, 10.8.1960.
31. *Petroleum Intelligence Weekly*, 15.1.1968. Under the 1964 settlement between the majors and the O.P.E.C., the fixed discount deducted from price was $6\frac{1}{2}\%$ both in 1966 and 1967, but then falls to $5\frac{1}{2}\%$, $4\frac{1}{2}\%$, $3\frac{1}{2}\%$, and 2% in subsequent years until 1971. The deductions are to be eliminated from 1972.
32. *Petroleum Intelligence Weekly*, 12.4.1965.
33. *Petroleum Intelligence Weekly*, 14.10.1968.
34. In 1963 the c.i.f. prices paid by these countries were $19.68, $19.65, $14.42, and $17.29, respectively, per ton. Only a small part of the difference can be explained in terms of freight differences. See *P.O.P.*, 3.12.1964, 9.8.1965. See also Table 17. In these four countries the percentage share of the majors in refining capacity in 1967 were $86 \cdot 8\%$, 100%, $34 \cdot 7\%$, and $52 \cdot 4\%$, respectively.
35. *Petroleum Intelligence Weekly*, 24.6.1968.
36. *P.O.P.*, 29.1.1959.
37. Recent attempts by Burmah Shell to Indianise a part of the equity capital and to bring both the marketing and refining company under one organisation

can be viewed as attempts to safeguard the marketing organisation from the threat of nationalisation. See footnote 2, p. 275.

38. P.I.W., 4.10.1965; 20.12.1965.

39. Government of India (1), p. 21.

40. *Capital*, 9.8.1962, p. 91, 9.5.1963, p. 581, 3.1.1963, p. 23.

41. *Capital*, 12.8.1964, p. 191, 9.5.1963, p. 581, 3.1.1963, p. 23.

42. P.T.P., 14.5.1965, p. 250.

43. P.O.P., 12.1.1966, and *Eastern Economist*, 15.1.1965, p. 121.

44. P.I.W., 28.1.1968.

45. P.I.W., 12.4.1965.

46. P.I.W., 20.11.1967. The agreement provides for a minimum of 40¢ discount off the posted price of light Iranian, subject to increase in the light of world oil price changes.

47. P.I.W., 20.5.1968.

48. P.I.W., 22.1.1965, 15.11.1965.

49. Penrose (4), p. 31.

50. See P.O.P., 22.7.1965, 21.10.1964.

51. P.I.W., 28.1.1968.

52. Adelman (1).

53. In the U.K. the ocean freight accounts for as much as the costs of refining, inland transporting, and marketing taken together, whereas in India it accounts for less than 15% of the landed price. See Grant and Luttrell.

54. P.T., May 14, 1965, p. 250.

55. P.O.P., 22.6.64, 23.6.67, 14.8.64, 1.10.64, 3.2.65, 26.7.65.

56. P.I.W., 20.11.1967.

57. See *Capital*, 15.11.1951, p. 583; 20.12.1951, p. 759; 2.4.1953, p. 447.

58. *Capital*, 20.12.1951, p. 759; *Indian Petroleum Handbook*, 1964, p. 16.

59. *Eastern Economist*, 15.1.1965, p. 121.

60. It was reported in 1965 that the major companies were willing to accept crude produced by O.N.G.C., abroad, as distinct from crude purchased by the Government from abroad, as a price for refinery expansion and in exchange for other guarantees with respect to taxes and repatriation. See P.I.W., 13.9.1965.

61. P.I.W., 12.8.1968.

62. P.O.P., 3.11.1965, P.I.W., 22.21965., 22.3.1965, 19.7.1965

CHAPTER 9

THE COST AND PRICE OF DOMESTIC
CRUDE OIL IN INDIA

EXPLORATION, DEVELOPMENT, AND EXTRACTION

In the oil world the word "crude production" covers exploration, development, as well as extraction of crude oil. "Exploratory activities" refer to the efforts made by the oil companies in finding new oil reserves. It normally begins with geological and geophysical surveys, and culminates in "wild cat" or prospective well drilling. If oil or gas is found, a number of "development wells" are bored around the original hole, in order to ascertain the vertical and horizontal limits, as well as the potential reserve of the oil field. "Extraction" involves the actual production from a fully developed field. In practice, the distinction between "exploration" and "development" is not always clear. Because of the migratory nature of this liquid fuel, it is sometimes difficult to establish whether a newly discovered reservoir is a new pool, or a mere extension of another known pool. The oil industry follows a number of conventions in this respect, but, like many other business practices, their economic significance is not always clear. For example, even if in the engineering sense the newly found pool is an extension of another pool nearby, it may need to be treated as a separate pool in the economic sense, if fresh exploratory investments had to be undertaken for its discovery.[1]

It has been shown by Professor M. A. Adelman that the marginal cost of producing crude oil, whether in aggregate, or in respect of its components, is an increasing function of output. The prospective oilbearing areas, at a given point of time, can be ordered in terms of their expected unit costs of exploration. The expected costs would be higher in deserts, marshy lands, or offshore waters, and in areas with a low probability of success. Given freedom of choice, an exploring company would begin with the expected low cost areas, and then would spread its efforts to relatively higher expected cost areas. The estimated costs of exploration in various alternative areas would be based on the current level of geological and geophysical knowledge, which may or may not be adequate. It is quite possible that an area with an expected high cost of exploration would turn out to be one with an exceptionally low cost, as a result of a prolific discovery. But such divergence between expected and actual costs would only influence future expected costs, and would require the cost function to be redrawn, probably at a lower level, without affecting the form of the cost function itself, at any given point of time.

Similarly, fields already discovered can be arranged in descending order of their costs, and developed in that order according to the crude oil needs of the company concerned. In the case of an individual field, with the intensification of the drilling effort, the newer wells are likely to be drilled nearer the edge of the field, and the proportion of dry wells will increase with output. Lastly, while at the beginning of the life of a well the crude oil is likely to flow automatically, with time and increased output, the pressure of gas and water inside the well will reduce. In such a case costlier recovery methods like the injection of gas, water, or mud would be required in order to maintain production.

While it is possible to relate, within a given margin of error, the investment on drilling and extraction to the realised crude oil output, given our existing state of knowledge, it is practically impossible to estimate probable costs of finding a barrel of crude oil reserve. It depends on whether there is in fact oil beneath the soil, if so in what amount and how the different oilfields are distributed all over the sedimentary area, and the respective sizes of these oilfields. If there is no oil underground, whatever the amount of effort employed in prospecting and drilling, no oil deposit will be found. If there is oil in existence beneath the soil, there is no guarantee that the drilling programme would succeed, but, with more extensive drilling, chances will continuously improve of ultimately finding these deposits. Again, the larger the size of an oilfield, the greater is the chance of its being located by drilling.

There are some practical difficulties in statistically calculating the odds in favour of a success in drilling, by adopting past discoveries and failures as a sample. Some well known petroleum engineers claim that the distribution of the size of oilfields usually follows "log normal" law of distribution. Professor Adelman argues, on the other hand, that mainly because of the migratory nature of oil, it is extremely difficult to designate with certainty the source of crude oil, and that there is not yet enough evidence in favour of "log normal" distribution to make its application for prediction useful in most cases.[2] In the United States, past exploratory results have been used as a sample for predicting results with a fair amount of success in those states where the exploratory activities were previously wide and extensive.[3] But this method is not going to succeed if the sample used for estimation, the past activities, is not large, and certainly not in India where so far only a small fraction of the total sedimentary area has been explored.

PAST EXPLORATORY EFFORTS IN INDIA

For various reasons very little work on exploration and prospecting was done in India before the 1950s. The only oilfield of India, Digboi (Assam), was discovered accidentally by a British railway company, which was also interested in coal and timber and, hence, neglected the development of this oilfield for a period because of its preoccupation with other activities.[4] This oilfield ultimately came under the ownership of Burmah Oil in 1921, the latter being practically the only concern active in exploratory work in India, but for a few small enterprises of little significance,[5] until the beginning of Stanvac operations in 1949.[6] But almost the entire drilling operation of Burmah Oil was concentrated in Assam and most of it in proving the extension of the Digboi oilfields[7] and, between 1889 and 1953, in sixty-four years, only fifty-five unsuccessful wells were drilled,[8] outside Digboi and Badarpur. Badarpur was a commercially unproductive oilfield, which was discovered in the Surma Valley of Assam in 1901, and came under the control of Burmah Oil in 1915. Its total production up to 1932, the year when it was abandoned, produced an aggregate of less than 250,000 tons of crude oil.[9] The production of Digboi oilfield never exceeded 500,000 tons annually.[10]

Exploratory activities were not undertaken seriously before Independence, for a number of reasons. First, the British Government was strongly opposed to any non-British company undertaking crude oil production in India. As early as 1902 two subsidiaries of the Standard Oil Trust, the Colonial Oil company of New Jersey and the Anglo-American Company of Britain, applied to the Government of Burma for a licence to prospect for oil. These applications were refused on the ground that "it is not desired by the Government of India to introduce any of the American oil companies or their subsidiary companies to India." Again, in 1917, Standard of New York's effort to prospect for oil was opposed on the ground that "a cardinal principle" of the Government policy was that "the licensee shall be and remain British or state subjects . . .".[11] Shell was refused permission to prospect Burma because of the fear that Standard Oil might enter through it and destroy Burmah Oil's virtual monopoly over India including Burma.[12] It was not until 1949, when Standard Vacuum began prospecting the West Bengal area, that any non-British company was allowed exploration rights in India.

Secondly, Burmah Oil, which enjoyed virtual monopoly over concession rights, was already producing oil in nearby Burma and Persia, and, given the state of geological and geophysical knowledge of that period, these areas were considered more attractive for investment than India.

Thirdly, Burmah Oil was already finding difficulty in marketing its own production in Burma and its affiliate's production in Persia, because of the restrictive marketing arrangements between the major oil companies. New discoveries in India might upset the balance between various interests in the markets of Asia, and might even lead to another price war. The overproduction and depression of the 1920s and the 1930s reduced the need for any further oil, from the point of view of the Burmah Oil company. The minimum amount of exploration work done by this company was necessitated by two compelling factors. Legally, it was bound to undertake a minimum amount of work to avoid forfeiting the concession rights. Commercially, it enabled this company to retain control over production from the fields of India and Burma, instead of surrendering the concession rights to its competitors. To quote the chairman of Burmah Oil, with reference to its investment in the Assam Oil company,

"That investment was thoroughly justified on marketing considerations alone, since in other unregulated hands . . . it would have cost us much more in the shape of 'cut' prices than we paid for it."[13]

In other words, their investment in India served a negative purpose, preventing others from discovering and producing crude and underselling Burmah Oil. No wonder the Geological Survey of India commented in 1942, "The search for oil in India, because of the expense in drilling operations, has been largely conducted by the big oil companies, who have their own geologists. Of late, there has grown up a feeling that the search for oil in India has not been as exhaustive as the importance of this substance warrants, and the possibilities of its occurrence justify."[14] A similar opinion was expressed on this subject by the "power subcommittee" of the National Planning Committee, set up by the Indian National Congress, under the chairmanship of Mr. Jawharlal Nehru.[15]

It is significant that both Nahorkatiya and Ankleswar were known since the 1920s as areas with good prospects for oil, although drilling did not begin in the former until 1952, and oil was discovered in the latter eight years after that. It is probably also significant that the drilling in Nahorkatiya followed the stoppage of supply from Burma after the war,[16] and the uncertainty created by the nationalisation of the Iranian oil industry in 1951 for the crude supply of the whole of the Middle East. The loss of two major sources of oil transformed the situation in the Eastern markets, from the point of view of Burmah Oil, and made further exploration in India a necessity, at least as a precautionary measure. One might suggest that the reasons which prompted the drilling work in Nahorkatiya in 1952 were similar to those which encouraged the major companies to agree to install refineries in India during the same period, and both were parts of a programme to diversify the areas of oil investment, following the Middle East crisis.

Oilfields of India

The oilfield of Nahorkatiya, situated about twenty-five miles south-west of Digboi in Assam, was discovered by Burmah Oil in 1953, at a depth of about 12,000 feet. This discovery followed fifty-five unsuccessful drillings in Assam,[17] and encouraged further exploration in this area. In 1956 another oilfield was discovered at Moran, situated about twenty-five miles west-south-west of Nahorkatiya, and for these two fields together the proved reserve was estimated at 45,000,000 tons, far higher than what was expected by any one connected with the oil industry. These discoveries exploded the popular hypothesis that the prospects for oil discovery in India were slim.

For a long time after this discovery, the development of the oilfields was delayed, because of disagreements between Burmah Oil and the Government of India. The former insisted on obtaining both marketing and refining rights, in addition to the exclusive right to produce crude from these fields, while the Government demanded the separation of the question about downstream facilities (which it sought to be kept under public ownership) from that of crude production. Finally an agreement was reached in 1959, when Oil India Limited was formed to take over the rights of Assam Oil, the subsidiary of Burmah Oil, over these fields. Originally one-third of the ownership was vested in the Government, but it was subsequently extended to 50% in 1961, in exchange for 1,800 square miles of additional area adjoining Nahorkatiya being given for further exploration to Oil India.[18] The other half of the equity is owned by Burmah Oil. The crude oil of Oil India is transported to the refineries of Nunmati and Barauni through a pipeline 750 miles long. Part of the crude not required by the public sector refineries is made available to the Digboi refinery.

Although the capacity of these fields is approximately 3,000,000 tons annually, the production has failed to reach this target even sixteen years after their discovery. It exceeded the 1,000,000 ton mark in 1964, and the 2,000,000 tons mark in 1966, but even in 1967 the production was 2·75 million tons.[19] The development of the oilfields was hampered by a number of factors, firstly, but the dispute between Burmah Oil and the Government about the ownership of the crude, then, by the dispute about the location of the refineries which would use this crude, and, lastly, by the failure of the refineries—both Barauni and Nunmati—to offtake crude because of technical troubles. Its aggregate production to date has been 10,000,000 tons, and out of 254 development wells drilled, about 78 % are producers.[20] Besides crude, Nahorkatiya fields also produce a certain amout of natural gas, but most of this is at present flared, in the absence of commercial opportunities.

The Oil and Natural Gas Commission of the Government discovered oilfields at Rudrasagar in 1962,[21] and at Lokhwa in 1964,[22] both situated in the Sibsagar region of Assam. Both of these fields are at present being developed and the trial production from the Rudrasagar field began in 1966.[23] Although the potential reserve of these fields is not yet known, they are expected to add at least another 20,000,000 tons to India's oil reserve.

The discoveries of oilfields in Gujrat has been a success story from the start. Oil was discovered in Lunez (Cambay) in 1958, from the first "wild-cat" drilling, although afterwards it was confirmed that there was more gas than oil in Cambay. Ankleswar was discovered in 1960, followed by Kallol in 1961, and Navagaum in 1965,[24] all these discoveries being made by the Oil and Natural Gas Commission with the help of experts from the Soviet Union. The aggregate amount of recoverable reserve from these oilfields has been estimated at 75,000,000 tons, of which Ankleswar alone contains about 53,000,000 tons.[25] Discoveries have also been reported at Dholka, Ahmedabad, and Mehsana, although these fields are yet to be developed.[26] The crude oil from these fields is transported to Koyali refinery by pipeline. The gas deposits of Cambay and Ankleswar, which can produce a minimum of 500,000 cubic meters per day, are now transported through pipelines to Dhuwaran and Uttaran power stations and also to Baroda.

For other parts of India the story of drilling is, so far, one of failure. Standard Vacuum drilled ten dry holes in West Bengal between 1957 and 1960,[27] and one drilled recently in that region by the Oil and Natural Gas Commission is still being tested.[28] Of the eight wells drilled in Punjab, Uttar Pradesh, and Bihar, so far, only one at Jwalamukhi, where gas seepages were known for a long time, has produced some gas. Only one of the three wells bored in the Cauvery basin has shown a minor flow of crude, and all are being tested further.[29]

Despite all these discoveries, the annual production of crude is still less than 6,000,000 tons, about two-fifths of the total oil consumption in India. According to the Energy Survey Commission, the estimated annual production of crude in India is not likely to exceed 10,000,000 tons, on the basis of our current knowledge about the oilbearing areas.[30]

However, in view of the fact that very little of the possible oil-bearing areas of India have so far been adequately investigated, it would be premature to base our judgement about the future prospect of oil discovery in India on past experience. Up to 1963, only 3% of the sedimentary area was mapped in detail, and less than a quarter per cent of the area was covered by gravity-magnetic surveys.[31]- Furthermore, of the 771 wells bored by Oil India, the Oil and Natural Gas Commission, and Standard Vacuum so far, only twenty-two or about 3% have been located outside Gujrat and Assam,[32] although these areas account for more than three-quarters of the total oil bearing areas, as is seen from Table 28.

TABLE 28

REGIONAL DISTRIBUTION OF SEDIMENTARY AREAS

Region	Thousand square miles
Assam	30
West Bengal	30
East Punjab, Himachal Pradesh and Jammu, and Kashmir	50
Rajasthan	46·5
Cambay-Cutch Area	68·5
Gangetic Valley	142
Madras Coast	17
Andhra Coast	9·5
Travancore Coast	6
Andaman and Nicobar Islands	3
Total	400

On the other hand, there are reports about promising structures offshore Cambay, and the Soviet experts, who carried out preliminary surveys, are highly optimistic about the outcome of further exploration.[33] Similar reports were submitted by the Soviet experts on Punjab and Rajasthan, but, as mentioned already, the drilling efforts have not been proportionate to the task required.

FACTORS AFFECTING THE COST OF DOMESTIC CRUDE

It is almost an impossible task to estimate the probable future cost of crude production in India. A large component of such cost would be that of exploration, which, as we have already observed,

P

it is not possible to calculate on the basis of past experience. It depends on the ratio of success in drilling, the size of the oilfields discovered, as well as the terrain in which these are located. In the United States, the success ratio is calculated as 11%, but in other countries (except possibly the Soviet Union), where the drilling is not even fractionally as extensive as in the United States, it has not been possible to work out any average ratio of drilling success. It is probably sufficient to point out that whereas in 1967 in the United States 36,883 wells were drilled, the corresponding number for India was only 100.[34] Again the distribution of drilling in India has so far been concentrated in only a part of the total oilbearing area. Because of the non-random character of the amount of drilling done so far, the success ratio in India has fluctuated violently from one period to another; it was less than 2% before the discovery of Nahorkatiya, then jumped to 5% when three out of five "wild-cat" drillings were successful in Assam.[35] Since then at least thirteen "wild-cats" have been drilled by Oil India without any luck.[36] On the other hand, the Oil and Natural Gas Commission drilled thirty-three exploratory wells up to 1965–66, of which seven have produced oil or gas, and another five are being tested, giving a very impressive success ratio indeed.[37]

Furthermore, any success with wild-cats is also a function of the amount of geological and geophysical work done before the actual work of drilling is undertaken. With better preliminary works, the chances of finding oil improve. For example, in both of the recently discovered oil producing regions of India, oil has been found under the alluvial blanket, where there is no surface oil-show or visible outcrops and the detection of oil by geological methods alone is difficult. The current emphasis on thorough preliminary surveys in offshore areas before undertaking drilling, is likely to improve the success ratio, provided of course there is oil beneath the soil.

The cost of exploration also depends on the terrain under exploration. A United Nations study published in 1962, showed how cost varied widely from one place to another—depending on whether the land was plain, marshy or desert-like, offshore or onshore.[38] In India, assuming other factors remain constant, the cost of prospecting is likely to increase over time, with the extension of activities to offshore areas and to the deserts of Rajasthan. As was proved during the drilling of the Jwalamukhi wells, it takes an unusually long time to drill in desert areas, besides the fact that the cost of prospecting there are three times higher. It took about two years to complete only 10,093 feet of drilling in Jwalamukhi, whereas in Nahorkatiya it takes only twelve to eighteen days,[39] to carry out the same amount of drilling.

Both wild-cat and development drilling are affected by the depth at which oil is discovered. The deeper reserve is more difficult to locate, and as the depth increases the reliability of the exploratory tools is expected to decrease. Accordingly, the cost increases because of the increasing number of dry holes drilled before a reserve is located. Furthermore, when the discovery is based on geophysical or sub-surface geological interpretation, the actual boundaries of the reserve become indefinite, which results in a larger proportion of dry holes also in development drilling.[40] The costs increase with depth also because of needs for higher grade and better protective arrangements for the equipment. The average depth of the Indian wells, at 6,489 feet, is higher than the world average, although comparable to the depths in the Middle East or North Africa. In Nahorkatiya the average is greater than 10,000 feet,[41] whereas in Gujrat the corresponding figure is 4,000 feet.[42] This fact explains to a certain extent the larger proportion of dry holes drilled in Assam compared to Gujrat. Other things remaining equal, the unit cost of development and exploration is expected to be higher in Assam than in Gujrat for this reason.

TABLE 29

AVERAGE DEPTH OF WELLS (IN FEET) IN 1964

Source: World Oil, August 15, 1965

Country	Depth	Country	Depth
India	6,489	Iran	7,986
World outside the			
Communist Bloc	4,510	Iraq	2,500
U.S.A.	4,325	Qatar	10,277
World outside U.S.A. and			
the Communist bloc	5,494	Saudi Arabia	5,285
Middle East	6,516	Neutral Zone	4,617
Kuwait	5,976	Venezuela	4,855
Abu Dhabi	7,794	Algeria	6,460
Bahrein	3,000	Libya	6,489

A large component of the cost of development of oilfields is the cost of drilling unsuccessful wells in proving the extension of the oilfields. As the table below indicates, about 40% of the total number of wells drilled in the world, both exploratory and development, are dry, which is a much greater figure than that for India—16% in 1964 and 30% in 1966.

This high proportion of success with drilling, although very impressive, does not tell us the whole story. As happens with any oilfield, at the beginning the development wells are expected to be drilled within the boundaries of the oilfield. But, as the field grows

THE PETROLEUM INDUSTRY IN INDIA

older, the newer development wells are drilled towards the edge of the field and the proportion of dry holes increases.[43] Hence, unless more and more new oilfields are discovered and developed, with the passage of time, the present economy in terms of drilling costs (because of the lower proportion of dry holes) will be wiped out by the more intensive drilling of the older oilfields.

TABLE 30

DRILLING ACTIVITIES IN 1966

Source: World Oil, August 15, 1967
(with 1964 figures in parentheses)

Country	Total No. of Wells Drilled	Oil	Gas	Dry	Others
India	100	62	8	30	107
	(128)	(93)	(8)	(22)	5
U.S.A.	36,883	16,216	4,321	15,193	1,153
	(44,149)	(19,905)	(4,694)	(17,694)	(1,856)
World (excluding the Communist Bloc)	44,513	20,059	5,075	18,132	1,247
	(52,432)	(24,397)	(5,453)	(20,627)	(1,955)

The cost of extracting oil, depends, among other things, on the number of wells and the system by which the pressure is maintained inside the well. A large number of wells would increase production from the field, but would also increase production costs as less will now be produced per well. At the beginning of its life, oil flows out of the wells automatically because of the pressure of gas inside the wells. But as the oilfield grows older, the pressures become less and the level of production can be maintained only with the help of artificial recovery methods. At present, all the new oilfields of India are passing through the initial period of flush production, and the period of flush production is likely to be longer than average in cases of Ankleswar and Nahorkatiya fields, because of the existence of associated gas deposits in the pools. In Digboi, as against this, only twenty-three out of 399 productive wells in 1964 were self-driven, and the rest were worked by pumps.[44]

Finally, the cost of oil production depends on the size of the oilfields. One important feature of crude oil production, which distinguishes it from other industries, is that the scale of production cannot be increased at will, since the economics of scale to be reaped are limited by the size of the field itself. The larger the size of a field, the brighter the prospect of its ultimate discovery, the smaller the proportion of dry holes in development drilling, and the smaller the extraction cost per well. The size of a field can compensate for almost any other factor affecting cost, including the inefficiency of the management. In the case of India, the fields discovered so far are still very small by world standards. The largest, Ankleswar, is not likely to exceed a production figure of 60,000 barrels per day, when it is fully developed, while the corresponding figure for Agha Jari of Iran was 808,142, and that for Kirkuk of Iraq was 823,175, in 1965.[45] Annual production of crude per well (in barrels) was only 58,138, (excluding Digboi) for India in 1964, whereas the figures for Iran, Kuwait, Venezuela, and the United States were 4,049,310; 1,497,643; 114,428; and 4,793, respectively.[46]

DOMESTIC CRUDE MARKET IN INDIA

A domestic crude market is conspicuous by its absence in India. All the producing companies are linked by long-term supply contracts to refining companies which, again, are partly or fully, directly or indirectly, owned by the producing companies themselves.[47]

As far as we can foresee, the domestic crude market will never be free in India. First, any competition from imported crude is ruled out by the Government's concern to save foreign exchange and the policy of limiting imports to what is needed for supplementing domestic crude supply. Secondly, the declared oil exploration policy of the Government is to separate the question of crude production from refining. If any company, exploring in India, discovers crude, it will probably have to supply it to a refinery indicated by the Government. Since in all future refineries the Government will have at least a majority share, the producing company, even if allowed to sell to a refining company of its choice, would be unable to take advantage of any competition between the refiners, in terms of prices. Thirdly, it is also likely that in all the future producing companies, the Government will have a large shareholding.[48] In other words, because of its control over both the refining and the producing sector, the Government will play a very important, if not decisive, role in the price and supply decisions of these producing companies.

THE PRICE OF DOMESTIC CRUDE

During the earlier stages of negotiations between Burmah Oil and the Government, it was agreed that the price of crude to the refineries would equal either the lowest price at which such crude could be secured at Calcutta by the refineries from any alternative source, or, the cost incurred by the company together with a reasonable commercial return, whichever was lower.[49]

The price formula was revised on July 27, 1961, to provide the following new formula[50]:—

(1) The price of crude oil would be based upon the c.i.f. price of an equivalent quantity of Middle East crude at Calcutta. However, if the f.o.b. element of the price at any time was not within the range of $1.52 to $1.68 per barrel, the c.i.f. price would be modified for the purpose of price fixation. The purpose of this provision was presumably to prevent wide fluctuations in O.I.L. crude prices.

(2) From the c.i.f. Calcutta price based on the Persian Gulf f.o.b. price, a certain amount would be deducted in such a way as to give Oil India Ltd. a net return of $10 \cdot 8\%$ on its paid up capital of Rs.280,000,000, after payment of all taxes including taxes on dividends.

(3) The price formula would be subject to review every year and the approval of the Government would be required for the price fixed. It was also agreed that in arriving at the rate of earnings, deduction would be made in respect of exploration and development costs, both past and present.

From 1962 O.I.L. is entitled to such profits in each year as will yield a return, after payments of all taxes, of not less than 9% and not more than 13% per annum. There is a provision for "retrospective adjustments" if the profit in any year is below the minimum or above the maximum limit of profits.[51]

TABLE 31

PRICE OF O.I.L. CRUDE: 1961–1964

Unit: Rupees per ton

Year	Assam Sales Tax	Retrospective Adjustment	Provisional Price	Total
1961	11.85	—	72.23	84.08
1962	11.79	35.37	67.44	114.60
1963	11.83	63.02	72.75	147.60
1964	11.85	55.10	71.00	137.95

The prices for Oil India crude paid by the Nunmati, Barauni, and Digboi refineries in 1961–64, given above, were much higher than the average of Rs.71 per ton paid by the refiners of Esso, Caltex, and Burmah Shell on their imported crude in 1962 and 1963, inclusive of landing charges, wharfage, transport into refineries, etc.[52] This difference arose because of the following reasons. (1) Whereas under the refinery agreements the private sector refiners were exempted from import duty on crude, the public sector refineries needed to pay about Rs.12 per ton as sales tax on the crude purchased.

(2) The price of Oil India crude was inflated by the "retrospective adjustment" item. Since the crude producing company was guaranteed a minimum return, the price of crude oil varied inversely with the amount of oil produced. Because of the slow rate of increase in production of these fields, the price of crude oil required to satisfy the guaranteed return to Oil India was enormously increased.

Until 1966, the Government of India subsidised the refineries to the extent of covering the sales tax and "retrospective adjustments", and the refineries only paid a price comparable to that paid by the coastal refineries for imports.[53] The difference created by the sales tax involved a transfer of money from the Central to the State Governments, and "retrospective adjustment" was treated as a kind of exploration incentive, and also as payment for past exploratory activities undertaken by the Burmah Oil which had been unsuccessful.

In 1966, the Government decided to equate the price of domestic crude with the landed cost of Persian Gulf crude at posted prices, which implied a 20% increase in domestic crude prices. At the same time a 20% import tariff was imposed on the landed price of imported crude. The allowance for "retrospective adjustment" was made unnecessary by 1967, as a result of increased production by the oilfields of Assam to a level of 2·75 million tons. In future, Oil India expects to repay the amount received on this account from the Government in the past.[54] The price of O.N.G.C. crude is fixed on par with the Oil India crude.

As things stand at present, the domestic crude is priced higher than the landed price of imported crude, subject to discounts. The reasons for the higher cost of domestic crude production are many, such as the heavy payments for past failures, and the small size of the oilfields. But not the least important are causes such as the slow development of the oilfields, and the lack of proper maintenance and employment of drilling equipments, which were pointed out by a team of Soviet experts.[55] While it takes on average three to four years to develop a field it took more than sixteen years to develop Oil India fields for reasons discussed above. The Ankleswar and Kallol fields, particularly the latter, seven to eight years after their discovery,[56] have yet to be developed to their optimum capacity. The drilling rigs have normally been slow to move from one place to another, and the drilling effort seems to have slackened over the past few years. The drilling target for 1967–68 was 1005·24 thousand meters and 507 wells, although during the first six months the total figure was 71·33 thousand meters only, and only twenty-seven wells were drilled.[57] From this, it does not follow that Indian crude will always involve a relatively higher cost of production. Much depends on the scale of future discovery, and, in view of our limited past experience, the future for India is unpredictable. On the other hand, it can be pointed out that many of the large oil producing areas of the present time were in the past dismissed as having little prospect for discovering oil, and India's records of drilling success to date is at least brighter than the record of some of these countries. For instance, it took Canada twenty-eight years and 133 failures before oil was discovered in vast amounts, its 1963 production being 53,000,000 tons. The existence of oil in Nigeria was known from the early years of the present century, but the first commercial discovery did not take place before 1958, although, had it not been for the tragic civil war, this country might now be counted among the foremost oil-producing countries of the world.[58] A more recent example is provided by Australia, where huge amounts were spent without success from 1900 until the discovery of Moonie fields a few years ago.[59] A further discovery in 1968 in offshore Bass straits is considered to be among the largest in the world, and has led to the surrender of the exploration incentive allowance of $1 per barrel by the producing companies.[60]

OIL EXPLORATION AND THE PUBLIC SECTOR

For a long time after Independence, the Government of India took no serious interest in oil exploration. The chances of finding oil were reckoned to be slim, the expenses and risks involved correspondingly large, and the technical expertise required for the task was also considered to be beyond the Government's abilities. More attention was given to the refineries, where efforts could be directly linked with output.

The discovery of Nahorkatiya, and then Moran, in Assam, helped to destroy the assumption that the probability of success in prospecting in India was limited and encouraged the Government's interest in this aspect of the oil business. The Government demanded a share in the crude production from these fields, and declared a policy of separating the business of crude production from the downstream activities. As we have seen before, the agreement of 1959, which led to the formation of Oil India, allowed the Government a share of one-third in the crude producing company and this share has subsequently been raised to half. But most of the drilling activities of this new company are devoted to the extensions of the fields already discovered, and, from the point of view of the Government, the investment is secure and productive, like investments in refining operations.

The Government began taking direct interest in prospecting from 1955, when an Oil and Natural Gas Division was created to specialise in oil exploration. At the beginning, the only area selected for prospecting was Jaisalmer in Rajasthan, and the budgeted amount was only Rs.45,000,000. But very soon Hosiarpur in Punjab and Kangra in Himachal Pradesh were included and the budget was expanded to Rs.100,000,000 to be spent over five years. In 1955, a team of Soviet experts came to study India's sedimentary area and produced a highly optimistic report, and suggested the formation of a statutory body for undertaking oil exploration, which encouraged the Government to revise the estimated expenditure under this heading during the Second Five Year Plan from 110 crores to 300 crores. The Government planned for Rs.2,020,000,000 expenditure during the Third Five Year Plan on this item.

The entry of the Government in the oil exploration business was criticised from many directions, not least from the financial press of India, which equated it to a gamble with taxpayers' money. Mr. Malviya, who was in charge of the Oil Ministry from the mid-fifties until 1963, was not deterred by this opposition to his policy, and enthusiastically took up the task of exploration, with the active support of the Soviet Union. The success in Gujrat, as also in Sibsagar (Assam) justified his stubbornness, as was admitted by many of his adversaries afterwards.[61] He enlisted the support of the French Petroleum Institute in prospecting the Jaisalmer area, and also the support of foreign experts from Italy, West Germany, Canada, and Rumania, in addition to the Soviet Union, in prospecting in various parts of the country.

The performance of the Oil and Natural Gas Commission has been criticised in the past on a number of grounds. The development of the oilfields has been extraordinarily slow, as has been pointed out already, the programme of prospecting having been interrupted by the slow movement of the working teams, and the equipment, and the lack of proper maintenance of the machineries which has inflated the costs. But, as things stand today, the Commission owns a substantial proportion of the oil deposits discovered to date, and accounts for about 6,000,000 tons of potential annual productive capacity, within the country, and another 1,000,000 tons from offshore Iran. In addition, the Government owns half the 3,000,000 tons annual capacity of Oil India, and the total public sector ownership is expected to become 75% of the annual crude production in India by 1971. This is despite the fact that the Government expected the private sector to grow along with the public sector, and had no intention of supplanting the latter, Mr. Malviya believed that oil was such "a potentially expanding field in India that the entry of the public sector has not and need not squeeze out the private sector. There is room for both and more."[62]

In 1959 the Government revised the petroleum legislation of 1949 and formulated an exploration policy for the private sector. The sedimentary areas were classified into two groups: those where the private companies were allowed to work on their own, and those where it was conditional on their acceptance of the participation of the Oil and Natural Gas Commission. The latter areas consisted of the following: the Kutch-Saurastra sedimentary belt, the Jammu-Punjab-U.P. foothills and plains, and the mesozoic tertiary sedimentary basin of the east coast of Madras. The Government left the details of the exploration agreements to be worked out through negotiations between the oil companies and the Government, although it implicitly expressed preference for those companies which were willing to accept the Government's majority share in the crude producing company and were prepared to leave the refining and marketing of the crude exclusively to the Government. The Government was inclined to bear a part of the expenditure undertaken for explorations which did not succeed.[63] The Government launched a campaign for persuading the foreign oil companies to undertake exploration in India, and distributed a booklet containing information about the sedimentary areas, oil legislations, and taxes.

In 1960 reports appeared in the press indicating that a number of foreign companies, including Shell, Caltex, Gulf, E.N.I., and Esso, were interested, but in the end no agreement was signed. Most of the oil companies were reluctant to engage in crude production alone without any share in marketing and refining. The Petroleum Press Service commented that "It is pointless for a company not already in the country to spend a lot of money looking for oil which it might be compelled to sell as crude at unprofitable levels to local state-owned refineries."[64] There was also opposition to a majority share to be given to the Government. To quote the same journal again, "What company is going to risk its money on the highly speculative job of exploration in a foreign country on a minority basis?"[65] Both these comments reflect the views of the oil press on this question, although they need not be accepted as statements of fact. A number of companies have in the past accepted concession agreements which stipulate that the entire risk of exploration would be borne by the company concerned, if oil were not discovered, while in the event of the discovery of oil, the Government would be entitled to purchase up to a 50% share, in exchange for the payment of a proportionate amount of costs of exploration, in the crude producing company.[66] Again, many of these companies specialise solely in oil exploration and production in one country, and export crude to refineries, situated in another country. But an important reason for the private oil companies' lack of interest in exploration in India at that time, unless under the most suitable terms, was the comparatively greater attraction of North Africa and the Middle East, with proved oil deposits in large amounts, for investment. The failure of the Indo-Stanvac exploration in West Bengal immediately before the publication of the new policy also contributed to the apathy of the oil companies towards India. The recent offer by Teneco, a U.S. independent, for exploring offshore Cambay at its own risk, and its agreement to accept Government majority ownership in the event of oil being found,[67] to a large extent reflects a brighter opinion about the prospects of oil discovery in India in the world oil industry, following the successes in drilling in Gujrat and the optimistic reports appearing about offshore Cambay. But as yet very little response has been received from the larger companies, despite the best intentions of the Government of India to secure their participation.

PUBLIC SECTOR "VS" FOREIGN OIL COMPANIES

The appearance of the Government in the field of exploration has been strongly attacked from many quarters, including the oil companies, the business world, the oil journals, as well as the World Bank. The main emphasis in all the criticisms has been placed on the costly nature of the undertaking as well as the high degree of risk associated with it. The experience of countries like Ecuador, Peru, or Guatemala, which have spent millions of dollars without success, has been mentioned, in order to underline the risk of loss, and the awesome burden which the taking of such risk involves on the limited financial resources of poor countries. Even when the search for oil is successful, the critics point out, the costs of development are also very high and would require the company concerned to meet deficits for a period of at least five or six years, at a time when either the required amount of foreign exchange is not available, or such an amount might be more fruitfully employed in other undertakings. Since most of the poor countries cannot afford to gamble with their limited resources, the efforts of their Governments should be directed towards less risky and less costly ventures, instead of being sunk in oil exploration.[68]

On grounds of comparative costs, most of the critics would like countries like India to abandon any idea of building a domestic crude producing industry. Given the present state of knowledge, the domestic crude of these countries is likely to be more expensive than the cost of imported crude and would force the Governments either to provide a subsidy to the crude producing companies or to restrict imports to the level required for supplementing domestic production.

Sometimes the actual amount of subsidy given to the crude oil producing companies is concealed, when a large part of it takes the form of tax reliefs, special loans, and other forms of subvention and privileges. All these require resources to be withdrawn from other sectors of the economy, which is not always justified in terms of the gains from their employment in oil exploration. When subsidies are not given, and imports are restricted, the cost of energy increases, thereby increasing the production cost of the industrial outputs and exports. This argument, although not often realised by those who advance it, is largely independent of the question about the nature of the ownership of the domestic crude oil production. Even large international oil companies demand protection and subsidy when the cost of domestic crude oil exceeds the landed cost of imports, and receive privileges and subventions during exploration work which are not normally available to the other industries. The Indo-Stanvac agreement, for example, provided for special income tax relief, as well as the right to import goods at reduced rates, and Oil India Limited, which is half-owned by Burmah Oil, receives with pleasure the benefits of protection and guaranteed net income.

While the comparative cost argument rules out a domestic crude industry, the critics would prefer crude production and exploration undertaken by the international oil companies to those being put under the ownership of the Government, despite this argument, in the event of such an industry being established, The arguments in favour of the foreign international oil companies, as against the Government owned companies, are given below.

Firstly, the foreign companies would bear the risk of failure. If the exploration was successful, the country would get the benefit of crude production, and if the venture were to fail, the economy would not lose. In addition, during the period of exploratory activities, the companies would help increase the foreign currency holding of the economy to the extent that they would spend a part of their investment in local goods and services. On the other hand, the fund for public sector programme would come from the domestic taxpayers, and would involve diverting resources from the other sectors of the economy.

Secondly, the risk of failure would be higher in the case of the state-owned companies than in the case of the international companies for two reasons, even if financial difficulties were overcome. Because of their long experience in the oil business, and technical expertise, the foreign companies would be less likely to make errors. Furthermore, even if the technical expertise is identical in the case of the foreign companies and the state-owned companies, the former would get the benefit of diversified judgement, as one of a number of oil companies in operation with different approaches. The state-owned companies, when operating as a monopoly, would be handicapped by their centralised administration.

All these arguments are based on assumptions which, to say the least, are disputable. While it is true that the foreign companies enjoy superiority over the Indian enterprises in their technical knowledge and experience, this fact alone is not a sufficient ground for handing over equity ownership to them. It is possible to hire the technical services of a number of international oil companies, like C.F.P., E.N.I., as well as the Soviet Union and Rumania, without also conferring ownership of crude on them. In fact the Government of India made the use of the services of a number of foreign companies in the past, and two of the recent offers on offshore Cambay provide for contract services. It is also wrong to exaggerate the importance of this "technical know how" argument. A number of small companies, including Arabian Oil of Japan, have earned success without much experience or technical knowledge. The growing experience of the Indian engineers is narrowing down the technological gap which existed before. The cost of technical service will decline in future with time and reduce this gap. On the other hand, it can be argued that the foreign companies, because of their lack of interest in any training programme for Indian personnel, would perpetuate the technological gap, at the existing level, between the Indians and the personnel of the international companies.

Although it is true that the establishment of a monopoly leads to the centralisation of the decision-making process, what is not clear is the argument that such centralisation adversely affects the probability of success in exploration. The centralisation of administration also implies centralised collection and analysis of information, and offers greater scope for comparing detailed geological and geophysical data relating to various regions, before working out the drilling programme. Where a number of companies are operating, each with its own technical staff and without access to the data collected by others, the decisions on drilling taken by those companies individually are likely to be based on insufficient data. There is no reason to conclude that a diversified exploration programme based on incomplete data has a greater probability of success than a centralised effort which relies on more extensive data, assuming no difference in the scale of operation. This argument applies equally to both kinds of monopolies—those under the public sector and those under the private sector. The success achieved by the Soviet Union's state-owned oil exploration enterprises, which has ranked the country among the three main oil producing regions of the world, should settle the argument against the assumption of inverse relationship between state ownership and success in exploration. The main oil producing countries of the Middle East were, until recently, under the monopoly of the large international majors, who were at one time among the chief exponents of the benefits which flow from such market structure in terms of the rational use of both resources and data for the exploration and development of oil deposits.

There is an implicit assumption in the arguments employed against the state-owned oil undertakings of the poor countries, that the foreign oil companies are capable of and willing to mount exploratory operations on a scale, larger than those which the limited resources of the former would allow it to undertake. While the capabilities of the major oil companies to launch large programmes are beyond doubt, their willingness to take such measures has not been demonstrated in the past. Until 1958 there was no state oil company for exploration in India, and the laws of the country were highly favourable to the foreign oil companies until the mid-fifties. But yet the amount of exploratory and drilling efforts undertaken by the foreign companies were insignificant. There are reasons for such behaviour on their part. Being international oil companies, these bodies seek and own concessions in a large number of countries, some of which contain known large deposits, and others with small amount of proved reserve. Given a certain sum budgeted for exploration, such companies are likely to spend more in those areas where the chances of success are relatively higher, and less on those where the prospects are less certain.

The extent of precautions taken by the major companies before committing a large sum for exploring uncertain prospects is illustrated by Standard Vacuum in West Bengal. Although the prospecting of this area began in 1949, it took five years to complete, and the company waited for another three years to sign a contract with the Government for various concessions and subsidies, before any hole was bored. All this happened during a period when literally thousands of wells were being drilled by the parent companies of Standard Vacuum all the world over, particularly in the Middle East. These international companies are prepared to bear "risk" in the Middle East or North Africa, because the extent of risk is small in those areas, and are unwilling to sink their exploration fund in India because, from their standpoint, it is still not very attractive compared to other alternative investment opportunities. The fact that the Government has received in recent years a number of offers—from Ashland and Teneco—for drilling offshore Cambay, can be explained by the extremely good reports produced by the prospecting work, and the drilling success of the state-owned Oil and Natural Gas Commission in mainland Gujrat. There is no doubt that the discovery of giant oilfields by O.N.G.C. in future would make exploration in India more worthwhile from the point of view of the foreign oil companies, but such a discovery would also make the participation of the foreign oil companies superfluous, as they would bear little risk and still take a share in oil production. The experiences of countries like Libya or Nigeria show that discoveries of large deposits have been preceded by long years of exploration at a very slow rate, and have been followed by a rapid expansion of activities by the already existing companies and also by the entry of many newcomers. There is no reason to believe that India's experience would be different.

Much has been written in the business press of India and the World about the discouraging effect of the present exploration policy of the Government on the foreign international companies. But, as the recent offers in the Middle East show, the oil companies are prepared to work under more stringent conditions, like bearing the entire risk of exploration in case of failure, and agreeing to hand over majority ownership to the state-owned company after the drilling succeeds, apart from paying more than 50% of the sales proceeds in the form of income taxation and another $12\frac{1}{2}\%$ as royalty, provided the deposits expected to be discovered are large enough to offset these payments. So long as oil prospects are comparatively less bright in India, even a fully free-market exploration policy would not lead to any large exploration programme. On the other hand, once large oil deposits are located in India, even a state-owned oil company would be able to arrange for a larger sum for exploration. Not only would the Government then be more willing to commit vast sums of money to this item in preference to some other projects, but credit would also be available from the foreign sources for a further exploration programme. The substantial increases in the exploration budget, following O.N.G.C.'s success in Gujrat, and also the financial help of the French and Italian Governments, are indications of such possibilities in the event of a spectacular success. Whereas the foreign companies would be willing to "bear risk" on a large scale after such a discovery, the scale of effort is likely to be small without such a discovery, no matter what policies are adopted by the Government towards foreign ownership.

Even assuming that the international oil companies are willing to explore in India, once the Government policy of claiming majority ownership in crude production and exclusive ownership in refinery operation is revoked, and also assuming that such efforts succeed in locating oilfields, there is still no guarantee that these would be developed according to the needs of the Indian economy. Being international firms, they are capable of meeting their crude requirements from a large number of oilfields, which are spread over many countries, and the amount lifted from a particular field under their ownership depends on a wide range of factors. From the point of view of such a company, the Indian production is worthwhile up to the point where its marginal cost equates the cost of production of one of its foreign crude producing affiliates, plus the transport charge and protective duties. Additional requirements would be met from imports, which are cheaper from their point of view though involving foreign exchange costs to the economy. There are examples where the foreign oil companies have participated in oil exploration and production, not so much to produce oil, but in order to prevent other oil companies from producing oil from these sources and thereby sharpening competition in the world market. The huge shut-in capacity in the Middle East bears testimony to this policy, while the companies holding concession rights in that region are also exploring in more costly areas. It is important from their point of view to diversify their crude sources and to own a large potential capacity, while the amount actually produced from a field depends upon marketing factors, and on political decisions. The fact that since the June War of 1967 the major oil companies have lifted more oil from non-Arab Iran than any other country also underlines the political content of their decisions.

Let us now analyse some of the arguments normally advanced against the state-owned oil companies. Firstly, the argument that the latter receives subsidies and concessions from the Government is without any importance, since, as has been already mentioned, even the foreign oil companies insist on such "public support" before undertaking exploration in a country like India. If this argument applies at all, it applies against domestic production, irrespective of the ownership of crude, when its cost exceeds the delivery price of foreign crude. Secondly, it is contended that funds used in risky enterprises should be provided voluntarily, but, whereas the investments made by the private firms are contributed voluntarily by the shareholders, the Government funds are raised involuntarily from the taxpayers.[69] But, as a close examination of the balance sheets of the large international oil firms shows, very little of their investment funds is raised from the shareholders, and they rely overwhelmingly on monopolistic pricing, which is no less involuntary than taxation, for financing. Thirdly, it is argued that the sum spent on exploration by the Government might be spent on activities which are not associated with so much risk. It is undeniable that the risk of loss is considerable in exploration, although some risk is inherent in every economic activity. But, as the private companies, when undertaking a new line of business, take the risk of making a loss which can be supported by earnings from other businesses, the Government is entitled to assume the risks of oil exploration if the possible benefit resulting from success, far outweighs the possible risks of loss, in terms of the output of the alternative activities to which the resources used in exploration might be diverted without such a programme. Whether investment in oil exploration is a worthwhile activity, in preference to other activities, cannot be judged in isolation from its impact on the rest of the economy. Whereas a private company would judge the performance of an activity from the point of view of individual profitability, the unit of operation for the Government is the entire economy.[70]

It is claimed that the exploration activities of the foreign companies help to bring into the host country foreign currencies which might not be otherwise available. The oil companies employ local personnel and purchase local raw materials, and the amount paid for the goods and services by them constitutes a net addition to the country's foreign exchange reserve. It also spares the Government the task of risking precious foreign exchange for exploration. On the other hand, a state entity would require to divert foreign exchange resources from alternative uses for the purpose of exploration. The need for such resources would be greatest during the short term, even if the programme succeeds ultimately, since a huge expenditure would be required for this purpose which would not produce oil for quite some time. The economy would require to meet the foreign exchange cost for this activity at a time when the development needs for the economy as a whole would put enormous pressure on the dwindling foreign exchange reserves.

The above argument is entirely valid in cases where the operations undertaken by the international oil companies fail to discover oil deposits. In those cases, the companies bear the risk, and also pay for the local goods and services in foreign currency. But the amount of such payment is not likely to be of much significance in the case of a large economy like India, although it may contribute significantly to the tiny economy of a country like Libya. As we have already seen, the activities of the oil companies are likely to be on a small scale until the discovery of a large deposit. Moreover, when the exploring companies are already active in the country in other fields—like marketing or refining—the fund for exploration may not actually be imported from abroad, and may originate from the profits of other such fields of activity. To the extent that a part of such profits was not going to be remitted outside the country, and also to the extent that such profits were normally taxable but exempted from taxation when used for exploration, no addition to foreign reserve takes place from the activities of the foreign companies. Again, a large component of the expenditure on exploration—about half— is related to the imports of equipments, which needs to be deducted from such an estimate of foreign exchange. On balance, the quantitative implication for such foreign exchange help is not likely to be very significant for a country like India.

The discovery of large oil deposits would almost certainly encourage many more companies to queue for exploration rights, and the pace of activity would most certainly quicken. Besides, the foreign oil companies would participate in the development of the deposits for production. In the short term, the foreign ownership of the crude production, therefore, would relieve pressure on the dwindling foreign exchange reserve of the country. In the long run, however, the economy would have to pay the cost of foreign participation in the initial stage in terms of regular profit remittances, and the benefits of import substitution would be reduced to the extent of those remittances. On the other hand, the state ownership of crude production would require a diversion of essential foreign exchange resources from other projects in the initial stage, while it would not be required to meet regular demands for foreign exchange from foreign participants once the project got under way. Once the degree of uncertainty usually associated with crude production largely disappears, the arguments for state ownership are similar to those advanced in cases of other projects of similar long gestation period, such as steel, irrigation, or fertiliser. Much depends on how one values the future needs in relation to the present ones. The emphasis given to the current foreign exchange shortage by the critics of state ownership presents a point of view which considers the short term problems to be more crucial than the long term ones, an opinion to which not every one would subscribe.[71] Furthermore, as has already been pointed out, there is a risk that the foreign companies might not increase domestic production to the point which is economically worthwhile from the point of view of the Indian economy, if such a production conflicts with their global interests. In such a case the amount of saving possible in foreign exchange through import substitution under Indian ownership, would exceed what is possible under foreign ownership.

To summarise, there is insufficient evidence to justify the presumption that the risk of failure would be higher in the case of the state-owned companies, or that the liberalisation of the exploration policy would lead to a large exploration programme being undertaken by the international oil companies. Whereas the participation of the foreign oil companies in exploration would relieve the foreign exchange problem in the short run, in the long run their profit remittances would constitute a regular outflow from India. The arguments against the international companies are their international character and the possibility that their world-wide interests might conflict with India's own interests, the oilfields under their ownership might not be used to the fullest extent, and the exploration work might not be taken very seriously by them in a country like India. The passion for secrecy of these private companies is prejudicial to a proper evaluation of the geological and geophysical characteristics of the sedimentary area, and their operation hinders the technological progress of the Indian personnel. The services they give in financing and applying technical experience, may be hired in the world market without also conferring equity ownership.

Lastly, let us examine the argument that countries like India should not produce crude oil, and should instead put their weight as consumers of oil on the side of reducing crude oil prices in the world market. Any protectionist policy in favour of domestic crude, whether in the form of tariff, subsidy, or concessions, according to this argument, inflates the cost of energy and inhibits international trade. It is not necessary here to go through the familiar arguments about the relevance of a protectionist policy, and we shall confine ourselves to the points specifically relating to the oil industry. A domestic industry helps to reduce the dependence on foreign crude oil sources, which is so important both for economic and military reasons. It also helps to iron out fluctuations in supply from the world market. Besides this, it reduces the foreign exchange cost of energy, which, given the importance of foreign exchange constraint in development planning, is more relevant as a policy variable than the domestic market price for energy. It can also be added that even a large world oil producer like the United States has been forced to adopt a protectionist policy towards oil imports, as also most other countries of the world, because of the high foreign exchange cost of oil imports.

NOTES

1. Adelman (3).
2. Adelman (3), pp. 59–63.
3. Kaufman, A., "*Statistical Decision and Related Techniques in Oil and Gas exploration.*"
4. See Metre (2) and Assam Oil Company (1) for details.
5. Another British company, Whitehall Petroleum Company, did some exploration work and drilled three wells in Assam between 1920 and 1927. One P. K. Sen, a well-known industrialist of Calcutta, drilled two wells in Assam in 1909. See Metre (1), Metre (2), Metre (3), and P.T., 18.10.30, p. 613.

6. Stan-Vac drilled ten unsuccessful wells between 1957 and 1960, in all a total of 98,000 feet, inWest Bengal. One quarter of the total expense was borne by India. See *World Oil*, 1958 to 1961 (August 15 numbers).

7. *Records of the Geological Survey of India*, relevant years.

8. Metre (1), p. 84.

9. *Ibid*, Metre (2), and also *Records of the Geological Survey of India*, 1917–1933.

10. *Ibid.*

11. U.S. (2), p. 41.

12. Henrigues, pp. 484–486.

13. *Petroleum Times*, 10.6.1933, p. 599.

14. *Geological Survey of India, Bulletin No.* 1, "Mineral Wealth in India", 1942, p. 19.

15. National Planning Committee, "Power and Fuel", 1947, p. 30.

16. Due, first, to the war, and then to the civil war, Burma has been reduced to the status of an oil importing country. See P.T., 26.12.1942, p. 620, and also P.T., 14.7.1950 (supplement).

17. Apart from Badarpur, two other oilfields were discovered at Masimpur (1927–1930) and Patharia (1930–1932). Both were abandoned soon after their discovery. See *Records of The Geological Survey of India* of relevant years.

18. *Capital*, 26.2.1959, p. 256, 23.1.1958, p. 123, *Eastern Economist*, 26.5.1961, p. 1244.

19. E.P.W., 7.9.1968, p. 1362.

20. *Eastern Economist*, 5.7.1968, p. 28.

21. *Capital*, 26.6.1962, p. 75.

22. *Capital*, 17.12.1964, p. 901.

23. *Report of the Ministry of Petroleum and Chemicals*, 1966–67.

24. *Petroleum Times*, 9.3.1962, p. 162; 5.3.1965, p. 120; *O.G.I.*, March, 1964, p. 65.

25. O.G.I., June, 1967, pp. 66–67.

26. Ministry of Petroleum and Chemicals, *Annual Report*, 1967–68.

27. 25% of the drilling cost was paid by the Government. See *World Oil*, August 15 numbers of 1958 to 1961.

28. *Eastern Economist*, 29.12.1967, p. 1258.

29. *Ibid.*

30. *Capital*, 3.12.1964, p. 827.

31. *Indian Petroleum Handbook*, 1964, p. 10.

32. *Eastern Economist*, 29.12.1968, p. 1258, 5.7.1968, p. 28.

33. E.P.W., 12.11.1966, pp. 528–529.

34. *World Oil*, 15.8.1967, p. 41.

35. Metre (1), p. 84.

36. Six wild-cats were mentioned by Metre (see Metre (2), pp. 108–109), two in 1963 and five in 1964 were reported in *World Oil*, 15 August numbers of 1964, 1965.

37. This may be an underestimation.

38. United Nations (1).

39. Metre (2), p. 108; *World Oil*, 15.8.1968, pp. 92–99.

40. Hall.

41. Metre (3), p. 86.

42. *Oil Statistics*, October–December, 1964, p. 3.

43. See Adelman (3).

44. *World Oil*, 15.8.1965, pp. 194–200.

45. O.G.I., February, 1966, pp. 42–43.

46. *World Oil*, 15.8.1965, pp. 194–200.

47. *Indian Petroleum Handbook*, 1964, pp. 7–8.

48. *Capital*, 3.12.1959, p. 776; 10.12.1959, p. 811; 24.12.1959, p. 892.
49. *Capital*, 23.1.1958, p.123.
50. Government of India (8), p. 14.
51. Government of India (8), p. 14.
52. Government of India (2), p. 37.
53. Government of India (2), p. 38.
54. *Eastern Economist*, 5.7.1968, p.28.
55. E.P.W., 1.1.1968, pp. 828–829.
56. Even by the end of 1966 the production from Kallol was about 100 tons per day. See Ministry of Petroleum and Chemicals, *Annual Report*, 1966–67. The production of Ankleswar was about 18,000 barrels per day in 1967, far less than its 60,000 barrel per day optimum capacity. See O.G.I., Feb., 1966, pp. 42–43.
57. *Eastern Economist*, 29.12.1968, p. 1258.
58. United Nations (1), p. 11.
59. P.I.W., 19.7.1965.
60. P.I.W., 13.5.1968, 21.10.1968.
61. *Eastern Economist*, June 28, 1963, p. 1439.
62. *Ibid*, 19.2.1960, p. 453.
63. *Capital*, 10.12.1959, 24.12.1959, 7.4.1960, 16.6.1960.
64. P.P.S., June, 1961, p. 216.
65. P.P.S., July, 1957, p. 266.
66. See the oil journals of the recent years.
67. E.P.W., 2.9.1968, p. 1359–1360.
68. See Levy (2) for a good exposition of the points of view of the critics.
69. See Penrose (4), pp. 235–246, for detailed discussion on this point.
70. *Ibid.*
71. *Ibid.*

CHAPTER 10

PARTICIPANTS IN THE OIL INDUSTRY OF INDIA: SOME COMMENTS

The last decade has witnessed a rapid decline in the relative position of the major international oil companies in the Indian oil industry. Until the mid-fifties the majors owned the entire refinery output, the entire crude oil production, and almost the entire import trade and marketing network. In comparison, at present the amount of oil products marketed by these companies is limited to their own refinery output in India, they have been denied participation in lucrative import trade in oil products, and no refinery has been allocated to their ownership since 1958. On their own option the majors have limited their exploratory activities to those undertaken by Indian Oil, as a protest against the exploration policy of the Government. On the other hand, the enterprises under the ownership of the Government, which have been formed over the past decade and half, have come to occupy a dominating position in the oil economy of the country. With time and further expansion of the oil industry, the relative position of the majors is likely to weaken further.

For the present state of affairs only the majors are to blame. The Government of India, despite its public pronouncements of "socialistic pattern of society", has always been friendly to foreign capital. The refinery contracts of 1951 and 1953 were made by the Government, in clear violation of the spirit of the 1948 Industrial policy resolution, in order to appease the major oil companies. As evidenced from the Indo-Stanvac contract for exploration, as well as the exploration policy documents of the late-fifties, the Government was eager to secure the participation of private foreign capital, and was willing to offer various incentives. The Government was, however, also interested in joint-ownership of some kind as well as in lower import prices for oil. It can be said that the total lack of sympathy of the major oil companies to the Government's concern for import-substitution, lower foreign exchange bill, and some Indian participation in ownership, left the latter with no option but to look for other sources of aid.

Whereas in the Middle East and a number of other places these major international oil companies played a historical role in the development of the oil industries of those areas, in India their main preoccupation was importing and trading. The development of Indian oilfields or refineries was never accorded a place in their list of priorities. They were reluctant to build refineries in India, until the Abadan crisis of 1951 forced them to reassess their global policy with respect to refinery location. Their present enthusiasm for refinery building is a direct consequence of the Government policy of limiting import of refined products to an amount necessary to bridge the gap between domestic demand and domestic refinery output. On the other hand, the majors are still unwilling to surrender the precious advantages which they gained through the refinery agreements of the early-fifties. Their limited interest in oil exploration has been discussed in detail in the previous chapter.

The role of the major international oil companies in the Indian market can never be isolated from their role in the world market as a whole. Each of these vertically integrated and internationally organised enterprises tends to programme its activities in various sectors and in various countries in accordance with the profit goal of the entire organisation, and the global objectives of these giant undertakings, not infrequently, tend to come into conflict with the economic interests of particular countries. Because of the vertically integrated nature of their organisation, these companies are capable of manipulating the profit-loss figures for different branches of their operation. In their effort to minimise taxes, these companies prefer to show higher book-keeping profits in crude-producing activities, and lower profits (sometimes losses) from downstream activities such as refining, marketing, or transporting. Such a book-keeping policy, although consistent with the profit motive of these companies, also implies for the crude-importing countries, such as India, a higher level of foreign exchange costs, and a lower level of taxation of the downstream activities of these major oil companies. It is against this international background of the oil companies, that one is required to judge the complaints these companies are constantly making about the non-profitability of their Indian operation. When Esso complains about the business loss it is incurring in the Indian market, it is only relating part of the story, the other parts being that these are "book-keeping losses", and that its entire operation in India—including sale of crude oil to Esso refinery by its parent companies—makes a very good profit, and that these manipulated "losses" also involve a loss of tax revenue on the part of the Indian Government.

The origin of all the major conflicts between the Government and the major oil companies can be traced back to the latter's international character. So long as the majors are capable of producing enough crude oil from the Middle East on their own account at a relatively lower cost, they are not likely to be interested in exploration in India. Crude oil produced in India under their ownership (perhaps at a higher cost) would only replace their own crude imports from the Middle East, without conferring any extra advantage. From the point of view of the Indian Government, on the other hand, each barrel of crude flowing out of the wells located within the country implies a certain amount of saving in terms of foreign exchange expenditure. Where an economy is operating under foreign exchange constraint, it might be prepared to accept a higher energy cost as a price for the substitution of crude imports. There are also other areas of conflict. As a consumer of crude oil, India would benefit from a purchase contract which involves a low price for crude and a suitable payment arrangement, no matter what the source of the crude, other factors remaining equal. On the other hand, a refinery, located in India but owned by the majors, would, unless forced by the Government to do otherwise, continue to purchase from its parent company irrespective of the price and payment arrangements. Here again, the interests of the Government of the oil consuming country on the one hand, and the interests of the major international oil company, have become irreconcilable. The "naphtha controversy" can also be explained in the same way, as a conflict between a Government which is intending to minimise its foreign buying by recommending the use of surplus naphtha produced inside the country for the fertiliser industry, while the interested oil-cum-fertiliser corporation is finding it cheaper to buy its surplus liquid ammonia from its Middle Eastern affiliate.

During the British period, the conflicts between the national economic interests of India as an oil consuming country and the world-wide organisation of the major international oil companies were always resolved in favour of the latter. The leading oil company, Burmah Oil, was also a British-owned company, and the profits which accrued to it also benefited the British Empire, of which India was a part. So long as a sufficient amount of oil was being produced from within the empire, the British Government was not likely to have any particular interest in the oil production from India. The international oil companies operating in India were left very much on their own, so long as British economic interests were not affected. The international oil companies, on the other hand, had much to gain from a market-sharing arrangement, and a uniform price structure, which minimised the risks of price war while yielding good profit to the participants. After 1905, the Indian market was neatly divided among the major competitors on a geographical, as well as a percentage basis. Whereas about a quarter of the kerosene market was reserved for the American interests, Burmah Oil was allowed to import as much as it could from Burma subject to the American share. Whatever was left of the Indian market went to the oil producers of the Far East and Persia. These arrangements were modified after the entry of Bahrein (owned by Caltex) into the market, and the Second World War forced the oligopolists to accept the reality of the economic conditions in the form of large imports from Persia, which is geographically so close to India.

The market sharing arrangements existing in India came under pressure from time to time, and the conflict of interests among the majors occasionally led to ruthless price wars amongst themselves. But, because of the international character of these companies, these price wars frequently spread to the other markets of the world, and injured all the contestants without giving any of them a conclusive victory. Although each price war led to a fresh agreement about market-sharing, it normally only confirmed the existing arrangement, and, from the point of view of the Indian consumers, involved no downward change in prices. Sometimes modifications were made to the existing market-sharing arrangement without an accompanying price war, for example in the case of Caltex in the late-thirties, if these were in keeping with the global interests of the oligopolists as a group. There was another kind of price war fought in India during the thirties, which almost always led to the elimination of the weaker contestant from the market—through merger, outright purchase, or bankruptcy—when the latter consisted of small Indian importers, who received their supplies from the non-major trading companies of Rumania and the Soviet Union. Whereas the majors had the common interest of preserving the existing price structure in different markets, the independent importers could only hope to take away the trade of the bigger companies through lower prices, and their presence in the market was going to have a disruptive impact on the price structure.

So long as the Government remained either ignorant or indifferent, the Independence of India produced no significant difference to the oligopolistic market behaviour of the major companies. The two sides—the Government and the majors—came to a conflict first on the issue of the development of the Nahorkatiya oilfield, and then on several other issues such as Soviet crude imports, the price of crude imports in general, the product prices, and so on. By the time the Government of India came to take a serious interest in the oil industry, the power and influence of the majors had been undermined by the emergence of a number of important competitors in the world market. But, despite their international weakness, the majors fought to the last minute the attempts of the India Government to impose price ceilings or to introduce Indian Oil as a rival trading company. The collusive market system of the oligopolists in India enabled them to maintain the import parity system of pricing in its pure form for quite some time after this system had been abandoned or modified in many other countries. A modified version of the import parity system based on Persian Gulf is still in operation in India, despite the fact that the country imports only a marginal amount (and most of that from the Soviet Union). This is largely due to the refusal of the majors to renegotiate the refinery agreements of the early-fifties. On the other hand, the majors have now reconciled themselves to the dominating role of the Government enterprises in the Indian market, and have accommodated Indian Oil as an integral part of their oligopolistic market structure.

In contrast to the international majors, the Governments of many countries have found it easier to work with the minor international companies, known as independents. The latter have shown more willingness than the majors to build new refineries, and to accept Government majority participation in those refineries. They have also displayed a greater flexibility in their approach, by offering crude oil at lower prices than the level at which the majors would agree to part with their crude, and consenting to work under the price ceilings fixed by the Governments. Being smaller in size, the independents also cause less fear of economic domination than the majors with their mammoth establishments and network of innumerable affiliates.

However, a proper evaluation of the role of the independents in India would be impossible without stressing that—like majors—the independents are also large (although not so large as the majors) international oil corporations, with vertically integrated organisation and many affiliates. The affiliates of the independents in India are as much responsive to the global policies of their parents as those of the majors. The independents are as keen to obtain high prices for their crude and products as the majors are, and, along with the major international oil companies, they have a vested interest in an orderly world market structure. The powerful influence of the international character of their operation, as also of their vertical integration, was clearly seen when the Indian affiliate of Standard Oil of Indiana refused to build a fertiliser factory based on naphtha from Indian sources, and insisted on importing liquid ammonia from its Middle Eastern affiliates. The major difference in the market behaviour between the majors and the independents lies in the fact that the latter have yet to develop adequate outlets for their crude of North Africa and Middle East, which have been located over the past ten or twelve years. Like good businessmen, they are offering better terms and concessions, and participating in refinery building, because it is only by doing these things that the independents can hope to replace the majors in part of the world market.

So long as the independents are treated as outsiders by the majors, they are forced to adopt aggressive marketing policies in order to make the entry to new markets possible. But, in the long run, after having achieved their objective of securing a stable outlet for their crude in the markets of the Eastern Hemisphere, these companies would prefer to come to terms with the majors. With a comparatively large and established market of their own, the independents would have more to gain, and less to lose, from stable high prices. In fact, some of the independents have already entered into deals with majors for buying and selling crude oil in various places. The arrangement for Philips in India to buy crude from Standard Oil of California in order to meet the requirements of the Cochin refinery is one such example.

Like the independent international oil companies, in recent years, the trading establishments of the Soviet Union have made deep inroads into markets which were previously regarded as the exclusive preserve of the international majors. The sales promotion activities of the Soviet Union have been facilitated by the generous credit terms it was willing to offer—low interest and local currency payment—in addition to the low prices of its merchandise. In many cases, oil deals have been linked with agreements covering other commodities and the package as a whole has proved attractive to its partners. Most of these negotiations have taken place on a Government-to-Government basis, and the Soviet technical help in building refineries or in locating oil deposits, as well as commercial help in terms of trade in crude and various oil products, have been given without asking for equity participation in any of the enterprises. All these were in marked contrast to the known practices of the international oil companies at the time when these were first offered.

There have been attempts by many to underline the political side of the trade activities of the Soviet Union in oil. Being a Government monopoly, they say, the Soviet oil establishments are in a position to ignore commercial considerations, and to absorb losses on a long term basis, if it is in accordance with the political objectives of the state. However, while it is certainly true that the gains made by the Soviet Union in the field of oil trade have not been confined to the economic sector alone, and these have their obvious political implications, it is not necessary to explain their behaviour in political terms. Even if there were no politcal considerations involved, the only way open to the Soviet Union in order to expand its trade in the markets of Asia, Africa, and Europe, was to make its offers look more attractive than those of its competitors. On the other hand, there is no evidence that the Soviet Union is aiming to destroy the oil oligopolies even at enormous commercial loss to itself. In fact, in a number of markets in recent years the Soviet Union has been outbid by the majors when applying for crude-supply contracts. In recent negotiations with the Indian Government, the Soviet Union has shown the same kind of commercial awareness as has been shown by the independents after having been established in the market. The discriminatory high prices which the Soviet Union still charges to the captive markets of the Eastern Europe, compared with the low prices at which its oil is sold to the rest of the world, shows the responsiveness of its commercial policies to measurements of elasticity. On the other hand, given the political nature of the customers of the Soviet oil, it is unlikely that the Soviet Union would succeed in expanding its share of the market, relative to the share of the other interests, beyond a certain point. Most of the Governments which are now importing Soviet oil would be reluctant to depend exclusively on Soviet oil, oil being such an important commodity in war. Given this limitation, and also the fact that the Soviet Union has already a large market for its crude and refined oil products, it has more to gain, and less to lose, as in the case of the independents, from an understanding, implicit perhaps, with the major oil interests, on the question of oil prices. In other words, along with the independents, the Soviet Union is expected to adopt a conformist position with regard to the world oil price structure in future years.

It is important to remember at this stage, that the oil from the Soviet Union (or Russia before the revolution) has always played an important role in the history of the oil industry of the Indian sub-continent. The price wars of 1895–1905 were fought following the invasion of the Indian market by the Russian oil, as also the price wars of 1908, 1911, 1922, and 1927–28. Because the supply from this source occasionally stopped for various internal reasons, Soviet oil always had a de-stabilising effect on the price structure in India and elsewhere. After the revolution in 1917, the major oil companies were denied direct access to this large source of oil, but some of them agreed to act as the agencies through which the Soviet oil reached the rest of the world. A part of the Soviet oil, along with a large quantity of the Rumanian oil, however, came to reach the world market through "unregulated hands", that is non-major companies, and although the amount involved in those transactions was small, it succeeded in producing a more than proportionate impact on the price and market structure in India and elsewhere.

The contribution of the Soviet Union, along with Rumania in the creation of the public sector in oil in India cannot be overestimated. Both of these two countries agreed to build refineries based on the newly discovered oilfields of Assam, when the western companies were not willing to cooperate with the Government's public sector programme. In both of these projects, as also subsequently in the case of Koyali refinery, the Indian engineers were allowed to participate in designing the refineries, and then in operating the refineries on their own. These countries also encouraged the Government to participate in exploration at a time when the western experts took a dim view of the oil prospects of India. Their contribution in meeting the deficit in oil products at a low price has already been mentioned.

One of the important developments of recent years has been the growth of state enterprises in oil in the producing countries of the Middle East. Until the sixties there were very few areas of direct contact between the Governments of the oil producing countries on the one hand, and those of the oil consuming countries on the other. There were many factors working against the development of such contact at the Governmental level. In the producing countries, the task of producing and selling oil was left in the hands of the international oil companies, and it was the latter who arranged exports to the oil consuming countries through their own marketing networks. Even the amount of crude oil available to the Governments of the oil producing countries as a part of their share was sold though the international oil companies at agreed prices. It was not until some of these Governments undertook production of crude oil on their own account, in collaboration with the independent international oil companies, that they took a close look at the prospects for marketing to other countries on a regular basis crude oil, produced by themselves.

There are two forms in which at present they encourage cooperation with foreign Governments. The first is to build refineries, in partnership with the independent international oil companies, and the Governments of the host countries, in the oil importing countries. The recently built Madras refinery, jointly owned by the state enterprise of Iran with the Standard of Indiana and the Government of India, is one such example. The second is to invite the state enterprises of the oil consuming countries to participate in oil exploration in the Middle East, in partnership with the state enterprises of the oil producing countries. The state enterprises of Italy, Spain, and France, have been active in recent years in such collabora-

tion arrangements in the Middle East. The Iranian offshore concession, which is jointly owned by the state enterprises of India and
Iran, along with Philips and E.N.I., is one such example. In some
cases, the oil producing countries have also agreed to allow the oil
interests of the oil consuming countries to participate in the production from oilfields which have already been developed, in return
for an assured outlet for the crude from such field on a long term
basis in the markets of the latter, such as the reported agreement
between Pakistan and Saudi Arabia.

Although the above examples of cooperation between two sets of
poor countries—one mainly producing, and the other mainly
consuming, oil—are encouraging, these by no means fully describe
the extent to which such cooperation can take place. The enlargement
of economic links between these countries can cover other non-oil
industries, such as fertiliser. Whereas the oil exporting countries
possess surplus capital, but little skilled manpower, and India
possesses a large supply of engineers and technicians while starving
from foreign exchange shortage, there is virtually no end to possible
fields of cooperation between them. Even in the field of oil, a closer
economic association between them, independent of the international
oil companies, would help the oil exporting countries to receive
higher prices for their crude, while also enabling the oil consuming
countries like India to buy crude oil at a cheaper price.

We have already discussed the important place the state enterprises
occupy in Indian oil industry. The Government establishments are
active in almost every important sphere of the oil industry—from
exploration and production, to refining pipeline transporting, and
marketing. The only important sectors of the oil industry which have
been left untouched by the Government are ocean transport and
coastal shipping trade. The private Indian interests are active in
coastal shipping, and would not respond favourably to the extention
of the public sector in this field. It is clear from our discussion about
ocean freight structure, that the Indian Government is still unaware
of the high prices oil imports pay through the present system of ocean
transport. Of these various activities, refining and marketing have
now been brought under the Indian Oil Corporation, but exploration
and crude production still take place under different Government
establishments. It is not known whether the Government ever
considered the idea of bringing all the public sector activities
connected with oil under one vertically-integrated enterprise.

One special feature of the growth of the public sector is that it
grew bit by bit in an un-planned manner. The exploratory activities
began in a very small way to investigate two known surface outcrops
of oil. Subsequently three more areas were brought under public

sector operation in order to spread the risk associated with exploration. It was only after the encouraging reports given by the Soviet technicians about the oil prospects in India, and the discovery of oil in Cambay soon afterwards, that the Government enlarged the budget for oil exploration and undertook a sizeable drilling programme. Similarly, the marketing activities under the public sector began at first solely in order to meet the large needs of the state transport enterprises in various states, with the help of Soviet imports. The growth of refinery capacity under the Government ownership in subsequent years, and the state monopoly of import trade in oil products, have contributed to the growth of Indian Oil in a way, which was not foreseen at the time of its establishment. One can find correspondence between the Government objective of building refineries under state ownership when these are based on domestic crude, and the construction of Nunmati, Barauni, and Koyali refineries. But the decision to build refineries based on imported crude under the public sector, was taken only after the public dispute between the oil companies and the Government on the question of crude oil prices. In a sense, the major international oil companies contributed to the development of the public sector by their negative attitude towards questions which vitally affected Indian interests.

Another significant feature of the state oil undertakings is the extent of the help received by the Indian Government from the socialist countries in their formation. But in this case also the decision to accept Soviet help was a direct outcome of the refusal of the western oil interests to aid in the construction of the public sector projects. Where non-socialist interests have shown willingness to participate in joint projects, the Indian Government has generally preferred those to socialist help. It is important to note that, despite Soviet help in other fields, the Government has yet to build a public sector refinery which is based on imported crude from the Soviet Union, although it has so far constructed two import-based refineries in collaboration with non-major international oil companies.

As we have noted already, the state enterprises have so far not functioned satisfactorily in India. The operations of the refineries of Nunmati and Barauni have been affected by technical troubles on a number of occasions, the development of the oilfields has been slow and the exploratory activities have not kept pace with the needs of the industry. Most of these difficulties reflect the average level of efficiency of the Indian Government, but some of these are created by purely political factors, such as the demand for the location of an additional oil refinery in Assam. On the other hand, the recent years show unmistakable signs of declining interest in drilling activities on the part of the Government. The public sector in oil in India is largely the creation of K. D. Malviya, and with his exit from the Indian cabinet in 1963 the pace of development of the public sector has been considerably slowed down. Furthermore, whereas in the mid-fifties or in the early-sixties the Government could afford to ignore the opposition of the World Bank and the United States to its public sector policy, its position *vis-à-vis* these two bodies is not so strong today.

Nevertheless, it needs to be emphasised again, that the growth of the oil industry of India over the past two decades owes a great deal to the leading role played by the state enterprises in various fields. It was the Government-owned Oil and Natural Gas Commission which, with the encouragement of the Soviet Union, and despite widespread scepticism and stiff opposition from the business press, took the initiative in exploring for oil in Gujrat and in proving the oil potential of the country. The fact that at least the theoretical possibility of India becoming self-sufficient in crude production is now recognised by several experts bears witness to the success of the Government in this direction. The enormous economic gains which India is realising in terms of foreign exchange saving, as a result of the substitution of a part of crude imports by domestic production, could never have been possible without the participation of the Government in exploration. As seen from the previous chapter, the private foreign interests were, and still are unlikely to maintain a close interest in locating crude in India, and the private Indian businesses were neither willing nor able to mount such investment on a large scale, particularly when there were other alternative ways of making quick gains from less risky ventures. On the other hand, the Government participation has enabled the Indian engineers and geologists to acquire invaluable skill and knowledge in oil technology, which were previously denied to them by the foreign companies. The growth of the oil industry, under the umbrella of the public sector, has also created favourable conditions for the development of other industries which are based on oil, which would in the long run contribute significantly to the industrial progress of the country. The main criticism against the Government is that it is inconsistent in its attitude towards the public sector and foreign oil interests, and that, after the exit of Mr. Malviya from the cabinet, it has failed to continue a high rate of expansion of the public sector. Whereas the share of the majors in the oil industry has declined, they have been allowed to expand enormously the capacities of the refineries already in their possession. Although there are several precedents in the history of world oil, the Government has not taken the logical stand of unilaterally cancelling the agreements of the

1951–53 period, which were signed under vastly different conditions. In view of the pricing policies of the majors, and their lack of sympathy with the national interests of the country, some political circles have advocated the nationalisation of the enterprises under the major international oil companies. Leaving aside the political implications of such a move, it can be said that the major oil companies are at present not carrying out any important economic function which cannot be performed by the Indian enterprises themselves.

BIBLIOGRAPHY

(A) WORLD OIL INDUSTRY

ADELMAN, M. A., (1) "Oil Prices in the Longrun (1963–75)", in the *Journal of Business of the University of Chicago*, 2.4.1964; pp. 143–61. (2) "The Supply and Price of Natural Gas", in *Journal of Industrial Economics*, 1962. (3) "The World Oil Outlook", in Marion Clawson (Ed.), "Natural Resources and International Development", 1964, pp. 27–125. (4) "Oil Production Costs in Four Areas", *Proceedings of the Council of Economics*, Annual meeting of the American Institute of Mining, Metallurgical and Petroleum Engineers (1966).

ASHTON, A. S., "Financing of the World Oil Industry", (February 11, 1965) [a mimeographed note, with charts, distributed in a seminar on oil at the L.S.E.].

AUSTRALIA, (1) "Tariff Board's Report on Petroleum Products", August, 1953. (2) "Tariff Board's Report on Motor and Aviation Spirits", June 7, 1956. (3) "Tariff Board's Report on Petroleum Refining Industry", 1959.

BITTNER, R. E., BAUMANN, G. P., and CROSSBY, A. R., "Recent Developments in the Design of Small Refineries", [a paper read at the U.N. Conference on the application of science and technology for the benefit of less developed areas, 1962].

BURN, DUNCAN, *Structure of the British Industry*, (vol. 1, 1958), chapter on "The Oil Industry".

CASSADY, RALPH, (jr.), (1) *Price Making and Price Behaviour in the Petroleum Industry*, (Petroleum Monograph Series, Vol. 1, 1954). (2) "Price Warfare in Business Competition—a Study of Abnormal Competitive Behaviour". (Occasional Paper No. 11 (1963) of Bureau of Business and Economic Research, Graduate School of Business Administration, Michigan State University.)

DE CHAZEAU, M. G., and KAHN, M. E., *Integration and Competion in the Petroleum Industry*, (Petroleum Monograph No. 3, 1959).

DECHERT, CHARLES R., *Ente Nationale Idrocarburi—Profile of a State Corporation*, (1963).

FRANK, H. J., *Crude Oil Prices in the Middle East: A Study in Oligopolistic Price Behaviour*, (1966).

FRANKEL, P. H., (1) *Essentials of Petroleum*, (1966). Reprinted by Frank Cass & Co. Ltd., 1969. (2) "1958 and its Implications for the Oil Industry" in *Institute of Petroleum Review*, (June, 1959, pp. 173–176). (3) "Taxation of Petroleum Products and Its Impact on Consumption", [a paper presented to the U.N. Regional seminar on Techniques of Petroleum Development, 1962].

FRANKEL, P. H., and NEWTON, W. L., (1) "The Location of Refineries", in *The Institute of Petroleum Review*, (July, 1961, pp. 197–201). (2) "Current Economic Trends in Location and Size of Refineries in Europe" [a paper submitted to the Fifth World Petroleum Congress, Section IX, paper no. 10, pp. 85–95]. (3) "Recent Developments in the Economics of Petroleum Refining", [a paper submitted to the Sixth World Petroleum Congress, Section VIII, paper no. 20].

GERRETSON, F. C., *History of the Royal Dutch*, four volumes, (1953–1957).

GRANT, J. McB., "The Petroleum Industry" in *The Economics of Australian Industry*, by Alex Hunter (ed.), 1963.

HAGEMANS, K. E., and INGALL, R. E., *Design, Erection and Operation of Small Refineries in Developing Countries*, (1962).

HALL, ROBERT G., "Payout and Profitability in Deep Well Drilling" in *Economics of the Petroleum Industry* (International Oil and Gas Educational Center, Texas), 1963, pp. 82–187.

HAMILTON, DANIEL C., *Competition in Oil* (1958).

HARTSHORN, J. E., *Oil Companies and Governments* (1962).

HENRIGUES, ROBERT, *Marcus Samuel—First Viscount Bearstead and and Founder of the "Shell" Transport and Trading Company*, 1853–1927, (1960).

HIDY, R. W. and HIDY, M. E., *Pioneering in Big Business*, 1882–1911, New York, 1955–56.

ISSAWI, C., and YAGANEH, M., *Economics of Middle East Oil*, London (1963).

JAMES, MARQUIS, *The Texas Story—The First Fifty Years*, 1902–1952, (1953).

JAPAN, Industrial Review of Japan (1965).

LEEMAN, W. A., *The Price of Middle East Oil* (1962).

LENCZOWSKI, GEORGE, *Oil and State in the Middle East* (1960).

LEVY, W. J., (1) "The Past, Present and Likely Future Price Structure for the International Oil Trade", in *Proceedings of the Third World Petroleum Congress*, 1951 (Section X, pp. 112–132). (2) "The Search for Oil in Developing Countries", prepared at the request of I.B.R.D., November, 1960.

LIVINGSTON, S. M., "Economics of Refinery Location in the United States", Section IX, paper 9, pp. 75–84, of the *Proceedings of the Fifth World Petroleum Congress*.

LONGHURST, HENRY, *Adventures in Oil—The Story of British Petroleum* (1959).

LUBELL, HAROLD, (1) *Middle East Oil Crisis and Western Europe's Energy Supplies* (1962). (2) *The Soviet Oil Offensive and Inter-Bloc Economic Competition* (1961).

LUTTRELL, W. F., *Factory Location and Industrial Movement* (1962) [Section on Oil Refinery, pp. 652–659].

MCLEAN, J. G., and HAIGH, R. W., *The Grown of the Integrated Oil Companies* (1954).

NEWTON, W. L., (1) "The Longrun Development of the Tanker Freight Market'', in *The Journal of the Institute of Petroleum*, September, 1964. (2) "Freight Indicators" (a mimeographed note). (3) "The Structure of the Tanker Market" (mimeographed).

ODELL, P. R., *An Economic Geography of Oil*, London (1963).

PANKHURST, E. SYLVIA, *The Truth About the Oil War* (1922).

PENROSE, EDITH T., (1) "Profit Sharing Between Producing Countries and Oil Companies in the Middle East", in *The Economic Journal*, June, 1959. (2) "Middle East Oil: The International Distribution of Profits and Income Taxes", in *Economica*, August, 1960. (3) "Vertical Integration with Joint Control of Raw Material Production", in *The Journal of Development Studies*, April, 1965, pp. 251–268. (4) *The Large international firm in Developing countries* (1968).

PRATT, WALLACE E., and GOOD, DOROTHY (eds.), *World Geography of Petroleum* (1950).

SHELL INTERNATIONAL OIL COMPANY, *International Oil Prices* (1964).

SOCONY MOBIL OIL COMPANY, "Socony Mobil Oil Company, A History in Brief" (a mimeographed note), 1963.

STANDARD OIL COMPANY (Indiana), *Toward New Frontiers*, 1889–1959 (1959).

STOTT, BERNARD T., *World Oil Trade and International Payments* in *Fifth World Petroleum Congress* (Section IX, paper no. 7, pp. 53–65).

TARBELL, I. M., *The History of the Standard Oil Company* (1904).

TORRAY, PAUL D., MOORE, C. L. and WABER, GEORGE, H., "World Oil Resources", in Sixth World Petroleum Congress, Section VIII, paper 9, pp. 83–99.

UNITED NATIONS (U.N.), (1) *Petroleum Exploration: Capital Requirements and Method of Financing* (1962). (2) *The Price of Oil in Western Europe* (1955). (3) *Techniques of Petroleum Development* (1964).

UNITED STATES (U.S.), (1) *Commercial Relations of U.S.* (Consular Reports of 1882–1890). (2) *International Petroleum Cartel* (Federal Trade Commission, 1952). (3) *Report of the Commissioner of Corporations on the Petroleum Industry.* Part I (1907).

WORLD PETROLEUM CONGRESS PROCEEDINGS, (1) London, (1934). (2) Paris, (1937). (3) The Hague, (1951). (4) Rome, (1956). (5) New York, (1959). (6) Frankfurt, (1963).

(B) INDIA

ASSAM OIL COMPANY (1) "Burmah Oil in India", (1961). (2) "The Oilfields of Assam", (1958).

CAPITO, CHARLES ERIC, "The Oil Wells of Assam" [a small pamphlet, undated, found in the India Office Library].

DHAR, P. N., *Petroleum Industry and the Third Plan* (1960).

EVANS, P., (1) *Petroleum in India.* (2) *Exploration and Development of Petroleum Resources of Upper Assam* (1958).

GOVERNMENT OF INDIA, (1) *Report of the Oil Price Enquiry Committee* (1961). (2) *Report of the Working Group on Oil Prices* (1965). (3) *Index Number of Indian Prices, 1861–1931,* (1933). (4) *Report of the Railway Fuel Economy Enquiry Committee* (1953). (5) *Report of the Expert Committee on Coal Consumption in Railways* (1958). (6) 103rd Report of the Estimates Committee to the Second Loksabha on "Oil and Natural Gas Commission". (7) 28th Report of the Estimates Committee to the Third Loksabha on "Indian Oil Company", (1962–63). (8) 34th Report of the Estimates Committee to the Third Loksabha, on "Indian Refineries Ltd." (1962–63). (9) *India—A Handbook of Commercial Information,* vol. 1, 1963. (10) *Handbook of Commercial Information for India* (1937). (11) *Report of the Committee on Distribution of Income and Levels of Living,* Part 1, (1964). (12) *Programmes of Industrial Development*; 1951–56, 1956–61, 1961–66.

INDIAN TARIFF BOARD (1) *Report of the Indian Tariff Board Regarding the Grant of Protection to the Oil Industry* (1928). (2) *Oral Evidences Recorded During Enquiry Regarding the Grant of Protection to the Oil Industry* (1928). (3) *Representations Received by the Indian Tariff Board in Connection with the Board's Enquiry Regarding the Grant of Protection to the Oil Industry* (1928).

METRE, W. B., (1) "Petroleum Industry in India", in *"The Quarterly Journal of the Geophysical, Mining and Metallurgical Society of India"*, December, 1956. (2) "The Future of the Petroleum Industry of India", in *The Quarterly Journal of the Geological Survey of India"*, September, 1957. (3) "Review of Work in Oil Exploration and Planning for Self-Sufficiency in Oil", in *Indian Minerals,* April, 1961. (4) "Role of National Government in the Oil Industry in India", pp. 175–184, in William Bonini, Hollis, D. Hedberg and Jorma Kalliokoski (ed.), *The Role of National Governments in Exploration for Mineral Resources* (1963).

MONEY, VAL, D. J. S., *Oil Problem* (1930)

NATIONAL COUNCIL OF APPLIED ECONOMIC RESEARCH (N.C.A.E.R.) NEW DELHI, (1) *Utilisation of Primary Energy in India.* (2) *Domestic Fuels in India* (1959). (3) *Dieselisation and Diesel Oil Taxation* (1960). (4) *Demand for Energy in India* (1960). (5) *Demand for Energy in Southern India* (1962). (6) *Demand for Energy in Eastern India* (1963). (7) *Demand for Energy in Western India* (1965). (8) *Domestic Fuel Consumption in Rural India* (1965).

NATIONAL PLANNING COMMITTEE, *Power and Fuel* (1957).
SINGH, SARDAR SWARAN, "Progress in the Production of Minerals in India", *Asian Review*, January, 1963.
STANDARD VACUUM, "Stanvac Story" (mimeographed note sent to me in 1964).
WATT, GEORGE C., (1) *Dictionary of the Economic Products of India*, vol. 6, part 1, pp. 156–180 (on Petroleum Industry). (1885–1894). (2) *The Commercial Products of India* (1908).
WESTERN INDIA OIL DISTRIBUTING Co., *A Note on the Proposal of the Bombay Government to Fix Petrol Prices*. (1939).

(C) FOREIGN OIL JOURNAL (Abbreviations used given in parentheses)

British Petroleum Statistical Review (Annual).
Oil and Gas Journal (Weekly) (O.G.J.).
Oil and Gas International (Monthly) (O.G.I.).
Petroleum Intelligence Weekly (P.I.W.).
Petroleum Press Service (monthly) (P.P.S.).
Petroleum Review and Mining Laws (1904–1910).
Petroleum Times (Weekly) (P.T.).
Platts Oilgram Press Service (Daily).
Platts Oilprice Handbook (Yearly).
Skinner's Oil and Petroleum Yearbook (Yearly).
World Energy Supplies (United Nations—Annual).
World Oil (Monthly).

(D) INDIAN PERIODICALS (Abbreviations used given in parentheses)

Commerce (Bombay) Weekly.
Capital (Bombay) Weekly.
The Eastern Economist (Delhi) Weekly (E.E.).
Economic Weekly (Economic and Political Weekly) (Bombay) Weekly (E.W./E.P.W.).
Indian Petroleum Handbook (Petroleum Information Service, Delhi) Annual.
Oil Statistics (Petroleum Information Service, Delhi) Quarterly.
Records of Geological Survey of India (Annual General Report on the Work Carried out by the Goelogical Survey of India).
Reserve Bank of India's Annual Report on Currency and Financing.

(E) GOVERNMENT OF INDIA PERIODICALS (Abbreviations used given in parentheses)

Annual Statement of the Foreign Sea and Airborne Trade of India (Accounts relating to the seaborne and navigation trade of India).
Indian Customs Tariff (Annual).
Indian Trade Journal (Weekly) (I.T.J.).
Monthly Statistics of Foreign Trade.
Review of Trade of India (Annual) (R.T.I.).
Statistical Abstract of the Indian Union (Annual).
(Statistical Abstract for British India).

(F) Various other journals, annual reports of various companies, reports of different ministries, and other relevant publications.

SUBJECT INDEX

AUTHOR INDEX